PREVENTING MASS ATROCITIES

What can be done to warn about and organize political action to prevent genocide and mass atrocities?

The international contributors to this volume are either experts or practitioners, often both, who have contributed in substantial ways to analyzing high-risk situations, recommending preventive policies and actions, and in several instances helping to organize remedial actions. Whereas current literature on the prevention of genocide is theoretically well-grounded, this book explores what can be done, and has been done, in real-world situations. Recommendations and actions are rooted in a generation of experience, based on solid historical, comparative, and empirical research and with a grounding in quantitative methods.

This volume examines historical cases to understand the general causes and processes of mass violence and genocide, and engages with ongoing genocidal crises including Darfur and Syria, as well as other forms of related violence such as terrorism and civil conflict. It will be key reading for all students and scholars of genocide, war and conflict studies, human security, and security studies in general.

Barbara Harff is Professor of Political Science Emerita at the US Naval Academy and was distinguished Visiting Professor at Clark University's Strassler Center for Holocaust and Genocide Studies. She co-founded the Genocide Prevention Advisory Network and served for a decade on the US Government's State Failure (later Political Instability) Task Force. In 2013 she received the Raphael Lemkin Award from the Auschwitz Institute for Peace and Reconciliation.

Ted Robert Gurr was Distinguished University Professor of Political Science (Emeritus) at the University of Maryland; Founder and Consultant of the Minority at Risk Project; Former Senior Consultant to the US Government's Political Instability Task Force; and Former Olof Palme Visiting Professor, HSFR, Uppsala University.

ROUTLEDGE STUDIES IN GENOCIDE AND CRIMES AGAINST HUMANITY

The Routledge Series in Genocide and Crimes against Humanity publishes cutting-edge research and reflections on these urgently contemporary topics. While focusing on political-historical approaches to genocide and other mass crimes, the series is open to diverse contributions from the social sciences, humanities, law, and beyond. Proposals for both sole-authored and edited volumes are welcome.

Edited by Adam Jones, University of British Columbia in Kelowna, Canada.

Constructing Genocide and Mass Violence
Society, Crisis, Identity
Maureen Hiebert

Last Lectures on the Prevention and Intervention of Genocide
Edited by Samuel Totten

Perpetrating Genocide
A Criminological Account
Kjell Anderson

The United States and Genocide
(Re)Defining the Relationship
Jeffrey S. Bachman

Perpetrators and Perpetration of Mass Violence
Action, Motivations and Dynamics
Edited by Timothy Williams and Susanne Buckley-Zistel

Preventing Mass Atrocities
Policies and Practices
Edited by Barbara Harff and Ted Robert Gurr

For more information about this series, please visit: https://www.routledge.com/Routledge-Studies-in-Genocide-and-Crimes-against-Humanity/book-series/RSGCH

PREVENTING MASS ATROCITIES

Policies and Practices

Edited by Barbara Harff and Ted Robert Gurr

LONDON AND NEW YORK

First published 2019
by Routledge
2 Park Square, Milton Park, Abingdon, Oxon OX14 4RN

and by Routledge
711 Third Avenue, New York, NY 10017

Routledge is an imprint of the Taylor & Francis Group, an informa business

© 2019 selection and editorial matter, Barbara Harff and Ted Robert Gurr; individual chapters, the contributors

The right of Barbara Harff and Ted Robert Gurr to be identified as the authors of the editorial material, and of the authors for their individual chapters, has been asserted in accordance with sections 77 and 78 of the Copyright, Designs and Patents Act 1988.

All rights reserved. No part of this book may be reprinted or reproduced or utilised in any form or by any electronic, mechanical, or other means, now known or hereafter invented, including photocopying and recording, or in any information storage or retrieval system, without permission in writing from the publishers.

Trademark notice: Product or corporate names may be trademarks or registered trademarks, and are used only for identification and explanation without intent to infringe.

British Library Cataloguing-in-Publication Data
A catalogue record for this book is available from the British Library

Library of Congress Cataloging-in-Publication Data
Names: Harff, Barbara, 1942- editor. | Gurr, Ted Robert, 1936- editor.
Title: Preventing mass atrocities : policies and practices / edited by Barbara Harff and Ted Robert Gurr.
Description: Abingdon, Oxon ; New York, NY : Routledge, 2019. | Series: Routledge studies in genocide and crimes against humanity | Includes bibliographical references and index.
Identifiers: LCCN 2018019031| ISBN 9781138956001 (hardback) | ISBN 9781138956025 (pbk.) | ISBN 9781315665931 (ebook)
Subjects: LCSH: Genocide--Prevention. |
Crimes against humanity--Prevention. | Humanitarian intervention. | International relations.
Classification: LCC HV6322.7 .P74 2019 | DDC 364.15/1–dc23LC record available at https://lccn.loc.gov/2018019031

ISBN: 978-1-138-95600-1 (hbk)
ISBN: 978-1-138-95602-5 (pbk)
ISBN: 978-1-315-66593-1 (ebk)

Typeset in Bembo
by Taylor & Francis Books

 Printed in the United Kingdom by Henry Ling Limited

CONTENTS

List of illustrations	*vii*
List of contributors	*viii*

1	Introduction *Barbara Harff*	1
2	Genocide and mass atrocities: Can they be prevented? *Yehuda Bauer*	11

PART I
Risk Assessment, Early Warning, and Early Response   25

3	Countries at risk of genocide and politicide after 2016 – and why *Barbara Harff*	27
4	Atrocity crimes as a disease: A statistical approach to early detection *Birger Heldt*	40
5	Preventing genocides and mass atrocities: Evidence from conflict analysis *Ted Robert Gurr*	60

vi Contents

PART II
Mobilizing International, Regional, and Local Responses   71

6 Ending the silence on war crimes: A journalist's perspective   73
Roy Gutman

7 Preventing mass atrocities at the local level: Using village
committees for conflict prevention in Mauritania   93
Ekkehard Strauss

8 In the absence of will: Could genocide in Darfur have been
halted or mitigated?   105
Eric Reeves

9 Atrocity prevention from Obama to Trump   113
James P. Finkel

10 Prevention through political agreements: The community of
Sant'Egidio and the Central African Republic   135
Andrea Bartoli and Mauro Garofalo

11 An African regional perspective on prevention: Experiences
from the Great Lakes region   144
Ambassador Liberata Mulamula and Ashad Sentongo

12 Roots of ambivalence: The United Nations, genocide, and mass
atrocity prevention   156
Edward C. Luck

13 Who is in charge?: Emerging national and regional strategies for
prevention   176
Andrea Bartoli and Tetsushi Ogata

14 Guidelines for prevention of genocides and other mass
atrocities: An overview   187
Ted Robert Gurr

Index   *194*

ILLUSTRATIONS

Figures

4.1	Civilian conflict-related fatalities in Darfur, July 2003–December 2004	50
4.2	Predicted versus observed number of half-monthly periods for a certain number of civilian fatalities, Darfur July 2003–December 2004	51

Tables

3.1	Risks of new onsets of genocide and politicide after 2016 *cases*	34
3.2	Countries with high risks of genocide and politicide if they should have major conflicts or state failures	36
4.1	Distributions of German V1 and V2 bombs hitting south London	47
4.2	Predicted versus observed number of half-monthly periods for a certain number of fatalities, Darfur July 2003–December 2004	51
5.1	Types of internal conflicts leading to geno/politicides and other mass atrocities, 1955–2015	61

Boxes

9.1	Calculated decisions rather than lack of political will	124
9.2	Watch lists	126

CONTRIBUTORS

Yehuda Bauer is Professor of Holocaust Studies (Emeritus) at Hebrew University; Honorary Chairman of the International Holocaust Remembrance Alliance; and Member of the Israeli Academy of Science.

Barbara Harff is Professor of Political Science Emerita at the US Naval Academy and was distinguished Visiting Professor at Clark University's Strassler Center for Holocaust and Genocide Studies. She co-founded the Genocide Prevention Advisory Network and served for a decade on the US Government's State Failure (later Political Instability) Task Force. In 2013 she received the Raphael Lemkin Award from the Auschwitz Institute for Peace and Reconciliation.

Birger Heldt is Senior Evaluator, Office of Internal Oversight, at the Organisation for Security and Co-operation in Europe (OSCE) in Vienna. This chapter was authored in a private capacity and is not intended to represent the views of the OSCE. Before joining the OSCE in September 2013, Heldt was Research Adviser (2003–2008) and later Director of Research (2008–2013) at the Folke Bernadotte Academy, a Swedish government agency. He has also been Chair of a multi-national specialist team within the NATO Science & Technology Organisation (2012–2013), representative of Sweden in expert working groups within the EU (2011), Research Project Leader at the Swedish National Defence College (2000–2003), and Post-Doctoral Fellow at Yale University (1997–1999) and Uppsala University (1997, 1999). He holds a Ph.D. in Peace and Conflict Research (Uppsala University, 1996), and is Associate Professor (by title) in Peace and Conflict Research since 2003.

Ted Robert Gurr was Distinguished University Professor of Political Science (Emeritus) at the University of Maryland; Founder and Consultant of the Minority at Risk Project; Former Senior Consultant to the US Government's Political Instability Task Force; and Former Olof Palme Visiting Professor, HSFR, Uppsala University.

Roy Gutman has reported on war and peace, human rights, and war crimes, for more than four decades and won most of the leading journalistic prizes. He covered East–West relations during the Cold War, starting with Willy Brandt's Ostpolitik; reported from Tito's Yugoslavia for Reuters; and covered the revolutions of Eastern Europe, the unification of Germany, and the break-up of Yugoslavia. His reporting on the "ethnic cleansing" of Bosnia, including the first accounts of death camps, won the Pulitzer prize in 1993 and a host of other honors. He reported for UPI, Reuters, Newsday, Newsweek, and McClatchy Newspapers and was foreign editor at Newsday and McClatchy. From 2011 to 2017, he reported on the Middle East, from Baghdad and Istanbul, focusing particularly on the war in Syria. He has written three books and co-edited *Crimes of War: What the Public Should Know*, published in 12 languages.

Ekkehard Strauss is a human rights lawyer and UN official.

Eric Reeves is Senior Fellow at Harvard University's François-Xavier Bagnoud Center for Health and Human Rights. He was Professor of English at Smith College and for a number of years has maintained close connections with opposition groups and leaders in southern Sudan. His detailed reports on human rights abuses in Darfur, and elsewhere, have been widely circulated; see his website: www.sudanreeves.org.

James P. Finkel left federal service in May 2013 after almost 35 years, the last 20 of which provided him with a bird's eye view of US policy towards the prevention of genocide and mass atrocities. He was a participant in President Obama's PSD 10 study and was a frequent attendee during the first year of Atrocity Prevention Board meetings.

Andrea Bartoli is the Dean of the School of Diplomacy and International Relations at Seton Hall University. He works primarily on peacemaking and genocide prevention. Dr. Bartoli has been involved in many conflict resolution activities as a member of the Community of Sant'Egidio. His most recent book is *Negotiating Peace: The Role of Non-Governmental Organizations* (2013).

Mauro Garofalo is the Head of International Relations of the Community of Sant'Egidio. An archaeologist by training, he has led the process in Central African Republic (CAR) with the United Nations and the African Union that produced the recent "Entente de Sant'Egidio." Recently, he has been involved in peace processes in South Sudan, Libya, Uganda, and Mali.

Ambassador Liberata Mulamula is former Permanent Secretary, Ministry of Foreign Affairs and International Cooperation, Tanzania, and former Executive Secretary of the International Conference on the Great Lakes Region on Peace, Stability, and Development. She is a Visiting Scholar, Institute for African Studies, at the George Washington University.

Ashad Sentongo is Director for African Programs, Auschwitz Institute for Peace and Reconciliation, New York.

Edward C. Luck is the Arnold A. Saltzman Professor of Professional Practice and Director of the Specialization in International Conflict Resolution, School of International and Public Affairs, Columbia University. He served as the United Nations' first Special Adviser on the Responsibility to Protect from 2008 to 2012.

Tetsushi Ogata is Lecturer in Peace and Conflict Studies at the University of California, Berkeley. He is also the convener of GPANet.

1

INTRODUCTION

Barbara Harff

The dawn of comparative genocide research: Historians/ sociologists/psychologists/political scientists

Let me begin with a brief overview of the evolution of genocide studies that has led to this project. I suggest that if we understand the obstacles that faced the early community of scholars, we may have some idea of why we have made only limited progress in anticipating and preventing the next genocide. The journey began in the late 1970s, followed by a number of meetings in the 1980s, including a dozen or so people who called themselves genocide scholars—I was one of them. We were later called *Pioneers of Genocide Studies* by Samuel Totten and Steven Jacobs, in their 2002 book of that title. In the early 1980s, at a meeting in New York—hosted by Helen Fein at the John Jay School of Criminal Justice—about ten of us met to discuss how each of us defined genocide, and how to differentiate among war crimes, crimes against humanity, and other forms of deadly conflict. We shared ideas about "causes" and what to do to prevent future genocides.

We—the scholars of the seventies and eighties—came from different disciplines, which both added to and detracted from delineating and understanding the phenomenon of genocide. We focused on different levels of analysis and competed with each other for attention from our larger scholarly communities. Each of us brought our own experience and baggage, which created some professional animosities and perceived proprietary rights. For example, I was a gentile German-born scholar on a mission to restore a modicum of dignity to Germans as a result of the Holocaust. Among us, we had refugees from Nazi Germany and others who had lost many relatives in the death camps. More professional exposure brought more problems, especially when other scholars became aware that we treated the Holocaust as the archetypal or most horrendous episode of genocide, rather than as a *sui generis* historical event. Our standard retort was that we were the scholars who accorded it its rightful

2 Barbara Harff

place in the annals of human misery—namely, as one of the worst events in modern history, but not the only one. And, self-evidently, from a systematic perspective only comparison to other cases would allow us to test hypotheses and thus begin to understand what "caused" these events.

Definitions: Genocide and mass atrocities

The core definition of genocide, according to the 1948 UN Convention, is mass killings by a state intended to destroy, in whole or in part, an ethnic, religious, or other communal group. Many scholars have elaborated on the core definition: Jones (2011: 16–20) lists 22 definitional variations. Bauer told the Stockholm Forum its focus should include, first, genocide as defined by the 1948 Convention, and

> second, politicide, that is mass murder for political or social, economic … reasons, … third, so-called "ethnic cleansing" … and fourth, global or trans-national genocidal ideologies that not only threaten mass killings but actually engage in them …
>
> *(Bauer 2004: 21).*

This brings me to the currently popular concept of "mass atrocities." Though this book deals with both genocide and mass atrocities, we should remember that these are distinct phenomena—albeit related. Mass atrocities can precede genocides, but do not always. Ideally, the concepts should not be interchangeably used. And we should not label something "mass atrocity" or "genocide" for convenient or political reasons if we are not entirely clear what was or is happening and with what intent.

Victims of mass atrocities typically have multiple identities, sometimes identities invented by their perpetrators. Often, but not always, the victims are members of ethnic, religious, or racial minorities or political opponents of a regime. What sets them apart from the victims of geno/politicide is that there is no evident intent to destroy the group(s) to which they belong. In contrast, genocidal victims should belong to an identifiable group as defined in the Genocide Convention. Operationally, in empirical analysis, 1000 victims in a year constitute a mass (Ulfelder and Valentino 2008:2), whereas genocidal victims can number in the hundreds or fewer. Numbers matter, if only to differentiate among unintended casualties of war or other conflicts. But does it constitute a mass if all villagers are killed in an area that is sparsely populated? What if the villagers are victims of one massacre, as happened in Vietnam—a war crime, yes; a genocide, no?

Death during a murderous campaign defined as a mass atrocity is not accidental but planned—how different this is from intentional or systematic death is still open to discussion or, worse, unclear. Key is that states are not obliged to act when these events occur. There is no convention that specifically mentions mass atrocities as events that should galvanize the United Nations or regional organizations into action. Though the Human Rights Convention and the Geneva Conventions address war crimes and other more general violations of human rights, unless there is specific mention of mass atrocities, no criminalization ensues and no penalty is attached to the crime.

And now there is R2P, the Responsibility to Protect doctrine—another great idea that carries no obligation for states, the UN, or regional organizations to act. But it sounds and feels good to talk about something we ought to do.

Differentiating between genocide and mass atrocities and its relevance for prevention

Prevention of genocide is nearly impossible if we use the conditions spelled out in the Convention. From a legal perspective, we have to know that a genocide takes place, or that there is a high degree of certainty regarding the intent to commit that crime. In reality, that means genocide has already taken place, or at the very least is well underway. Essentially, we are stuck with a post-genocide scenario that allows the international community to bring perpetrators to justice. Yet, even here we encounter a problem: there is no automatic or specific punishment attached to the crime of genocide. Courts invest enormous time and effort to collect information on individual perpetrators, and punishment is not guaranteed. The Nuremberg Trials should serve as a reminder that war crimes, criminal warfare, collective responsibility, general human rights violations, genocide, and now mass atrocities are hard to delineate in these types of conflicts. Complicating the issue further is the questionable legal status of the Genocide Convention in public international law. International law is essentially case law, based on precedent, not necessarily on morality and ethics, but also not wholly devoid of essentially normative propositions. What would law be without justice? Today, it is understood and accepted by legal scholars and policymakers that an individual's fundamental rights still exist even if states are engaged in criminal warfare. Yet there is no penal code attached to human rights laws, including genocide. As of today, preventive action relies essentially on decisions made by enlightened policymakers.

There exists an enormous literature about the nature and purpose of law—I have written a dissertation and monograph about it (Harff 1984). But, this debate gets us nowhere we want to be when it comes to the usefulness of the concept of mass atrocities.

Typically, "mass atrocities" is as an umbrella term that includes genocide/politicide/ethnic cleansing, war crimes, and crimes against humanity. Scheffer (2006) argues that these inclusions may sharpen the definition of these specific conflicts, but I argue that they equally well could obfuscate even further their meaning. Conversely, he argues for the usage of "mass atrocities" to describe pre-genocidal situations. This allows states to take steps such as diplomatic missions and other soft interventions to stop escalation to a fully-fledged genocide. Essentially, he thinks that using a less intimidating concept (mass atrocities) as a possible precursor or indicator of genocide would free states to take action. I cannot see how such a label is less intimidating to potential intervenors. I agree, however, that the indiscriminate use of the term "genocide" can lead to obfuscation and procrastination in responding to victimization. What to do? I argue that the concept of genocide is pretty well-defined, despite the wide range of alternative definitions proposed. When one looks closely, the basic ingredients of genocide are near enough to a consensual understanding. An umbrella term such as "mass atrocities" that includes a number of specific conflicts may sharpen the specific definitions of genocide/politicide/ethnic cleansing and war crimes, but equally well could obfuscate even further the meaning of genocide. Furthermore, adding yet another term to human rights law could result, if the concept were to achieve legal status, in just another ignored label in public international law.

In conclusion, I see three distinct problems when one uses Scheffer's argument. First, if we use "mass atrocities" as an umbrella term for war crimes, genocide, crimes against humanity, and ethnic cleansing, it waters down each specific crime, potentially providing a back door for reluctant states to do nothing to prevent escalation. Second, if we use "mass atrocities" to describe a situation in which genocide is likely or imminent, essentially treating mass atrocities as a warning signal, a precursor, indicator, or antecedent in the hope that states may take preventive measures, we leave it up to politicians to decide what is or is not genocide. Do we really believe that the term "mass atrocities" carries less moral weight than "genocide"? Third, we would inevitably loosen the definition of genocide by giving it the preliminary label of mass atrocity, which in turn may lead to denial or minimization of what is happening.

What to do? It is essentially up to scholars and relevant private or governmental organizations to provide risk assessment and early warnings that are good enough to be acted upon. I venture to say we have it today, as recommended by Albright and Cohen (2008), who specifically mentioned the State Failures Task Force's work (and my risk assessment) as an actionable example

I suggest, then, that the best way to use "mass atrocities" is to give the term enough meaning that it can be used as an instrument to prove *intent* to commit genocide—that is, as a key early warning indicator. This is what I have done in part in our efforts to identify "causes" of genocide.

The genocide debate, past and present: Re-discovering the wheel

The following are just a few examples of the many different explanations of genocide, and the obfuscations, that have developed over time and, to some degree, remain today.

A psychologist among us said that unfortunately all of us (potentially) could be murderers. This was hard to swallow for those of us who believed that only some people are genetically and culturally predisposed to evil. Some of us believed and had written that empathy could be taught—a key disposition that would immunize people from acting on murderous impulses.

Some of our sociologists focused on group interaction as a causal key that motivates potential perpetrators. Of course, all genocide scholars, because of the language of the Convention, took group membership very seriously, but typically only in the process of identifying real or potential victims. But there was doubt about how important group membership was in regard to the motivations of potential perpetrators. Just because a person joins a political movement that promotes a racial, ethnic, or religious agenda, this does not make him/her a potential egregious human rights violator. Then and now, I think that, without an ideology that binds people together, group membership is fluid and unstable and by itself, with the exception of race, has little explanatory power.

The historians among us began to unravel the Holocaust in all its dimensions, and dissected other "genocides" such as the Armenian genocide and the Ukrainian *Holodomor*. Faced with the vexing question of which was the worst episode that befell mankind, as mentioned above, some of us opted for the Holocaust as the paradigmatic case. Why was there so much reluctance to compare the Holocaust to other genocides? Maybe it was safe to think of a particular people and culture as being uniquely susceptible to committing such a crime. See, for example, Goldhagen (1996), who argued that because of latent and enduring anti-Semitism, Germans were more likely to perpetrate the Holocaust than any other nation in Europe—an explanation that is nonsense in light of the 46 cases of geno/politicide committed post-World War II (Harff and Gurr 1988). In retrospect, I think the concern reflected a fear that the suffering of Holocaust victims would be minimized if compared to other genocides. I would argue the opposite: when we compare, we detail who were the primary victims and why they were chosen to be annihilated rather than decimated. Thus, we have a choice to say whether one genocide was more horrible than another—but we have no choice but to remember all.

Political scientists like myself thought that structures of society, political leadership, and certain ideologies predisposed certain societies and leaders to commit genocide. Thus, democracy appeared as a cure-all for preventing genocides. I also thought that we should focus on nineteenth- and twentieth-century cases, rather than genocides that happened as a result of European conquests of the Americas or Africa. Why? The international political system, having undergone tremendous changes during the last 100 years, bears little resemblance to the past. Thus, with the end of slavery, decolonization, and advances in knowledge and technology, we might witness more death given sophisticated weaponry, less death on account of advances in civilization, or more exclusion, discrimination, and ethnic cleansing because of the birth of the nation-state system in Africa, the Middle East, and Asia.

All of us thought that education was the key to building better, more tolerant societies. The optimists among us thought that civilized and democratic societies could deal rationally with intergroup differences based on religion, culture, race, and ethnicity. We strongly believed that post-Holocaust Europe would be immune to a repeat. And then Bosnia and Kosovo happened.

Armed with tighter and mutual agreeable definitions, some of us started to count and identify all cases in the twentieth century, because we were simply unaware of how many times genocides had happened during this period. Data was key to answering the "why" question.

Data on victims of geno/politicide

Millions were killed in the Soviet gulags, the Chinese Cultural Revolution and the Great Leap Forward. The numbers are staggering, and we will never know the exact number of victims. Rudolph Rummel and I were the two people counting as best as we could victims who numbered more than 10 million in each of these episodes (Rummel 2005, Harff and Gurr 1988, Harff 2003). Then there was the Cambodian genocide committed by the Khmer Rouge, in which between 1.2 and 1.5 million people were killed out of a total population of 7 million. In Africa, atrocities happened against ethnic rivals, religious minorities, and others in a number of countries—often repeat offenders, as in Rwanda (where 800,000 people were killed in 3 months in 1994), Burundi, Sudan, Congo/Zaïre, and others. And what about the Americas? American native populations were systematically decimated in the eighteenth and nineteenth centuries and earlier, as they were in Australia and Canada as well as Central and South America. In the twentieth century, fascist regimes committed geno/politicides in Guatemala, El Salvador, Argentina, and Chile. And in the Middle East, Syria is a repeat offender.

Political scientists, sociologists, and to some degree psychologists understood that we needed hard data (we were after all positivists in the midst of the behavioral revolution) to test any kind of general explanation. Historians were more skeptical. But aside from counting victims, what kind of data was required? Of course, we had to identify which countries had committed genocide (the repeat offender hypothesis). Furthermore, we needed to identify types of victimized groups, considering that the Convention obliges us to count as victims of genocide only those people belonging to an identifiable group.

I developed the first dataset that could be used for systematic analysis—it took 7 years. Thanks to the US government's State Failure Task Force, later known as the Political Instability Task Force, of which I was a member, we were able to generate data on all kinds of variables aside from those already-existing data-sets that experts thought were potentially significant in explaining genocide (Task Force reports; Harff 2003).

The road to explanation: Typologies and hypotheses

By the time the first lists of cases were identified by Kuper and Harff (Kuper 1981, Harff and Gurr 1988), we all had prepared case studies. And off we went to develop typologies—the mode of the day. I thought this was unnecessary, just a way to sort cases. But, as we realized later, that effort was useful in suggesting hypotheses.

After I had identified 46 cases since World War II, I realized that many did not fit the definition found in the Genocide Convention, because many victims had multiple identities or belonged to political groups not covered by the language of the Convention—so legally these were not genocides. Thus, I coined the concept of "politicide" to account for those victims who were killed primarily because they were members of a political or economic group deemed undesirable by the perpetrator.

These problems persist today. Some scholars follow the language of the Convention, while others have adopted my concept of politicide, and yet others call these events mass atrocities.

In a typology published in 1987, I identified one major "cause" as an antecedent of genocide—a concept defined later as "upheaval." This suggested two variables used in future multi-variable statistical analysis: the magnitude of political instability during the previous 10 years, and the occurrence of past genocide. Furthermore, in 1987 I thought that a state's colonial experience, postwar experiences (of international as well as civil wars), post-coup and post-revolutionary experiences, and conquests by outsiders would predispose states to use violence as a tool to resolve internal disputes. We tested the impact of colonial experience—the results were mixed or not encouraging. Much more important was the habituation to violence—that is, whether states experienced periods of great instability coupled with human rights violations, or had a history of deliberate discrimination against minorities. Our early findings, whether through case studies or typologies, led to a wealth of theoretical propositions that were tested once we were able to secure existing data or generate our own at the State Failure Task Force. We tested about 40 variables in many combinations—albeit mostly structural variables—that resulted in a best-fit model that endured and reportedly is used today in the US government and other organizations (Task Force reports; Harff 2003). Other variables that focused less on structure but (for example) on group characteristics were tested in my early warning work—more on that in my Chapter 3.

I venture to say that because of this and subsequent empirical research, we know enough about what "causes" genocide and political mass murder. The missing link is how we use that information effectively to halt or prevent these events.

The uses of risk assessments for prevention

The uses of risk assessments and early warning are discussed by some of our contributors in the following chapters. Others analyze the development of national, regional, and international mechanisms by which risk assessments and political action can be brought to bear on high-risk and ongoing conflict situations.

In Chapter 2, Professor Bauer provides a historical perspective on the evolution of the concepts of genocide, politicide, and mass atrocities. His insightful analysis focuses on three stages: how to detect mass murder, how to deal with current crises, and, when prevention has failed, how to reconstruct societies. Echoing my concerns, he thinks that although we have come a long way in discovering cases, "causes," and hotspots, we have a long way to go in mobilizing states to undertake remedial action. In his analysis of current crises, he suggests that religiously-inspired movements such as ISIL are the most dangerous groups we have to deal with. These groups take atrocities to another level, committing mass murder, mass rape, torture, and other sadistic acts, as dictated by their exclusionary ideology.

The uses of empirical analysis for warning and policy planning to deter genocide (and politicide) are examined in Chapters 3, 4, and 5. In Chapter 3, I sketch the

8 Barbara Harff

history of empirical attempts at global risk assessment and early warning. I also report my latest analysis of countries presently at risk. One advantage of this kind of analysis is its identification of the causal factors that generate the risks. In Chapter 4, Heldt uses a simple statistical procedure to determine whether killings observed in a country are random or systematic. It is an approach to early warning that does not require massive investment in events coding, but rather analysis of just one kind of event reports. In Chapter 5, Gurr uses the results of conflict analysis to address two issues. First, what is the empirical difference between genocides and (other) mass atrocities? Second, he surveys the outcomes of "upstream" and "midstream" attempts to avert or resolve civil conflicts before they escalate to genocidal killings, with special reference to identity conflicts in which the protagonists seek independence or regional autonomy.

In the book's second half, our contributors discuss paths to prevention, from local to international. In Chapter 6, journalist Roy Gutman traces the twentieth-century history of international efforts to contain humanitarian crises, including his own on-the-ground reporting of genocidal conflicts in Bosnia and, now, Syria. He thinks that international responses depend in good part on public pressure, which in turn is spurred by reporting. He proposes to establish networks of citizen journalists who can contribute this kind of first-hand reporting of atrocities.

In Chapter 7, UN official Ekkehard Strauss describes a program that uses village committees to defuse ethnic tensions in over 50 communities in southeast Mauritania. Strauss shows how local-level initiatives (under international auspices) can be successful in preventing outbreak of conflict in high-risk societies.

In Chapter 8 Eric Reeves identifies international measures (at six key junctures) that might have checked genocidal policies in Darfur. The Khartoum regime quickly learned from the lack of international action that it could pursue genocidal policies with impunity.

James Finkel, in Chapter 9, enlightens us about the bureaucratic wrangling of the Atrocities Prevention Board created by the Obama Administration in April 2012 to deal with genocides and mass atrocities. Despite good intentions, both the Clinton and Obama Administrations failed to prevent or deal with genocides, as we saw in Rwanda and now witness in Syria. The APB has one arguably successful intervention to its credit, supporting international peacekeeping in the Central African Republic. On the ground in CAR, the results were rather different, as described in Chapter 10. A highly-respected NGO, the Community of Sant'Egidio, worked for years to gain the confidence of a succession of CAR governments and a host of violent contenders, and in June 2017 secured a tentative peace agreement among them.

In Chapter 11, Tanzanian Ambassador Liberata Mulamula takes a critical look at East African regional efforts to prevent atrocities. Similar to Finkel's view, she contends that a focus on structures (building a spaghetti-bowl bureaucracy) can be detrimental to halting emerging crises. Yet there has been one regional success, in eastern Congo.

In Chapter 12, Edward Luck, the UN's one-time R2P adviser, reviews the UN's long-standing ambivalence about taking strong action against genocidal conflicts. He is also quite critical about R2P's usage. Is it providing cover for states to do nothing in emerging crises? Or is it a potential tool for states to intervene in the affairs of another state? We hope the latter is the case.

In Chapter 13, Andrea Bartoli and Tetsushi Ogata introduce us to GAAMAC (which stands for Global Action Against Mass Atrocity Crimes), a multi-state initiative to develop preventive architectures and national strategies to check mass atrocities and other related crimes against humanity, including genocide.

In the concluding chapter, Ted Robert Gurr synthesizes the lessons of the 12 chapters for international strategies for averting and containing genocides, politicides, and mass atrocities.

Editor's note

On November 25, 2017, we lost Ted Robert Gurr after a 3-month battle with pneumonia. Ted has written or edited more than 20 books and monographs, many of them translated into foreign languages including Arabic, German, and Russian. His many honors included an honorary doctorate from The University of Sofia (Bulgaria). He was a Distinguished University Professor Emeritus at the University of Maryland, held academic positions at Princeton, and was the Payson S. Wild Professor of Political Science at Northwestern University. In Yehuda Bauer's words, Ted was life himself: "gentle and forceful, never mind his seemingly endless knowledge." I lost my husband of nearly 37 years and my best friend; he will never be forgotten.

A special thanks to Adam Jones … friend and colleague whose support and careful reading of the manuscript has been invaluable.

References

Albright, Madeleine K. and William S. Cohen (2008) *Preventing Genocide: A Blueprint for US Policymakers*. Washington, DC: US Holocaust Memorial Museum, American Academy of Diplomacy, and the Endowment of the United States Institute of Peace.

Bauer, Yehuda (2004) "Address by Professor Yehuda Bauer," *Stockholm International Forum 2004: Preventing Genocide: Threats and Responsibilities*. Stockholm: Svensk Information for the Regeringskansliet.

Goldhagen, Daniel Jonah (1996) *Hitler's Willing Executioners: Ordinary Germans and the Holocaust*. New York: Knopf.

Harff, Barbara (1984) *Genocide and Human Rights: International Legal and Political Issues*. Denver: Graduate School of International Studies, University of Denver, Monograph Series in World Affairs, Vol. 20, Book 3.

Harff, Barbara (1987) "The Etiology of Genocide" in Michael N. Dobkowski and Isidor Wallimann, eds., *The Age of Genocide: Etiology and Case Studies of Mass Death*. Westport, CN: Greenwood Press.

Harff, Barbara (2003) "No Lessons Learned from the Holocaust? Assessing Risks of Genocide and Politicide since 1955," *American Political Science Review*, 97 no. 1, 57–73.

Harff, Barbara and Ted Robert Gurr (1988) "Toward Empirical Theory of Genocides and Politicides: Identification and Measurement of Cases since 1945," *International Studies Quarterly* 37 no. 3, 359–371.

Jones, Adam (2011) *Genocide: A Comprehensive Introduction*, 2nd ed. London and New York: Routledge.

Kuper, Leo (1981) *Genocide: Its Political Use in the Twentieth Century*. New Haven, CT and London: Yale University Press.

Rummel, Rudolph J. (1994). *Death By Government*. New Brunswick, NJ: Transaction Publishers.

Scheffer, David (2006) "Genocide and Atrocity Crimes," *Genocide Studies and Prevention: An International Journal*, 1 no. 3, 229–250.

Ulfelder, Jay and Benjamin Valentino (2008) "Assessing Risks of State-Sponsored Mass Killing, *"Report for the Political Instability Task Force*. McLean, VA: Science Applications International Corporation.

2

GENOCIDE AND MASS ATROCITIES

Can they be prevented?

Yehuda Bauer

The term 'genocide', coined by Raphael Lemkin, probably in 1943 and published in 1944,[1] is problematic. There is of course the definition in the Convention for the Prevention and Punishment of the Crime of Genocide (December 9, 1948), passed by the United Nations. It defines genocide, basically, as the intent and action to annihilate an ethnic, national, racial, or religious group as such, in whole or in part, and then describes five types of action, each of which constitutes genocide: killing members of the targeted group, causing physical and/or mental harm to members of the targeted group, creating conditions that make the survival of the group impossible, preventing births, and kidnapping children. (There is no gradation between these elements, and no other forms of genocide are mentioned.) Only UN member states can cause cases that may be genocidal to be investigated. Very importantly, incitement to genocide is considered to be part of the crime of genocide. And only the UN – i.e. the Security Council – can act to prevent genocide or punish perpetrators. No judicial process is mentioned in the Convention, which was not the result of scholarly investigation and deviated significantly from Lemkin's original proposal. It was the product of political horse-trading between the West, led by the US, and the Soviet-dominated East, with important input by some Latin American states.

The mention of racial groups may have made sense in 1948, when what we today call ethnicities or nationalities were called 'races' – a British race, a German race, a Russian race, a Jewish race, and so on. But there are no races. All humans are descended from *Homo sapiens* as it developed from earlier forms of primates, with an admixture of some 4–5% of some other, mainly Neanderthal, genes. We are all one race (all major religious belief systems agree on that), and the differences between types of dogs are greater than between humans: a marriage between an inhabitant of Papua New Guinea and a Harvard professor of different genders will produce healthy offspring. The mention of races in a UN document could be misinterpreted as racist, because, while there are no races, there is racism, which is a historical construct originating in the Iberian peninsula: the *Reconquista* of that area by Christian Spaniards from Muslims (*Moors*) resulted in discrimination on the basis of 'blood' – that is, descent from Muslims or Jews. The first such decree was issued in Toledo in 1449. With the penetration of Spaniards and Portuguese into North and West Africa, discrimination deepened, and was then exacerbated by the slave trade. Africans were enslaved by other Africans, and sold to mostly Arab traders, who brought the slaves to West African ports occupied by Europeans, who then shipped them to the Americas. Slavery was justified by the color of the skin of the victims, black skins being seen as evidence of a lesser humanity (the fathers of the US Constitution decided in 1787 that black slaves counted as three-fifths of human beings). Before the fifteenth century, no racism existed – ancient Egyptians, Babylonians, and so on, were not exactly blond and blue-eyed, whereas most slaves in the Roman Empire were Germanic, Celtic, or Greek, i.e. 'white.' There was no discrimination on the basis of color anywhere in the Ancient World. From A.D. 212 (Decree of Emperor Caracalla), every free man (but not woman) in the Roman Empire was entitled to be a Roman citizen, irrespective of his ancestry or color of skin.

The five types of genocide described in the Convention are no less problematic. It is impossible to measure the extent of physical, and even less so of mental, harm. Prevention of births – when women were slated to be totally extinguished, as in the case of Jews during the Holocaust, does that count as prevention of births? And when children are kidnapped, but not killed, is there not a chance that when they grow up, they may return to their original families and/or communities? Can kidnapping, evil as it is, be compared to murder?

But the most crucial problem is that prevention and punishment can only be activated by the UN – that is, by the only body the UN has that can actually act, namely the Security Council (SC). For any action, the SC needs the unanimity of the five veto-wielding powers, plus the votes of three of its ten non-permanent members. This is very difficult to achieve, as states are not usually motivated by moral considerations but by economic, political, military, or other interests. Therefore, the SC has not acted, directly or indirectly, against genocides or threats of genocide except in very rare instances (for instance, in Kenya in 2007/2008, Macedonia in 2001, and Timor Leste in 2007).[2]

It would be a major mistake to ignore the Convention, despite these problems; it is, after all, part of international law, provides a basis for possible future action, and could perhaps be used to greater effect in the future. But the controversies regarding the definition of genocide appear not to be very useful. In 2006, and later, David J. Scheffer suggested the use of another term – 'mass atrocities' – to include war crimes, crimes against humanity, ethnic cleansing (when the purpose is to annihilate a group as such), and genocide. Scheffer's proposal keeps the four types of crimes that he mentions as valid descriptions of reality, but recognizes the fluidity of the borderlines between them[3]. We are, after all, dealing with a continuum of a certain type of human group behavior; our definitions are, of necessity, abstractions from a reality that is much more complicated than our definitions can encompass. There are therefore many borderline cases in which the categories that we invent do not adequately reflect reality. Some are obvious: the Holocaust was clearly a genocide – indeed, it was a major cause for drafting the Convention. Was Rwanda a genocide? Hutu and Tutsi are actually not ethnic, but social, groups. They speak the same language (Kinyarwanda), follow the same cultural customs, and go to the same churches (there is a small Hutu Muslim minority). Tutsi were the landowning aristocracy in the old Rwandan kingdom, whereas Hutu were the peasants. The Belgian colonialists solidified the differences between these basically social strata in order to rule both groups more easily, as all colonialists would do, by introducing (in 1934) identity cards defining every person as Hutu, Tutsi, or Twa (a small indigenous group). Thus, it is possible to argue that the massacres of 1994 in Rwanda were not genocide, because the groups were not ethnicities or nationalities. But of course they were genocide – the problem lies in the definition, not the event.

What about groups that do not fit the Convention's definition, such as political, social, economic, or ideological groups? Barbara Harff[4] introduced another term to include all these: 'politicide', which has come to be accepted by many academics and politicians, but is not of course part of international law.

In the end, what most of us mean when we use the term 'genocide' is the intent and action to annihilate a human group as such, in whole or in part.

The question arises of whether genocide, and genocide-like acts (some use the term 'genocidal massacres'), are modern phenomena of the last two centuries, or whether they are ancient. As a result of research that has accumulated in recent years, it is becoming increasingly evident that groups of humans occasionally killed other groups of humans in prehistoric times. Two of many examples are the discovery of some 34 skeletons near Talheim (not far from Heilbronn in Germany), and about 100 such remains in a mine near Schletz in Austria, both dating from 9000–5000 BC.[5] Both groups were killed by other humans. It seems that when two human groups meet on the same real (or sometimes virtual) territory, there are five options: one, to combine, as this may strengthen both groups; two, for the stronger group to enslave the weaker one, or assign it a lower position on the socio-economic and political ladder; three, to expel the weaker group from the territory; four, to kill the group, in part or in whole – which happened innumerable times in history, and presumably in pre-history. But there is a fifth option as well: to compromise and find a way to co-exist, and even to form an alliance between two or more formerly warring groups. Thus, England (not Scotland) and France were bitter enemies for hundreds of years, and a permanent alliance between the two was unthinkable as late as the latter half of the nineteenth century. Today they are close allies. The same applies to France and Germany who fought against each other until 1945, and are now very closely allied within the EU. Paraguay and Brazil, Uruguay and Argentina were bitter enemies and fought a disastrous war (1864–1870), whereas today an armed clash between these countries is unthinkable. There are many other examples.

The idea of creating broad alliances of states and international norms that would in essence further what is called here the 'fifth option' existed in embryo before modernity, but received its first formulations in the work of Hugo de Groot (Grotius – 1583–1645) and the agreements that resulted from the Peace of Westphalia (1648). Efforts to maintain peace among states by international agreements based on accepted norms continued after that, but were only very partially successful. The eighteenth century was a century of wars and brutal colonial expansions accompanied by mass atrocities, creating a series of global crises, including genocides and genocide-like events, in the Americas and in Africa. The Treaty of Vienna of 1815 established some kind of peace based on a reactionary, semi-feudal European supremacy, while the US developed into a major force, joining the colonialist powers with its supremacist policies in Central America and the Far East (the 'opening' of Japan from 1853, war against Spain in 1898, and the exercise of supremacy in the Philippines and elsewhere, accompanied by the genocide of Native Americans and the continued enslavement of Blacks). The American Civil War cost the US more casualties than all its later wars combined. World War I marked the end of attempts to achieve something like international agreements based on accepted, traditional, norms, despite the establishment of the International Red Cross (founded in 1863) and the Hague agreements on the limits of warfare, in 1899 and 1907 (including the establishment of the Permanent Court of Arbitration, to settle international disputes peacefully).[6]

In the wake of World War I, at American initiative, but in the end without American participation, the League of Nations tried to establish an international order based on accepted international law. It proved to be inefficient, and as the totalitarian regimes arose, in and outside Europe, the League disintegrated. However, its legacy was, in essence, to try again, with better groundings. The United Nations, established in 1945, sought to avoid the mistakes of its predecessors, and serves as an indispensable forum for all attempts to reach globally-accepted international norms. Its performance is very far indeed from satisfactory, its bureaucracy is byzantine, but it is the best United Nations we have.

Background to genocide

The basic question is, why have groups of people been murdering other groups of people since 'time immemorial'? One approach is that based on anthropology. Humans are, clearly, mammals and, equally clearly, predators. Our ancestors were most certainly not vegetarians, and most of us live by eating the flesh of other mammals (and of fish). We no longer hunt mammoths, but we pick the meat of the animals that we kill from the shelves in supermarkets or groceries – which amounts to the same thing. We are still hunters and collectors, except that we raise animals in order to kill them, and the killing instinct is as deeply ingrained in us as it is in any pack of wolves or hyenas. Does that mean that we cannot avoid what is called here 'mass atrocities' and genocides, because we are programmed to kill? Not quite; we are also collectors of the fruit of the ground, the bush, and the tree (bears also are killers and collectors, for instance). Thus, some of us have learned that there is a type of green grass that turns yellow and grows little kernels on it, which we pick and grind, and turn into flour, out of which we make bread and other edibles. Like cattle, therefore, we actually eat grass – and other products of the earth, such as potatoes, taro, rice, and so on. The same applies to products of the bush and the trees. But all this, whether killing or collecting, cannot be done by an individual acting alone; like many other kinds of predators, we are social animals that cannot really exist outside of a social, collective framework. In order to be able to exist, we have developed characteristics, some of which we share with other animals, and some that are the result of many thousands of years of changes, adaptations, and development, and differ, sometimes radically, from the behavior of other predators. Among these is the conscious capacity to cooperate, collaborate, and sympathize, something that other predators also evince in considerable measure; but with us it is a conscious kind of behavior. A natural instinct of attachment has developed into human love and even into willingness to risk one's wellbeing, even life, to rescue another human or group of humans. This may include people whom we do not know at all. There are over 26,500 people commemorated as 'the Righteous' by Yad Vashem, the Israeli Holocaust memorial center: non-Jews who rescued Jews during the Holocaust out of non-materialistic motives. During the Armenian genocide in World War I, there were individual Turks, Kurds, and Circassians who rescued Armenians with no ulterior or ideological motives. The same applied in Rwanda, especially among the small minority of Moslem Hutus and in many, but not all, other genocides or genocide-like events.

It would seem clear, therefore, that humans have two opposing inclinations, instincts, or characteristics – the result of very long developments, from faraway primate ancestors to the past 200,000–300,000 years or so, after the emergence of modern humans in East Africa. A killing instinct that most probably derives from the fact that humans are predators exists alongside the equally essential development of norms that maintain humans in families, clans, tribes, nations, and so on, and thus enables them to survive. A development towards societies or a society that will limit, or in the very long term possibly even eliminate, tendencies to commit mass atrocities, including genocide, appears therefore to be a possibility. It is not a certainty by any means, and perhaps it is even a remote possibility. We should beware of positivistic imagery that sees human behavior as inexorably leading to greater achievements, whether political, social, economic, or moral. But we should equally avoid the kind of cultural pessimism that in the past has led to weakness and non-action in the face of human aggression, which can be found today, in the twenty-first century, in very many places.

The obvious question that arises is how to strengthen one set of characteristics, or instinctual behavior, versus the other. A number of strategies have been and are being tried. One is to exercise moral influence, whether by emphasizing the humane aspects of religious beliefs (and, usually, ignoring the fact that any given religious beliefs are also, in many instances, murderous ideologies), or by moral teachings that are part of most, if not all, human cultures (and, usually, ignoring the fact that most human civilizations also contain calls to war and murder). Actions by individuals and societies are obviously motivated by a mix of individual and collective attitudes. These usually reflect material or political interests, real or imagined. However, moral norms are also very important. Such norms may differ across societies. Moral norms may reflect pragmatic interests, but sometimes morals and interests clash, and this creates serious social and political tensions.

Trying to influence human collectives by moral preaching is an admirable exercise, but its practical effects are limited, although it is not totally without impact. In the post-Holocaust world especially, the Holocaust is often invoked as a warning to politicians to avoid what is called the slippery slope of an anti-liberal tendency, towards authoritarianism, disregard of human rights, gender equality, discrimination, persecution, and dehumanization, all of which may (but need not, necessarily) end in mass atrocities and genocide. There is logic to that warning. The Holocaust was indeed such a genocide, though some of its characteristics have no parallel with other genocides, while others border on the universal.

Collective moral norms are enshrined, since 1948, in such documents as the Universal Declaration of Human Rights (December 1948, building on precedents formulated before World War II). Groups such as the recipients of the Nobel Peace Prizes, and similar efforts (such as the UN General Secretary's committee of eminent personalities, nominated in 2012) tried and continue to try their best to influence political decision makers. However, I know of no evidence that would show that a collective denial of human rights – or worse – has been stopped because of such well-meaning interventions. In the end, moral sermonizing has little effect.

The alternative might be to attempt to yield to the demands of states, mainly but not only the major ones, and ignore acts and attitudes that stand in glaring contradiction to moral norms accepted by liberal and democratic societies, or to international law. This indeed is a slippery slope, and inevitably ends in accepting the opposite of such norms. However, to ignore economic, political, military, and other state interests leads us to being ineffective and irrelevant in contemporary global politics. While yielding to interest-directed power politics threatens to turn us into scoundrels lacking moral values, we need to recognize the game of political interests without succumbing to it; all our efforts need to undergo reality checks. We may well need to engage in what I would call 'morally-motivated political cynicism.'

What does this mean? It means, at least in this explanatory effort, that interests of states, justified (or justifiable) or not, have to be analyzed to see whether their pursuit can be squared with striving for the maintenance of international law, moral norms, and, mainly, the saving of human lives. This is the overriding purpose of all attempts to diminish, and possibly ultimately eliminate, mass atrocity crimes, including genocide. It would then seem legitimate to propose political options that might both satisfy such state interests, in whole or in part, if they advance efforts to save lives. To give an example: there is little chance of stopping the ongoing genocide in Darfur without exerting effective pressure on the Khartoum regime, and there is little chance of such pressure as long as the Sudanese government is supported by China and Russia (to an extent also by the US, for reasons connected with the so-called 'war on terror'). Chinese support is based, it seems, on the fact that most oil concessions in Sudan are owned by Chinese interests, and China needs oil in order to maintain and develop its economy. Sudanese and South Sudanese oil is therefore a vital Chinese interest. It is a principle of current Chinese politics not to intervene in the internal affairs of other states, if possible. As long as the (North) Sudanese government advances the export of oil through its only port, Port Sudan, which is also where the oil pipeline from mainly the southern oilfields ends, China will not exercise pressure on the Khartoum government. But the oil flows only in part (3 billion dollars in 2015) out of a much larger potential (almost all of it goes to China), because of Khartoum's genocidal policies in the southern parts of North Sudan, and because of the fratricidal and genocidal war in South Sudan. It has proved useless to appeal to China in the name of humanity and moral norms. But an approach that will seek to guarantee the flow of oil to China in return for China's support to force Sudan to cease the mass killing of populations in Darfur, the Nuba mountains, and aid in arranging a compromise between the warring South Sudanese ethnicities, may turn out to be a more promising option, or at least an option worth trying.[7]

There are efforts that may be called 'work in progress.' International law (IL) and international moral and legal norms are an example. The problem with IL is that it is observed, in the main, by states and communities in which the danger to human lives through mass atrocities, including genocide, is low or non-existent. On the other hand, major powers, and even smaller states, ignore IL when it is viewed as detrimental to their real or perceived interests, and when they can get away with not observing it. It is not likely that Russia will be called to defend its murderous policies in the Northern Caucasus or Syria before an international court of law. We have just examined the problem with Sudan; Chinese policies in Tibet, or the Taliban's attack on the Shiite Hazaras in Afghanistan, or Israel's occupation of the West Bank, were and are not likely to be dealt with in accordance with IL. That does not mean that efforts at strengthening IL should be abandoned: quite the contrary. The work to expand the effectiveness of IL is an essential part of any program trying to avoid genocide and mass atrocity crimes generally. What is regrettable is the tendency by well-meaning politicians and others to regard IL as something that is actually working, and is respected by all and sundry. One wishes that were the case.

Part of today's effort to deal with these situations involves organizations such as the International Criminal Court (ICC). Its foundational document, the Rome Statute (agreed upon in 1998, ratified in 2002, now [2017] signed by 124 member states), is an excellent example of the kind of thing the world needs to fight impunity and establish the rule of law. The problem is that the major powers – the US, Russia, and China – are not members, and neither are some of the more problematic states (Iran, Libya, Israel, and others). The ICC has no effective executive powers – in other words, it is a paper tiger. Again, this is not an argument against the ICC, but should be an incentive to provide the tiger with teeth. A contrary example, in some measure at least, is the special courts established at the Hague to bring to justice persons accused of committing crimes against humanity, war crimes, and causing genocides or genocidal attacks. Of course, the special courts established to prosecute alleged perpetrators of mass atrocities in the former Yugoslavia, Rwanda, and elsewhere act, by definition, *after* the traumatic event that prompted their creation. They are attempts to fight impunity and punish perpetrators in the name of humanity.

Dealing with mass atrocities appears to have three dimensions. First is how to prevent mass atrocities, including genocides and genocide-like events, in the first place; second, how to deal with such events if prevention fails and they are actually taking place; and then, the last stage, how to try and cure a society that has been traumatized by such acts. Prevention has to be based on theoretical considerations. At its base there should be the realization that perpetrators never act in inhuman ways; their acts are, unfortunately, very human indeed. Murder, mass murder, brutality, sadism, torture, rape are, as already pointed out, part of human history, the expression of a tendency found in all human beings, even when such a tendency is only embryonic and, unless developed, essentially harmless. The question that well-meaning moralists ask, 'How could they have done this?', is not only naive but dangerous, because it prevents counter-action based on realistic assessments of what humans as individuals, and human societies in the aggregate, have been doing all along. Such assessments can, in principle, be based on quantitative analyses, on a qualitative approach, or preferably on a mixture of both.

Quantitative analysis will be based on economic, political, military, cultural, historical, and other data pertaining to a certain country or region or society, and then regionalized and globalized; such data are then ordered and compared in accordance with advanced statistical models, and computerized. This enables us to make what is called global risk assessments of mass atrocity events. This is not futurology or prophecy, but it makes it possible to establish warning signals of potential developments, other things remaining equal – which, of course, they rarely do. Actual early warning – that is, predicting with some degree of accuracy when a potential threat will become realized – is almost impossible. All events are the result of an infinite number of intermingling causal chains, and because the number is infinite, we cannot know all the causes and therefore predict the outcomes. We might perhaps be able to identify some of the central causal chains and their interactions, and thereby increase the possibility that our warning may be realistic. Without quantitative analysis we cannot make any risk assessments, and therefore cannot approximate any early warning mechanism.

Obviously, then, quantitative analysis is essential, but it is not sufficient. What many of us call qualitative analysis must complement our approach. By 'qualitative analysis' we normally mean research into the historical, social, cultural, legal, political, and other background of a given state or society or region, on the basis of a variety of sources – archival, secondary, or contemporary (media-related and other). Global connections and impacts are equally important.

One of the major elements in qualitative analysis should be the sources, development, and importance of ideology in human behavior. Not every genocide, or genocidal massacre, or mass atrocity of some other kind, was guided ideologically. The destruction of Carthage in 146 BC was motivated by the blatant assertion that

Carthage's prosperity endangered Roman superiority in the Mediterranean basin. The notorious mantra of Cato the Elder, 'Ceterum censeo, Carthaginem esse delendam' ('Moreover, I believe that Carthage should be eliminated'), needed no ideological underpinning. But in many other cases, an ideology developed or was used to justify mass murder: people had to be convinced that murderous behavior towards a real or imagined adversary was just and proper. Historically, religious ideologies were and are one of the major factors that make for genocidal behavior. Belief in transcendental beings, or a Being that controls destinies and requires certain types of behavior, including the killing of those who do not believe in the perpetrators' religion, has been a motivation in many genocides. Monotheistic religions are, almost by definition, exclusivist, and whoever does not believe in their particular form of theism is condemned to damnation; only the believers reach a blessed afterworld. Today's radical Hinduism is not far behind, although its history is tolerant of other belief systems. Buddhism is in a different category, because the Buddha (Siddhartha Gautama, ca. 563–483 BC) rejected the worship of all kinds of transcendent beings and declared a law of nature that controls the world. Some of his disciples, especially of the Mahayana school, transformed his teachings into a religion with the Buddha as a kind of god, and Buddhist history is not free of committing mass atrocities and genocide-like transgressions. Chinese religious beliefs did not, apparently, have much influence on Chinese history.

It seems that in all genocides or genocide-like events, ideology, whether religious or not, was a cover, intentional or not, for pragmatic motivations underlying these mass atrocities. The Armenian genocide was caused, it appears fairly clear, by Turkish fear of a military conquest by Tsarist Russia, and by a nationalistic dream to establish a Turkic empire between the Dardanelles and Kazakhstan based on a unity of Turkic-speaking peoples. The fear of an Armenian autonomy or independence that would deny the Turks their heartland, Anatolia, and the desire not to permit any group with a different culture, language, and religion to rule any part of Turkey, were additional and very strong contributing factors. A further element was the aspiration of Turkish nationalists to wrest economic positions from the Armenian merchant class in Turkish towns and cities. In this mixture of pragmatic and ideological motivations, the very real, and very pragmatic, fear of an Armenian–Russian alliance led to the near-total annihilation of the Armenians in Turkey.

Similar analyses in more recent cases, for instance in Rwanda and Darfur, lead to similar conclusions. The same applies to the annihilation of the Caribbean Indians by Spain in the sixteenth century, the Native Americans by the Anglo-Americans in North America in the nineteenth century, and many other cases. The only non-pragmatic – in fact, anti-pragmatic – genocide one can think of is the genocide of the Jews (the Holocaust) in World War II. Thus, the confiscation of Jewish property was not the cause of the Holocaust, but its corollary. At first, when Nazi policies aimed at the expulsion of Jews in Germany, the expulsion was the central aim, and robbery was part of the policy of expulsion. During the mass murder, the murder was the Nazi German aim, the expropriation a 'natural' result. The collaboration of other – in fact, practically all – European countries, such as the Balkan states (with the exception of Albania), and to an extent also France, which had important local origins, became murderous because of Nazi initiative; its main motivations were robbery, plunder, and the nationalistic desire to establish an ethnically homogeneous society. This is even more true for Poland, the Baltic States, the Ukraine and to a lesser extent Belarus. The Nazi motivation was purely ideological: i.e., the view of the Jews as a satanic force that had to be destroyed – everywhere, not just in Europe. However, as the Holocaust was the result of human action, it can be repeated, though not in the same form, and hence was not unique, but unprecedented – which means that it was a precedent that may be followed by others, with variations, in other circumstances, with anyone as victims.

Religion, however, while certainly not the only ideological element, was one of the most potent ones in justifying mass atrocities. On the other hand, religion has also always been the ideological foundation of the best of human culture. There are no biblical prophets without the belief in God; no paintings in the Sistine Chapel without Jesus; no Oratoria of Bach without the New Testament; no Taj Mahal without Allah; and no Shwe Dagon in Yangoon without the Buddha. Murderous religious fanaticism can often only be met by non- or anti-radicals of the same religious persuasion.

The question of course arises as to what exactly we mean by religion. If we accept one of the definitions/approaches which says that any ideology that accepts transcendence and a decisive non-human impact on the natural and human world is a religion, then a theistic belief is not necessarily the only criterion for defining religion, and Marxism–Leninism and National Socialism can be seen as religions or at least as quasi-religions. The former posited a deterministic and immutable set of natural and social extra-human laws that controlled the world, whereas the latter believed in a god of nature who was on the side of the stronger, in both the animal world and in that of human societies. Both ideologies had clear genocidal implications.

I would suggest that Nazism, Bolshevism, and Radical Islam have some important common features. They all aspire(d) to world domination by violent, including genocidal, means; they all were/are radically, and on principle, opposed to elective democracy; they all were/are opposed to ethnic or national self-determination, although they may pay some lip service to them; they were/are anti-Jewish (in the case of Nazism and Radical Islam, genocidally so), and they may share other elements as well (a factual gender discrimination, for instance: there was one female minister in all the Soviet governments between 1917 and 1991, Polina S. Zemcuzina, Minister of Fisheries, 1930–1940; there were four female members of the Party Politburo in the early 1920s, and there are none in the Chinese Communist leadership. There was no woman among the Nazi elite, and of course no woman in the Radical Islamist leadership either).

Current crises

As to current crises, a qualitative analysis would show that, of the contemporary mass atrocity cases or threats, most are caused by ethnic, social, or political conflicts, or by clashes of economic, political, and military interests, but the most dangerous ones are obviously connected to Radical Islam. In past eras, Christianity was no less of a genocidal ideology, and Judaism has parallel ideological movements – though of course radical religious Jewish activists are members of a small people; they can certainly do a great deal of damage, but it will of necessity be local or at worst regional in nature. Radical Protestantism in the US and elsewhere may endanger the internal structure of their countries' democratic institutions, but they, as different from previous centuries, no longer have the genocidal potential of Radical Islam. Radical Hinduism does have a genocidal potential, but it is probably not as dangerous as its Islamic counterpart (in India itself, most of the Muslim population follows a peaceful interpretation of the religion). The extremely violent struggle over Bangladesh, considered by many to have been a genocide with millions of victims and a massive campaign of rape, mostly by the Muslim Pakistan Army (1971), was a Hindu–Muslim war with ethno-nationalistic overtones.

It is therefore essential to deal with religious ideologies justifying extreme exclusion of non-believers, up to intent and actions to annihilate them physically. Are these ideologies superstructures, as Marxist ideology would lead us to believe, produced by economic and social relations, or are they the product of long histories of cultural development? It seems that they are both. They are no doubt the result of long histories of intertwined social, economic, political, cultural, and intellectual processes, but they acquire, over time, lives and histories of their own. Human groups have very long 'memories' – that is, concepts, beliefs, and images, true to actual historical facts or not – that are transmitted, by word of mouth or, for the last few thousands of years, by written records and architectural structures. Radical Islamist ideology acts in the twenty-first century, but lives in the seventh, the time of the Prophet Muhammad. Christian civilization of our times lives and re-enacts, consciously and unconsciously, the first century. Jews celebrate the Exodus from Egypt (which almost certainly never happened) at every Passover festival. Hindus act the 'lives' of the Hindu gods. Ethnicities and nationalities live in a mix of present and real or mythical pasts.

Developments of present mass atrocities/genocides, as in the case of Radical Islamic movements, in the Middle East, in Africa, and elsewhere, cannot be understood in terms of what is called 'terror' – one movement's terrorist is another movement's resistance hero. Acts of violence, including mass murder, mass rape, torture, and sadism are, in the twenty-first century, in part at least, the immediate product of ideology, though that can be motivated by a plethora of economic, political, and other factors that can be analyzed by quantitative and qualitative research. Ideologies can only seldom be fought by force, and certainly not by force alone. In principle, the struggle for people's minds is as central as any political, economic, or military steps. In order to fight current murderous ideologies, an understanding of the historical background is absolutely essential. For all that, theoretical investigation is an essential aid or, as Barbara Harff has formulated, political action should be guided by 'theory-based practicality.' Once genocidal development takes place, as in the Middle East and parts of Africa, it may be necessary to employ force, but force is never a solution in itself. Even in a current crisis, diplomatic solutions have to be sought, except in a case such as radical Islam, where no negotiations are possible, but where, as has been pointed out, ideological 'warfare,' mainly by the use of modern technologies, is at least as important as the military kind. Alliances between major and minor powers who may differ radically in their interests but all of whom are threatened by ISIS, al-Qaida, the Taliban, and similar groups, should be sought. The practical possibilities of creating broad-based alliances of UN member States are discussed in another chapter in this book.[8]

Genocidal situations always start with words. At present, the so-called social media are full of hate speech calling for violence, for nationalistic, religious, or even personal reasons. A major task of any attempt to reduce mass atrocity crimes must be to find an international, consensual, legal solution to this situation.

Post-trauma reconstruction

There are several aspects to post-trauma reconstruction ('transitional justice'). One aspect, already mentioned, is that of trying to counter impunity by bringing suspected perpetrators to trial in international courts (e.g., those dealing with Rwanda, former Yugoslavia, Sierra Leone). Such courts can only deal with the most prominent figures, not with the mass of perpetrators. Only Rwanda has tried to bring large numbers of alleged perpetrators to trial, in traditional village and hamlet courts called the *gacaca*. It remains to be seen whether such proceedings, essentially trials with public participation, will heal the wounds. But under the semi-authoritarian (and very efficient) regime in Rwanda, mention of Hutu and Tutsi is forbidden; the *gacaca* trials deal with the actual killings, not with their motivations. There is, therefore, a unique combination of uncovering the deeds while hiding their background, thus in effect suppressing the trauma rather than facing it. This may or may not work, and can be explained by the fact that the Tutsi, though victorious in their war against the Hutu perpetrators, are a fairly small minority in their country, and, unless the memory of the Hutu ideology is suppressed, it may be revived.

There was no genocide in South Africa, but the brutal suppression of the black population created a chasm between blacks and whites that has been dealt with by a 'Truth and Reconciliation Commission,' which uncovers the perpetrators and their actions but promises a reconciliation at the end of the process. No systematic effort at rebuilding traumatized societies has been engaged in elsewhere – e.g., in Cambodia (where very few trials have been held), Zimbabwe (the *Gukurahundi* massacre of the Ndebele between 1983 and 1987), Sierra Leone, and so on. The exception here is the Holocaust: the masses of German perpetrators were not called to account, except during the last few years, when very old men were brought to trial – too little and too late. But instead, German society has been exposed, by most of its politicians and intellectuals, to massive educational programs, not only for the young, but for the whole of society. Antisemitism has not been eradicated, not by a long way; but it has been repressed, and the mass murder of Jews – and to a more limited extent of others, such as the Roma (and, going back into German history, the extermination of the Hereros and the Namas by the German Army in what is now Namibia in 1904–1907) – have all been exposed to a public that at first did not want to be confronted by it. The mass conversion, as one might call it, of a society from racism, genocidal thinking, and anti-democracy to a society tending towards opposition to the use of military force has not yet been properly investigated.

Dealing with post-genocidal traumas, especially in former European colonies, is still in its infancy. The genocidal atrocities committed by the Belgians in Congo, Dutch oppression in what is today Indonesia, and so on, are still being investigated, and the societies in these places still suffer from the after-effects of colonial rule. Japan still struggles with its history of mass atrocities in Korea and China in the twentieth century. Turkey adamantly refuses to recognize the genocide of the Armenians during and after World War I, and with the expulsion of Greeks and Armenians in 1923 (admittedly, after Greek aggression there). Historical investigation and overall, global analyses of these situations appear to be essential in order to repair the damage that humans inflicted, and continue to inflict, on other humans.

One should not underestimate the work done in the last few decades in the area of genocide studies – efforts at prevention, at stopping mass atrocities, and at rebuilding traumatized societies. After the 1948 Convention, nothing much happened until the breakthrough achieved by a number of scholars in the sixties and seventies. One of the prominent figures, but by no means the only one, was Leo Kuper, a South African Jewish social scientist, who fled from the apartheid regime to California, and published a number of most important books, beginning in the 1960s and culminating in his *Genocide: Its Political Use in the 20th Century*.[9] Real progress began in the eighties – that is, only three decades ago. Since then, there has been considerable development, first in the field of research, and subsequently in investigations of what genocide and mass atrocities mean and what motivates them. Academic centers dealing, usually, with what is called 'Holocaust and Genocide Studies,' have sprung up. Academic journals have been established, many books have been published, and vibrant controversies are taking place, unfortunately much less in Asia and Africa than in Europe and North America (and Israel). Possibly as a result of this, but possibly also independently, political efforts are being made to create an international consensus between states that might perhaps reduce the danger of genocidal developments. There appear to be the first glimmers of hope, despite justified skepticism regarding global politics. But we still have a very long way to go.

Notes

1 Raphael Lemkin, *Axis Rule in Occupied Europe*, New York: Howard Fertig, 1944.
2 The General Assembly can override the SC under the Uniting for Peace Resolution, which was done just once, and requires a two-thirds majority in the Assembly. I am grateful to Barbara Harff for reminding me of this.
3 David J. Scheffer, 'Genocide and Atrocity Crimes,' in *Genocide and Prevention*, vol. 1, 2006.

24 Yehuda Bauer

4 Barbara Harff, 'No Lessons learned from the Holocaust? Assessing Risks of Genocide and Political Mass Murder,' *American Political Science Review*, vol. 97, no. 1, 2003; Barbara Harff and Ted R. Gurr, 'Toward Empirical Theory of Genocides and Politicides,' *International Studies Quarterly*, vol. 32, 1988.
5 Stig Förster, 'Krieg und Genozid,' *Mittelweg*, vol. 36, no. 18. October–November, 2009, pp. 71–86.
6 Steven Pinker, in his *The Better Angels of our Nature* (New York: Viking Press, 2011), has argued that mass violence has over time, in fact, declined. His book was written before the Syria/Iraq disaster, the rise of ISIS, and the expansion of Boko Haram. I believe his argument is misleading, as these matters cannot be decided upon by short-term analyses. Mass violence in the twenty-first century may, on the whole, have caused less fatalities than, say, the Mongol invasions of the thirteenth century, but globalization of mass violence did not exist in previous centuries, so the comparisons are not very helpful.
7 Since the above was written, the genocide in Darfur appears to have ended in the victory of the perpetrators and the defeat of the Black tribal societies (Fur, Masalit, Zaghawa, and others) who had ruled the region for centuries.
8 See Chapter 13 by Andrea Bartoli and Tetsuchi Ogata in this volume.
9 New York: Penguin, 1981; New Haven, CT: Yale University Press, 1982.

PART I

Risk Assessment, Early Warning, and Early Response

3

COUNTRIES AT RISK OF GENOCIDE AND POLITICIDE AFTER 2016 – AND WHY

Barbara Harff

An introduction to quantitative analysis of risks of genocidal violence

I have written a dozen chapters and articles on risk assessment and early warning (EW) of genocidal violence, and thus it is hard to say anything new that is supposed to advance that project (for example Harff 2001, 2003, 2016). Should I talk about the need for good data-based systematic risk assessment and early warning to answer the few remaining academic pessimists, or the larger number of activists and even more numerous policy-makers who question the utility of systematic analysis? After several generations of data-driven analysis of conflict, the skeptics' chorus is getting smaller but no less vociferous. The skepticism, I think, has multiple causes. Partly, it is due to past practitioners' reliance on data-driven rather than theory-driven analysis, in which data are developed to fit theoretical concepts. The older practice has been dismissed as mindless number crunching. There also is discomfort with the probabilistic nature of statistical findings contrasted with the familiar details of field-based case studies. Furthermore, there are over-promises, systems whose proponents claim to be able to forecast – accurately, that is – anything from electoral outcomes to civil war. And there are flawed examples such as the early warning system employed by the UN, which includes a large number of indicators drawn in part from the genocide literature but even more so from general conflict theory. This effort is neither systematic nor data-driven, nor is it based on genocide theory; thus, it does little to create confidence in its general applicability or findings (if any are reported). These shortcomings may contribute to the inertia and lack of political will of UN members to take preventive action. If genocidal violence is hard to identify, why take costly and risky action to forestall it? The question remains: should policy be informed by empirical forecasts, case studies, or field reports – or a creative synthesis of all?

28 Barbara Harff

We think the latter. This chapter, though, focuses on empirical forecasts and their policy uses.

Risk assessment versus early warning

Risk assessment is based on the analysis of a country's background or structural conditions, such as ethnic divisions or type of political system, that may determine risk of genocide. Risk analysis can tell us, given the absence or presence of such factors, which countries are at high, medium, or low risk of genocide in the next several years (preferably the risk assessment should be updated every year). In contrast, early warning focuses on dynamic factors such as changes in political or ideological measures by (for example) increases in hate propaganda that may indicate killing campaigns are more imminent. In an ideal world, we should do both. For preventive action to work, policymakers need reliable information in time to make informed decisions about how to stop conflict escalation. The typical argument raised by those familiar with conflict situations is that EW adds only marginal value to situations already known. But, what is known? Knowing that a conflict is in the making or is underway does not tell us what kind of conflict it may turn out to be. Most but not all genocides have been preceded by violent conflicts, and not many such conflicts produced genocides. This is where theoretically-based models come into play. The dynamics of genocidal action are quite different from those ending in civil war or terror-based ethnic violence. Mass atrocities, however, are typically part and parcel of genocidal behavior. Yet, even in these situations, the killings of innocents may not evolve into genocides. Would it not be gratifying if policymakers had the option to mute or eliminate those factors known to contribute to an escalation to genocide? More on that later.

What causes genocide? Empirical theory

Of course, to talk about causes in conflict analysis is misleading; it is better to call them probable antecedents to genocide. My early empirical model (2003) identified six causal factors that jointly differentiate with 74 percent accuracy the 36 serious civil conflicts between 1955 and 2002 that led to episodes of genocidal violence and 93 others that did not. Accuracy increased to nearly 90 percent when temporal inconsistencies in the data were taken into account.

A clear definition is key to understanding any conflict phenomena. Although Adam Jones identifies 22 definitions (2011: 16–20), I argue that agreement among scholars on the essential characteristics far outweighs disagreements. The operational definition used here was developed in 1988 and introduces the concept of politicide now widely used in the literature:

> Genocides and politicides are the promotion, execution, and/or implied consent of sustained policies by governing elites or their agents – or in the case of

civil war, either of the contending authorities – that are intended to destroy, in whole or part, a communal, political or politicized ethnic group.

(Harff and Gurr 1988)

The 2017 risk assessment, in the final section of this chapter, briefly describes the variables used in the current model and how they are measured. All variables are anchored in the theoretical literature. These are: ethnic character of the ruling elite, exclusionary ideology, past geno/politicides, groups that are targets of systematic discrimination, and regime type. The original model, published in *American Political Science Review* (Harff 2003), included two other variables: the magnitude of recent political upheaval, and the international economic variable of trade openness. It did not include systematic discrimination, for lack of data; when this was compiled and added, it proved more significant than political upheaval. Also dropped, in the latest (2015 and 2016) analyses described below, was trade openness. The variable changes were introduced to get better results than the 74 percent accuracy of the first published analysis.

Regime type, meaning autocratic regimes, and specifically those whose elites ascribe to exclusionary ideologies, have been a recipe for disaster. Thus, these two variables proved to be robust in any re-testing of the original model. Publication of my 2003 model prompted many efforts to re-test the findings, for example by Wayman and Tago (2010) and Goldsmith et al. (2013). Some results were marginally better, hovering about 78 percent accuracy, but suggested no theoretical modifications. Moreover, prior to publishing the 2003 structural model, many alternative models were tested. In all, 65 structural variables in every conceivable combination were tested for significance when included in the 2003 model (some are discussed in Harff 2003: 63–65). Though some individual factors were significant in and of themselves, they faded in significance when tested in combination with others. Let me mention some factors thought significant in the theoretical literature that, when tested (empirically), lost their appeal. Political and leadership variables such as party fractionalization, party (il)legitimacy, neighboring countries in major civil or ethnic conflict, and Freedom House civil and political rights indices all proved to be less significant than thought. The same holds true for some economic and environmental variables such as recent change in GDP per capita, access to safe water, and trade openness. Environmental variables had some secondary significance. Thus, for example, in dire national emergencies such as earthquakes, regimes that could not provide for their citizens, either because of corruption or lack of economic capacity, often experienced some form of political upheaval – but seldom genocide. Demographic and societal variables that were singularly significant did not improve the level of explanation when tested with the other more robust variables. Thus, female life expectancy (essentially testing a consequence of economic and social development), percentage of population with primary education, and urban population growth rate were of less significance than I had anticipated.

I fully realize that structural variables do not tell the whole story – but, for preventive purposes, they offer enough information to develop response scenarios to

30 Barbara Harff

defuse crisis situations over the long run. When coupled with early warning indicators briefly described below, the policy community has enough ammunition to act proactively early on, rather than wait until genocidal violence is in full swing.

Structural variables and early warning indicators as guides to early action

Structural variables

Prior genocides: Past offenders often became repeat offenders, similar to the recidivism rate found in the US penal system. In most cases, criminals (perpetrators) become habituated to taking extreme measures when challenged by would-be contenders. Among genocidal perpetrators the risk is especially high when state authorities adhere to an exclusionary ideology that resonates with the population at large and can find supporters abroad (see, e.g., ISIS). This is not so different for the common criminal in the US who supports racist causes.

Autocratic governments sharply restrict public participation. Elite structures exercise power with few if any constitutional constraints. The more skewed the country is in terms of placing full control in the hands of the few, especially if the elite represents an ethnic minority, the greater the chances that future conflicts will lead to mass atrocities and genocide.

Elite ethnicity: The greater the ethnic, racial, and religious diversity in autocratic systems, the greater the chances that disadvantaged groups will mobilize to stake their demands. If one group disproportionally dominates the political system, and if demands, responses, interests, and security are defined in communal terms, violent ethnopolitical conflicts are likely and often provoke elite responses aimed at ethnic challengers (see the Afrikaner elite in South Africa during the Apartheid system, and Serbs, Croats, and Bosnians during the Yugoslav crises).

Systematic discrimination and exclusionary ideology may be precursors to more sinister forms of exclusion. Any form of exclusion increases the salience of a group's identity and its potential for mobilization and resistance. An ideology is a belief system that identifies some overriding principle or purpose that justifies government policies to restrict, persecute, exclude, or eliminate categories of people based on real or imagined criteria. Criteria for persecution may include ethnicity, race, religion (real forms of identity), and/or political status (imagined or assigned), or just about any group of people who are perceived as standing in the way of development or expanding settlement. I have identified certain belief systems in the post-1945 world that have justified the use of genocidal means to achieve their objectives. They include Marxist/ Leninism as practiced in China and North Korea, and fundamentalist Islam as practiced in Saudi Arabia and parts of Syria and Pakistan. Rigid anti-communism as advocated by fascist and militaristic states also features, as in Germany in the 1930s and Guatemala and Argentina in the 1950s and later. Another example is doctrines of ethnic superiority such as those practiced in South Africa and now in parts of the Middle East. In contrast, doctrines of strict secular nationalism as practiced in Turkey (more in the past than the present) as well as in Egypt are equally likely to justify violent suppression by elites.

What to do

It is not too difficult to develop response scenarios based on the structural factors identified above. Addressing the shortcomings of regimes on the brink of disaster is less challenging than is sometimes envisioned, given that the political interests of would-be intervenors are satisfied and states have the capacity to take action. Most states have an interest to avoid conflict and most states have some capacity to act in a decisive manner. These measures could be nothing more than providing good offices, diplomatic advice, aid, sanctions, or peacekeeping forces. The positive action by the Vatican in the Central African Republic, through its affiliate the Sant'Egidio lay movement, is a case in point. Here, its representatives accomplished a ceasefire in June 2017 that included virtually all warring groups in the CAR.

Of course, it would be desirable and tempting to spread the ideas of democracy through forceful intervention. But democracy is a process that has to have widespread support from the bottom up. It cannot succeed if introduced from above – see the Middle East.

I will cite only one more example of what could be accomplished to halt escalation: curbing the spread of exclusionary ideology through counter propaganda. When we see the spread of these ideologies through an increase of hate propaganda, we need to act, as Special Rapporteur Juan Mendez did on behalf of the UN in Ivory Coast. He pointed out that this kind of smear campaign was detrimental to the regime's international reputation, and some of the contending elites listened.

Early warning models

My early warning model included some ten variables measured by about 70 indicators – these were designed to complement the theoretically-based risk analysis (see Harff and Gurr 1988). These indicators, identified as accelerators, were operationalized to reflect their dynamic nature. In addition, the model identified deaccelerating factors or events and triggers that could reduce the severity of conflict development or contribute to its de-escalation. The accelerating factors included, first, internal actions that challenge the legitimacy of the regime (or ruling elite), such as declarations, riots, armed attacks, and refugee flows caused by internal unrest; and, second, any outside interference such as fact-finding missions, arms transfers, or armed intervention. A third category included threats against the regime not backed by action.

On the side of the potential victims (rebels and their supporters), I identified categories that manifested opposition groups' hostility toward the regime, such as increases in anti-government propaganda, militarization, threats, and armed attacks. We monitored any government activity that could be construed as hostile to opposition groups, such as verbal attacks, appearance of pro-government militias, and any increase of restrictive policies aimed at a target group, ranging from restrictions on civil service

32 Barbara Harff

participation and on economic activities to revocation of citizenship. In addition, we measured increases in life-integrity violations. Last, we tried to assess both increases and decreases in the capacity of regimes and opposition groups.

Nine triggers of genocide were identified – events that could singularly and negatively change the direction of a crisis, such as *coups d'état*, assassinations, or natural disasters. The last category consisted of 17 de-accelerating events that could singularly defuse crisis situations: examples include peace accords, cease-fires, release of political prisoners, instituting a new constitution, and so on. The idea was to pinpoint the timing of impending genocides. Key to this exercise was its potential usefulness for policymakers; it should buy time to allow for better planning once particular states or organizations decide to engage. And here is the dilemma – who should receive this early warning information? Friends and potential foes alike, i.e., potential perpetrators (who may be thus forewarned), or would-be intervenors who have the political will, capacity, and/or political interest to intervene?

The use of risk assessments and early warning models for prevention: Political considerations

Any kind of crisis warning is politically sensitive. Potential intervenors may have close political or economic ties that affect the wellbeing of their own citizens. There is donor fatigue in regard to states that are chronically beset by crises, corruption, and other preventable maladies. Costs of late intervention may be high and ineffective; thus, early interventionary measures are desirable, but little may be known about which actions work best in complex situations. Some states simply lack the capacity to intervene in any form other than lending verbal support to potential victim groups. Other states may be hindered by public pressure, law, and their own history of dubious self-serving interventions. Worse yet are threats that are uttered but not enforced – the line in the sand (uttered by President Obama in the case of Syria) is an unfortunate example. Such threats actually encourage would-be perpetrators and their supporters, as we see in Russia's acceptance (and supportive intervention) of Assad's horrendous human rights violations. Much better are low-profile diplomatic efforts, such as the Vatican's recent success (through its Sant'Egidio organization) in achieving a ceasefire in the Central African Republic.

Ideally, we should have response scenarios in place for different types of crisis situations, such as are routinely provided by the US and other militaries. It is well known that policies applied by multiple actors in a coordinated fashion (with a clear chain of command) are more likely to succeed than, for example, uncoordinated NATO actions such as we saw in the former Yugoslavia. Security assurances, providing venues for adjudication of disputes and equitable distribution of aid and public resources, are prescriptions that can work. Adam Lupel and Ernesto Verdeja (2013) and especially James Waller (2015) have provided us with excellent recipes for how to respond to genocides, politicides, and mass atrocities. Their discussion of options inform and sharpen debates about what to do.

Countries at risk of new genocides or politicides after 2016

The accompanying table reports the most recent of annual risk lists based on the results of Harff's 2003 analysis, described above. Risk lists have been prepared for most years since 2003, presented at GPANet meetings and posted on GPANet.org. This and the 2015 risk list use a different analytic approach than previous ones, which looked only at the risks for countries with serious internal wars or regime instability. The new risk lists are based on analysis of all country years from 1955 through 2015. The absolute risks are relatively low in any given year, but make it possible to identify the relative degree of risk among countries, including countries that are not now challenged by serious conflicts. As in the past, we report not only relative rankings, from highest to lowest, but also identify (in text boxes) the country characteristics that determine the risks.

How to interpret and use the results? First, the results technically refer to 2015, but we make the reasonable assumption that they will remain much the same for 2017 and subsequent years, unless and until there are changes in the driving variables. Second, it is inevitable that a statistical model that is "trained" on 60 years of patterns of genocide and politicide onset may involve false positives (i.e., false alarms in that the predicted percentage risk is too high), false negatives (i.e., missed alarms, in that the predicted percentage risk is too low), and true alarms (i.e., the risk estimate is accurate). This approach resembles how the epidemiology community regards early warning alarms from model-driven and automated disease surveillance systems – a warning may be a false alarm (data are wrong, model is correct), false alarm (data are correct, but model is wrong), or a true alarm (data and model are correct). Experts then look closely at each warning and ask how accurate it is, given the specific traits of each case, before they recommend responses. And this is precisely comparable to how these risk assessments for geno/politicide should be used. Some examples are found below:

Ethiopia, facing a low-grade insurgency by Oromos in the Ogaden, is second in risk only to Syria, which is already in a genocidal conflict.[9] Thus far, the Ethiopian regime has used conventional counterinsurgency techniques, and has also given Oromo opportunities – which many have taken – to participate in conventional politics. Moreover, the country is open to extensive international influence from donors and investors, and houses the headquarters of the African Union, which has taken strong stands against mass violence. Ethiopia should nevertheless be closely monitored for signs that the regime might overcome these restraints and resort to genocidal policies.

Israel, which ranks fifth on the list, also is likely a "false alarm". Its security services have been relatively effective in dealing with violent Palestinian attacks, despite criticism of human rights violations. Its internal democratic constraints against extreme policies are strong, and international constraints point in the same direction. Islamist ideology, however, calls for elimination of Jewish populations, a genocidal aim that justifies violent opposition for the indefinite future.

Central African Republic, Libya, and Yemen are countries with positive but relatively low risks that observers might judge to be "false negatives". All are experiencing civil

TABLE 3.1 Risks of new onsets of genocide and politicide after 2016 *cases*[1]

Countries and 2015 total risk score	Recent changes in geno/pol hazards	Current instability	Contention re. elite ethnicity[2] Risk score 1.54	Regime type 2015[3] Risk score 0.91	Targets of systematic discrimination[4] Risk score 2.35	Exclusionary ideology Risk score 2.26	Past geno/ politicides Risk score 0.36
Syria 8.99	Very high since 1958, no change since 1982	Civil war since 2011 ONGOING GENOCIDE	Yes: Alawite minority dominates	Full autocracy	Islamists, Sunnis, Kurds (*Shi'ites, Yazids, Christians*)[5]	No	Yes: 1981–1982, 2012–present
Ethiopia 6.170	No significant change in the last decade	Regional rebellion since 2006	Yes: Tigrean minority dominates	Partial autocracy	Oromo, Anuak	No	Yes: 1976–1979
South Sudan 4.53	High since independence in 2011	Civil war from 2013 between Dinka and Nuer	Yes, Dinka dominate	Mixed regime	Nuer	No	No
Egypt 4.20	Increase after 2013	Islamist terrorism since 2013	No	Partial autocracy	Muslim Brotherhood, Copts	No	No
Israel 2.17	Increase after 2013	Attacks by Palestinians domestic and from Gaza	No	Full democracy	Palestinians	Yes: right-wing nationalism	No
Sudan 1.90	Slight decline after 2009	Civil wars since 1982 ONGOING GENOCIDE	No	Partial autocracy	Darfuri, Nuba, Kordofan peoples	Yes: Islamist	Yes: 1956–1972, 1983–present
Turkey 1.65	Decline after 2008, sharp increase in 2015	Kurdish rebellion since 1979	No	Partial democracy	Kurds, political opposition	No	No

Russia 1.25	Slight increase after 2006	Chechen rebellions since 1994	No	Partial democracy	None	No	Yes: 1920s and 1930s
Ukraine 1.19	Increase since 2014	Secessionist war in Donbass	Yes: Ukrainian vs. Russian speakers	Democracy	None	No	No
Myanmar 1.17	Major decline after 2010	Regional wars since 1950s	Yes: Burman majority dominates	Partial democracy	Royhinga Muslims	Yes: Burman nationalism	Yes: 1978
Central African Rep. 0.98[6]	Significant since 2003	Civil war, communal massacres 2012–2017	Christian and Muslim elites contend for power	No effective regime	Muslims, Christians	No	Mass atrocities 2013–2016
Libya 0.90	Major decline after 2011	Violent contestation for power since 2011	No	No effective regime	None	No	No
Yemen 0.90	Medium since 2011	Civil wars since 2004	Houthi (Shi'i) and international coalition (Sunni) contend for power	No effective regime	None	Yes: Islamist	No
Burundi 0.81	Increase in 2014, 2015	Serious electoral violence 2014	Hutu vs Tutsi contention resumes	Shifting from democracy to autocracy	Bi-ethnic political opposition	No	Yes: 1963–1973, 1988–2005

TABLE 3.2 Countries with high risks of genocide and politicide if they should have major conflicts or state failures[7]

Countries and 2015 total risk score	Recent changes in risks	Current instability	Contention re. elite ethnicity	Regime type 2015	Targets of discrimination	Exclusionary ideology	Past geno/ politicides
Saudi Arabia 15.01	**Persistently high**	None	**Yes: Sunni majority, Sudairi clan dominates**	**Full autocracy**	Shi'i	**Yes: Wahabism**	None
Bahrain 10.25	**Sharp increase after 2010**	Mass protests by Shi'i majority	**Yes: Sunni Al-Khalifa clan dominates**	**Full autocracy**	Shi'i	No	None
Mauritania[8] 7.00+	**No change since 2009**	Social unrest due to fundamental-ist Islam	**Minority ethnic elite: Beydane (White Moors)**	**Partial autocracy**	**Black Moors, Afro-Mauritanians**	**Yes: Arabiza-tion policy in government, military**	*Passif humani-taire*, **mass atrocities of 1989–1990**
Uzbekistan 5.79	**No change since 1992**	Low-level Isla-mist terrorism	No	**Full autocracy**	**Tajiks, Islamists**	**Yes: Uzbek nationalism**	None
Cameroun 5.65	**No change since 1992**	None	**Majority ethnic elite: Christian southerners**	**Partial autocracy**	**Westerners, Bamileke, Bakassi**	No	None
North Korea 4.14	**No change since 1994**	None	No	**Full autocracy**	None	**Communism**	None
DR Congo 3.66	**Substantial decline after 2001**	Regional rebel-lions since 1962	No	**Partial democracy**	**Tutsis, Batwa/ Bambuti**	No	**Yes: 1964–1965, 1977, 1999**
Turkmenistan 3.53	**No change since 2003**	None	No	**Full autocracy**	**Uzbeks, Baloch, Russians**	None	None

Source: Barbara Harff and Ted Robert Gurr, June 2017

Risk of genocide and politicide after 2016   **37**

or communal wars. But in none of them is there a governing authority that might launch a campaign to eliminate its opponents. Moreover, none except Yemen harbors an exclusionary ideology, which is one of two strongest preconditions for genocidal killings. And neither Libya nor Yemen has a history of systematic discrimination against minorities – also a powerful predictor of genocide. In the longer run, the risks of mass killings in these countries depend on the character of whatever elite eventually gains power and re-establishes an effective regime. Another highly relevant factor is international presence, which in the case of CAR and Libya mitigates against mass violence by communal contenders or political rivals, or by any new regime. In Yemen, unfortunately, international involvement in the civil war by a Saudi-led coalition of Arab states – among others – exacerbates the conflict.

Nigeria is included in the table because observers might conclude that, in the face of two regional insurgencies, its military might resort to genocidal policies. In fact, military policies have been characterized more by incompetence and corruption than atrocities. Moreover, the country is democratic (17 on our 20-point scale) and lacks either a history of discrimination against minorities (Igbos might disagree) or an exclusionary ideology. So, the finding of low risk appears accurate.

Countries without severe civil violence or instability. The last section of the table shows results that are only possible using our new all-country, all-year hazard analysis. It highlights the eight countries that are at highest risk *if* major internal war breaks out or the regime collapses. The two highest risk countries, Saudi Arabia and Bahrain, have higher conditional risks than any of the countries in the first portion of the table – including Syria. And they share three of five risk factors: they have minority elites, practice discrimination against Shi'as (a minority in Saudi Arabia, a majority in Bahrain), and are autocratic – which means, among other things, that they lack democratic norms of accommodation and internal political or normative restraints on the use of massive violence against challengers. Mauritania is third highest. Its profile and estimated risk score have been updated based on information provided by our colleague Dr. Ekkehard Strauss, who has been conducting fieldwork in the country for several years (see Chapter 7).

All eight of these high-risk countries should be carefully monitored for evidence of possible instability, and plans for response made accordingly. If any causal variables in Saudi Arabia or Bahrain are susceptible to international influence, such influence should aim at reducing discrimination against Shi'as and to democratize their political systems, at least enough to permit conventional participation by minority leaders.

Notes

Technical notes:

1 Risks are calculated based on results of an analysis of the annual likelihood of onset of genocide or politicide in all countries from 1955 to 2015. Since outbreaks of geno/politicides are uncommon, most percentages are small. Their main effect is to show the *relative* likelihood of new geno/politicides (*unless this is a deliberate abbreviation*) breaking out in the near future. State failure is defined using the Political Instability Task Force's operational definition. It includes countries with ethnic or revolutionary wars underway and

those with rapid, abrupt changes in regime. Monty Marshall of the Center for Systemic Peace provided updated data for this analysis. Birger Heldt advised on the analysis using new and updated data on the five variables used in previous risk assessments by Barbara Harff. The last five columns in the table show the variables that have been strongly significant in predicting to the onset of past genocides and politicides. Trade openness, used in previous analyses, is not significant in the statistical analysis used here. Past genocides seem to inoculate states from resorting to it again in the short run, but after a decade or more they increase risks.

2 A three-category code is used: if the ethnicity (or religion) of the elite is politically contentious, the country is coded 1. If the elite in power represents a minority, like Alawites in Syria, the country year is coded 2. Otherwise, the country year is 0.

3 The Polity scale is used, converted so that a fully autocratic regime is 0 and a fully democratic regime is 20. Note that some states have no effective regime, and in the analysis are coded 0.

4 From the Minorities at Risk project survey of groups subject to state-led discrimination (through 2006, www.cidcm.umd.edu.mar/), updated using information from the Minorities' Rights Group's 2011 report on other groups subject to widespread discrimination and additional reports plus more recent academic and journalistic accounts.

5 Italicized groups are targeted as heretics by the proclaimed Islamic State (ISIS, Daesh) that controls parts of eastern Syria and western Iraq.

6 The State Failure/Political Instability Task Force data codes the recent conflict in the Central African Republic as a genocide. We regard it as mass atrocities committed by contending communal groups in a civil war. A negotiated settlement was announced in June 2017.

7 Countries that are not now experiencing failures – civil wars or regime instability – also have some of the factors that predict the onset of geno/politicide. The countries listed here are the non-failure states with the highest risks for geno/politicide if state failure were to occur.

8 Updated in mid-2017 based on current information provided by Dr. Ekkehard Strauss (see Chapter 7). The percentage risk factor based on earlier data was 4.63; 7+ is our estimate.

9 Our identifications of current geno/politicides differ from those in data prepared for the Political Instability Task Force. They do not treat the ongoing Syrian conflict as genocidal; we regard it as the site of two ongoing events: a politicide by the Assad regime against its opponents, and a genocide by ISIS against heretical minorities. We also characterize Sudan as the perpetrator of ongoing genocides against the peoples of Darfur and Nuba. The CAR conflict was not genocidal in our view; rather, it was a communal war between Muslim and Christian militias without any intent or direction by a regime or revolutionary authority. We also do not code conflict in Iraq as a geno/politicide, since it comprises mainly terror campaigns by ISIS and Sunni militants targeting the government and Iraqi Shi'a civilians. Because of these differences in categorization, we calculate and report here risks and the contributing variables for all these countries (except Iraq, whose risk score of 0.11 is far below the threshold used in the accompanying table).

References

Goldsmith, B. et al. (2013) "Forecasting the Onset of Genocide and Politicide: Annual Out-of-Sample Forecasts on a Global Dataset, 1988–2003". *Journal of Peace Research*, 50(4), 437–452.

Harff, B. (2001) "Could Humanitarian Crises Have Been Anticipated in Burundi, Rwanda, and Zaire? A Comparative Study of Anticipatory Indicators". In H. R. Alker, T. R. Gurr, and K. Rupesinghe, eds. *Journeys Through Conflict: Narratives and Lessons*. Lanham, MD: Rowman & Littlefield, 81–102.

Harff, B. (2003) "No Lessons Learned from the Holocaust? Assessing Risks of Genocide and Political Mass Murder since 1955". *American Political Science Review*, 97(1), 57–73.

Harff, B. (2016) "Detection: The History and Politics of Early Warning". In A. Lupel and E. Verdeja, eds. *Responding to Genocide: The Politics of International Action*. Boulder, CO: Lynne Reinner, 85–110.

Harff, B. and T. R. Gurr (1988) "Systematic Early Warning of Humanitarian Emergencies". *Journal of Peace Research*, 35, 552–579.

Jones, A. (2011) *Genocide: A Comprehensive Introduction, 2nd. edition*. London and New York: Routledge.

Waller, J. (2016) *Confronting Evil: Engaging Our Responsibility to Confront Genocide*. Oxford and New York: Oxford University Press.

Wayman, F. and A. Tago (2010) "Explaining the Onset of Mass Killing, 1949–87". *Journal of Peace Research*, 47(1), 3–13.

4

ATROCITY CRIMES AS A DISEASE

A statistical approach to early detection[1]

Birger Heldt

1. Introduction

One conservative estimate puts the number of civilian fatalities in intra-state armed conflicts over the period 1989–2015 at around 828,000, which includes the 1994 genocide of Tutsis in Rwanda, estimated conservatively at 500,000 fatalities.[2] Another estimated 305,000 fatalities were recorded as of "unknown status" in terms of being civilians, rebels, or government personnel. The same source conservatively estimates the number of deliberate killings of civilians – as opposed to collateral damage fatalities – in armed conflicts as close to 772,000, including the Rwanda genocide but also interstate conflicts that are linked to fewer than 5,000 civilian fatalities. Removing the 500,000 victims of the Rwanda Genocide, as well as the civilian fatalities linked to interstate conflicts, leaves approximately 323,000 civilian fatalities in intrastate conflicts, of which 267,000 were intentionally killed by rebels (181,000, or 69%) and by governments (82,000, or 31%).

Not counting the 1994 genocide in Rwanda, these estimates show that civilian killings in the context of civil wars are more than 80% intentional killings instead of "collateral damage", and that rebel groups were responsible for around two-thirds of the intentional killings. Whereas genocidal killings are intentional as well as systemic, intentional killings of civilians are not necessarily systematic. The latter occur when civilians are killed not as a consequence of a policy or a strategy, but foremost because of lack of discipline and decisions of individual combatants. In line with common vocabulary (e.g., Verdeja 2012), instances of genocides and intentional killings of civilians – whether systematic or not – are labeled "atrocity crimes" throughout this chapter.

Risk models and early warning models are bricks in the international atrocity crime prevention architecture. This chapter proposes an additional brick to that architecture. As a complement to risk models and early warning models, and sharing basic features with standard approaches and concepts in epidemiology and early detection mechanisms for disease outbreaks, this chapter outlines and applies in an illustrative manner a disease-oriented approach to the *early detection* of *systematic* atrocity crimes. The approach involves detecting whether civilian fatalities are unsystematic, in that they are randomly distributed across time or space – and thus statistically independent events though still possibly intentional – or whether civilian fatalities are non-random and interdependent events, and thus likely systematic.

The early detection approach outlined in this chapter can serve two functions. First, and as the name suggests, it is forward-looking or prospective in that it can identify systematic atrocity crimes in their early phases, and thus constitutes a de facto early warning mechanism, not only for genocides, but also for systematic atrocity crimes that are not genocidal in intent. Second, it may also be applied in a backward-looking or retrospective manner in terms of forensic analysis of past civilian fatalities to establish the extent to which the fatalities were not just intentional but also potentially systematic. In the latter capacity, it can complement other pieces of information – such as witness accounts or documentary evidence – used to assess the intentionality of killings of civilians.

Section 2 summarizes the current state of risk assessment and early warning of atrocity crimes. Section 3 briefly describes the basic approach to early detection as practiced by the disease surveillance community. The basic elements and principles of the suggested data analysis are presented in non-technical manner in Section 4, whereas Section 5 illustrates the approach by applying it to an emerging case of genocide and atrocity crime: Darfur in 2003–2004. The final and concluding section discusses the need to analyze extensions and complications of employing statistical approaches, and highlights the need for a thorough analysis of key concepts that may assist in more precisely specifying what to look for in data. This may assist in developing criteria for the statistical detection of atrocity crimes.

2. Risk assessments and early warning of atrocity crimes

Risk models of atrocity crimes – whether systematic or not – address the question of *where* outbreaks may take place, and focus on often slow-moving structural risk factors, such as regime type and level of economic development. In contrast, early warning models of atrocity crimes address the question of *when* atrocity crimes may break out, and focus on immediate or proximate causes in terms of fast-moving factors or triggers.[3] Risk models and early warning models are ideally used in a complementary manner, as they serve different functions. First, risk models are used to identify countries at risk that may then be placed on a "watch list". Second, early warning analysis homes in on when an outbreak may be imminent in the countries at risk.[4]

After the pathbreaking statistical study by Harff (2003), and to varying degrees related to Harff's statistical model, the number of published cross-national statistical studies attempting to predict the onset, occurrence, duration, or magnitude of genocides and politicides has grown, and this applies also to the number of statistical studies attempting to predict the occurrence and magnitude of mass killings (with or without genocidal intent, and whether systematic or not).[5] These studies constitute de facto risk assessments, as they focus almost exclusively on slow-moving factors.[6] There are meanwhile as yet no statistical studies that focus on triggers to predict the onset of genocides and mass killings, i.e., de facto early warning. A possible reason for this asymmetry is that historical data on slow-moving risk factors are easier to collect than data on fast-moving events and triggers, which in turn hampers the development of statistical risk models[7].

In contrast to the mentioned retrospective statistical studies, three projects generate public country-by-country risk forecasts on the basis of statistical models that have been validated by historical data. Barbara Harff and Ted Robert Gurr provide an annually updated list of a subset of countries predicted to be most at risk for genocides and politicides, whereas the Atrocity Forecasting Project at the University of Sydney provides countrywide multi-year forecasts.[8] Another forecasting initiative is the Early Warning Project at the U.S. Holocaust Memorial Museum that provides global risk assessments for all countries of the world and covers the broader category of mass atrocities, whether genocidal or not.[9]

One difference among these three projects is that, whereas the two former ones provide forecasts solely on the basis of statistical models trained on historical data, the latter approach complements forecasts from a statistical model with input from an expert opinion pool. Another difference is that the Atrocity Forecasting Project includes not only slow-moving risk factors, but also fast-moving potential triggers, such as election periods and political assassinations. As such, it is a risk assessment–early warning hybrid forecast model, and thus serves to illustrate Verdeja's (2016) observation of no "hard line" between risk assessment and early warning of atrocity crimes. These and other difference aside, as the three projects rely on broadly similar explanatory models, despite differences in how data are analyzed, they generate risk lists that overlap to a considerable extent, even though the relative risk rankings of individual countries may differ.

As outlined by Harff (2009), it is still the case in 2017 that, in contrast to these risk forecasts, purely statistical genocide/politicide early warning forecasts based on empirically validated statistical models, reliant on triggers/events alone, and providing numerical and replicable early warning assessments do not exist. The core reason is the absence of empirically validated statistical models on the subject matter. As a consequence, the genocide prevention community is currently better equipped for forecasting *where* rather than *when* state-led genocides, politicides, or mass killings may break out. Early warning is instead currently a practice based on analytical frameworks and expert judgements. For instance, the *Framework of Analysis for Atrocity Crimes* of the United Nations Office of the Special Advisor on the Prevention of Genocide Crimes lists 143 underlying and proximate factors to assess the risk of genocide, crimes against humanity, and war crimes.[10] In practice, illustrating Verdeja's (2016) observation of no "hard line" between risk assessment and early warning of atrocity crimes, the *Framework* combines fast-moving early warning factors with slow-moving risk factors, and appears to cover not just states but also nonstate actors as potential perpetrators. It meanwhile poses a daunting task for any analyst, as it requires the simultaneous assessments of 143 factors, or moving parts.

Current risk assessment models and forecasting projects, as well as early warning analysis of atrocity crimes, display some limitations. First, only a couple of statistical studies have assessed the risk of mass killings by rebel groups and other nonstate actors, despite the fact that targeting of civilians by rebel groups is common, as noted in the introduction to this chapter. Second, as pointed out by Ulfelder (2012), since genocides and politicides are – thankfully – relatively rare events, the empirical basis for developing accurate models of genocide onset is constrained: there are relatively few cases from which we can learn with confidence, and on which we can "train" statistical risk and early warning models. That is, the fewer the cases, the less the data, and by extension the less certain the conclusions from statistical studies. This observation raises, in turn, the question of how much more accurate statistical genocide/politicide risk assessment models and forecasts – and future genocide early warning models and forecasts – can become: even if methods, theories, and models become more refined, and the trigger data challenge for early warning models is addressed, the inherent challenge of predicting the onset of rare events will remain.

The larger number of instances of atrocity crimes – whether systematic or not – that are not genocidal or politicidal in intent means that predictive models that focus on this sub-category should in theory be able to attain a higher predictive accuracy than models that focus on the less-common genocides and politicides. However, whereas genocides and politicides may conceptually be regarded as processes with a distinct and discernible onset, the same does not apply to non-genocidal/-politicidal atrocity crimes. For instance, does 100, 1,000, or 10,000 civilians intentionally killed indicate that a larger amount of atrocity crime is to follow, and within what time period? This suggests that statistical models that focus on the onset of non-genocidal/-politicidal atrocity crimes face conceptual challenges.

Third, analytical early warning frameworks are labor-intensive as they contain many moving parts. Moreover, since they rely on expert judgements, they are also not systematized and replicable like the three aforementioned risk assessments, and they do not generate numerically precise, replicable, and empirically validated early warning forecasts. As such, they do not live up to standard early warning model criteria in terms of providing "timely, accurate, valid, reliable and verifiable" warnings (Verdeja 2016: 14).

This state of affairs raises the question of whether there exists a complementary approach to current early warning approaches that (1) sidesteps data challenges as well as the time-consuming and costly process of developing empirically validated early warning models, (2) avoids the labor intensiveness, non-replicability, and accuracy issues of analytical frameworks, (3) can cover state and non-state actors as perpetrators, (4) focuses on *systematic* atrocity crimes, (5) is simple and relies on standardized and well-known statistical diagnostics that do not require extensive statistical expertise, and (6) generates timely, replicable, and precise numerical scores.

44 Birger Heldt

One approach that meets these requirements focuses on early detection. In practice, the approach involves reconceptualizing atrocity crimes as a disease, and adapting standard tools from the disease surveillance community to the particularities of *systematic* atrocity crimes. Moreover, in contrast to possible future early warning models that will attempt to statistically forecast the timing of outbreaks by analyzing a series of key trigger variables, and early warning frameworks that may contain more than 100 variables, the systematic atrocity crime detection approach to be presented turns previous early warning analysis on its head by not including any predictor variables, and by using only a single moving part or variable: civilian fatality data.

3. Early detection in epidemiology

The complexity of the early detection of disease outbreaks is indicated by the multitude of data analysis techniques that have been developed and refined over the past 20 years (see Unkel et al. 2012). While employing different techniques, the shared goal is to detect statistically unusual or conspicuous clusters of disease cases in time or in space. As expressed by Wong et al. (2005), "The basic question asked by all detection systems is whether anything strange has occurred in recent events". By "strange" is meant that event rates are statistically unusual or unlikely in that they are beyond a certain threshold, whether in time, space, or both. Related to this is the concept of "clusters" that refers to "aggregations of relatively uncommon events or diseases in space and/or time in amounts that are believed or perceived to be greater than could be expected by chance" (Porta 2014). Similar to the early warning criteria cited by Verdeja (2016), disease surveillance systems are typically judged on a number of criteria, including sensitivity (proportion of accurate predictions of "onset", or true positives), specificity (proportion of accurate predictions of "no onset", or true negatives), timeliness, validity, and simplicity (Center for Disease Control 2007).

Automated disease surveillance systems depart from a baseline, continuously add data, and strive to detect whether the added data deviate too much from the baseline – that is, whether "anything strange" has occurred. Epidemiologists rely on a historically established normal incidence rate as the baseline, against which observed incidence rates are statistically assessed as normal or deviant, given some pre-established threshold beyond the baseline. An incidence rate over a certain period of time that exceeds a certain threshold *may* indicate that an outbreak is imminent. Some diseases have non-stationary rates that vary across time, and this means that the baseline varies across time. For instance, the normal or baseline rate of influenza infections varies across years. The wide applicability of this general approach for identifying anomalies is demonstrated by its application to a series of other non-disease related phenomena, including early detection of terrorism wave outbreaks and clustering of car crashes (Gao et al. 2013; Sparks , Okugami, and Bolt 2012). Since so-called count data are studied, reliance on the Poisson distribution is at the core of disease surveillance systems.

Typically, surveillance systems generate an "alarm" when observed rates deviate too much from the baseline, after which experts assess whether the alarm may be due to data and/or model errors (false alarm), whether the observed deviation may have natural explanations such as seasonality of data (false alarm), or whether a disease outbreak may be imminent (true alarm) (see, for example, Hulth et al. 2010). Surveillance system alarms are thus not accepted at face value, and are only acted upon after further expert assessments. Thus, the early warning systems are in practice regarded as, and used as a decision support for, experts. It may in this connection be noted that the Early Warning Project at the U.S. Holocaust Memorial Museum adheres to this principle in that it applies expert assessments to the country-specific statistical risk forecasts before the final risk assessment is issued. Meanwhile, expert assessments of the forecasts generated by Harff and Gurr, and the Atrocity Forecasting Project, are in practice left to potential end users of the forecasts.

Whereas epidemiology early detection approaches focus on deviations from a normal incidence rate, such a volume- or rate-centered approach is difficult to apply to the early detection of *systematic* atrocity crimes in civil conflicts. First, there are no "normal" or "natural" rates or volumes of civilian fatalities that can be used as baselines. Second, the goal is to detect outbreaks (forecasting) or the past occurrence (forensic analysis) of *systematic* atrocity crimes, not whether a systematic atrocity crime is ahistorically large, or whether atrocity crimes in general are taking place.

As will be developed in the next section of this chapter, instead of focusing on volumes of killings, an alternative early detection approach focuses on the pattern of killings. Such an approach has a number of benefits. First, it requires only minute amounts of data. Second, it is easy to apply, and the numerical findings are easily replicable. Third, it does not require an understanding of the causes or drivers of genocides and other atrocity crimes. Hence, there is no need for a costly and time-consuming development of causal models. Fourth, since the focus is not on the volume of violence but its distribution, systematic atrocity crimes can be detected in their early stages (forecasts) when data and other circumstantial evidence – such as documents or witness accounts – are limited and the violence is at a low level. Early detection can thus serve an early warning function. Fifth, it only requires one piece of data – fatality data – and there is no need for "big data". Finally, the approach is related to tried and tested approaches within epidemiology and disease outbreak surveillance systems. The latter means also that the further development of the approach may gain traction from already-existing disease surveillance detection practices and concepts.

4. Randomness in count data

The distribution of count data, such as the number of persons killed in war for a given temporal and/or spatial unit, may be in line with the Poisson distribution in which the variance is in theory equal to the mean (King 1989a, 1989b). This distribution is based on two core assumptions (*ibid.*): independence, in that events are independent of one another, and homogeneity, in that the rate of occurrence of an event is in theory constant across time. Translated to violence against civilians, the former assumption means that civilian fatality events are independent of one another across time or space, in that they are isolated – but still possibly common – events. That is, the violence is not systematic. The latter assumption means that the

46 Birger Heldt

underlying risk of civilian fatality events is constant across time or space, and means in practice that there is no so-called seasonality in the data.

The distribution of events may in reality be characterized by so-called under-dispersion or over-dispersion, which indicate either non-randomness in terms of events not occurring independently of one another other (*ibid.*), or seasonality in the data. The latter means that the assumption of an underlying constant probability of an event across time is violated. Under-dispersion means that the variance of the data is smaller than the mean, resulting in a pointier probability distribution; over-dispersion means that the variance is larger than the mean, resulting in a flatter probability distribution. In turn, over-dispersion may indicate positive contagion; that is, violence begets violence, in that violence occurs in clusters and is somehow linked rather than consisting of isolated events (*ibid.*; Richardson 1944). Meanwhile, under-dispersion may indicate negative contagion (e.g., violence begets non-violence) (*ibid.*). Again, these interpretations apply provided that the homogeneity assumption holds, in that there is no material seasonality in the data.

Incidentally, perhaps the earliest scientific study of war relied on the Poisson distribution, in this case to examine whether war onset was a random process (Levy 1982, Mansfield 1988, Richardson 1944). Richardson (1944) reported that the observed distribution of war onset from the year 1500 to 1931 did not deviate from the predictions of the Poisson distribution, thereby indicating that war onset during one time period was not contingent on war onset during the previous time period, but instead random: war onsets did not show clustering across time. Thus, a war diffusion process was not evident. Richardson's finding does not mean that war onset cannot be predicted, but only that onsets of individual wars were overall independent of one another: they were isolated events.

A study often cited in statistics textbooks or university statistics courses as a classical case and illustration of an application of the Poisson distribution is Clarke's (1946) famous single-page study that examined whether German V1 and V2 flying bombs fell in clusters over London, and thus hit London in a non-random manner.[11] Clarke's study focused on south London, which he divided into 576 squares measuring 500 meters. Clarke reported that 299 squares were not hit at all, that 211 squares were hit once, 93 squares were hit twice, 35 squares were hit three times, 7 squares were hit 4 times, and 1 square was hit 5 or more times. As it turned out, the observed number of hits per square was perfectly in line with the number predicted by the Poisson distribution.[12] As the observed numbers did not deviate from the Poisson-predicted numbers, the findings meant that the bomb hits were randomly distributed across the 579 squares, and did not fall in non-random clusters. Clarke's original table is reproduced as Table 1 below.

5. Early detection of systematic atrocity crimes in civil conflicts

As suggested by numerous scholars, and as follows from the definition of genocide in terms of being intentional, *systematic*, coordinated, and sustained, genocides should reveal themselves in the patterns of killings. To borrow from, among others,

TABLE 4.1 Distributions of German V1 and V2 bombs hitting south London

No. of flying bombs per square	Expected no. of squares (Poisson)	Actual no. of squares
0	226.74	229
1	211.39	211
2	98.54	93
3	30.62	35
4	7.14	7
5 and over	1.57	1
Sum	576	576

Source: Clarke (1946)

Rosenberg (2012), genocide is a process, not an event. Consistent with this conceptualization, Park (2011) discusses four direct and circumstantial pieces of evidence that can be applied on any of the five dimensions of the Genocide Convention to assess intent: statements indicating genocidal intent; the scale of the atrocities committed; *systematic* targeting of the protected group; and evidence suggesting that the acts were consciously planned. Related to this, Verdeja (2012) focuses on circumstantial evidence, and divides behavior into three dimensions that lend themselves to further analysis: level of lethality; degree of coordination (how *systematic*, coordinated, and sustained does lethal violence appear to be, such as the use of similar destructive tactics in a wide area); and scope (the extent to which coordinated lethal violence was applied against all or a substantial part of a victim group).[13]

Rwanda 1993 constitutes an illustrative example of the approach of assessing whether violence against Tutsis was systematic. The genocide in 1994 was preceded by violence against Tutsi civilians during 1991–1993. The exhibition at the Genocide Memorial Museum in Kigali describes it as a government dress rehearsal, as well as an attempt to assess the reaction of the international community to a planned mass killing of Tutsi civilians. A UN inquiry into human rights violations was launched and issued its report in April 1993 (United Nations 1993). According to team leader Mr. Bacre Waly Ndiaye, UN Special Rapporteur on the Commission on Human Rights, the team looked into the location and timing of violence, and found among other things that violence was located along major roads, and often preceded by local electricity blackouts.[14] Based on data covering October 1990 until December 1992, the team concluded that this pattern of seemingly interdependent events meant that the violence was not random, but systematic and co-ordinated.

The above insights on the systematic character of genocidal violence applies to the intentional killings of civilians that may not be genocidal or politicidal in intent but are still *systematic* instead of a consequence of random acts by government soldiers or rebels: if killings are systematic, then the pattern should be different as compared to when the killings are not systematic or random, though still potentially intentional. Speaking more broadly of systematic atrocity crimes instead of only genocides and politicides, and thinking in statistical terms: if they are systematic rather than essentially random – whether intentional or not – civilian killings, then the distribution of civilians killed across time and/or space should not evince randomness. This means in turn that the distribution – rather than the volume – of fatalities becomes of interest for assessments of whether systematic atrocity crimes have taken place.

The goal then becomes to detect whether killings are non-random and thus form a pattern or process of interdependent or clustered fatalities, rather than random (that is, non-organized) isolated fatalities that would be the case if decisions to kill civilians are taken by individuals without any co-ordination with one another. Similar to the approaches used by, e.g., Clarke (1946), Richardson (1944), and, for many years, in standard diagnostic tests of different types of count data, a basic formal test of whether fatalities are non-random is whether the distribution of fatalities across time and/or space deviates from the Poisson distribution in terms of showing over-dispersion. Over-dispersion indicates in turn that fatalities are not isolated occurrences, but instead interdependent and non-random. This means that a certain probability distribution (Poisson) rather than historical volumes of fatalities is used as baseline. A routine statistical package diagnostic procedure to assess whether an observed count data distribution adheres to the Poisson distribution involves a Pearson Chi-Square goodness-of-fit test that compares expected (Poisson) rates with rates across all observations, and assesses whether the fit is "good": if the observed data deviate too much from the Poisson predicted data, then it may be concluded that observed data are not randomly distributed.

For illustrative purposes, this early detection data analysis approach is applied in a forensic manner on the genocide in Darfur. The analysis is confined to July 2003 until December 2004, when evidence of a systematic character of atrocities against civilians was mounting but still contested in some quarters. The purpose of the application is to illustrate the early detection approach and demonstrate insights that can be gained from analyzing only fatality data. The purpose is not to enter into a debate on fatality figures.[15] Whereas the application is retrospective and thus forensic in nature, it could be used in a prospective manner by applying it to real-time data from ongoing conflicts to provide for real-time early detection and, in effect, early warning of systematic atrocity crimes. For instance, analysis could be carried out on continuously updated weekly, bi-weekly, or monthly data.

In June and July 2004, the United States carried out an investigation of the violence in Darfur through the Atrocities Documentation Project (ADP), the purpose of which was to assess whether genocide had been and/or continued to be carried out in Darfur (Totten 2006). During July and August 2004, the project collected interview data that covered the period from late 2003 until August 2004. In September 2004, and "based on a consistent and widespread pattern of atrocities (killings, rapes, the burning of villages) committed by the Janjaweed and government forces against non-Arab villagers", the United States Secretary of State Colin Powell declared that genocide had taken place in Darfur (*ibid.*). Similarly, in late 2004, the UN launched a Commission to "investigate reports of violations of

A statistical approach to early detection **49**

human rights law and international humanitarian law" in Darfur, with a report issued in January 2005. But in contrast to the declaration of Secretary of State Colin Powell, and while the Commission reported that serious human rights violations had taken place and was "alarmed" by "attacks on villages, killing of civilians, rape, pillaging and forced displacement", it did not consider that a genocide had taken place:

> [...] the crucial element of genocidal intent appears to be missing, at least as far as the central Government authorities are concerned. Generally speaking the policy of attacking, killing and forcibly displacing members of some tribes does not evince a specific intent to annihilate, in whole or in part, a group distinguished on racial, ethnic, national or religious grounds. Rather, it would seem that those who planned and organized attacks on villages pursued the intent to drive the victims from their homes, primarily for purposes of counter-insurgency warfare.
>
> *(United Nations 2005: 3)*

The question is whether the outlined statistical early detection approach for systematic atrocity crimes generates findings that corroborate the ADT's conclusions, or the UN report's conclusions. In this particular case, the outlined approach for assessing data could have been used as part of the UN's as well as the ADT's effort to analyze fatality data. For the analysis, the Darfur civilian fatality data can be arranged spatially with regard to some geographical grid system, or in accordance with, e.g., "natural" geographic areas.[16] In this case, civilian fatality data are arranged temporally, across time, and the analysis examines fatality patterns for the entire Darfur region.

The analysis covers a long period, 18 months, which entails risks of variations in fatalities as caused by seasonality – here with regard to effects of weather patterns in terms of the rainy season from June to September that may reduce the mobility of government troops and the Janjaweed in Darfur. Seasonality may in turn undermine the analysis and provide for faulty conclusions, as it would violate the theoretical assumption of an underlying constant probability of violent events across time. Hence, any observed over-dispersion in the Darfur fatality data could be due to systematic violence, but could also in whole or in part be due to seasonality in the data. Another factor that may possibly influence the fatality data is the ceasefire agreement of April 2004 and the deployment of the African Union Mission to Sudan (AMIS) in July 2004, which by October consisted of 465 personnel and by January 2005 of around 1,300 personnel (Human Rights Watch 2006). While this long period is selected to align broadly the analysis with the period covered by the UN report and the ADP project, the issue of potential seasonality will be returned to in the data analysis.

Over the period of July 2003–December 2004, the number of civilians in Darfur killed by the government or the Janjaweed is estimated at around 4,696.[17] For the analysis, data are arranged in half-month periods, generating 36 half-monthly observations, which entails an average of 130.4 civilian fatalities per half-month period.[18] In the graph in Figure 4.1, it is difficult to discern any obvious within-year seasonality in the data as being due to the rainy season. In 2003, civilian fatalities are high in July and August, which is the larger part of the rainy season, and the number of civilian fatalities in September (last month of the rainy season) are not materially different from the number of fatalities in October or November. In 2004, fatalities are actually higher during the rainy season than during many other months of the year. To the extent that seasonality exists in the data, it is difficult to link it to the rainy season. Finally, fatality levels for 2004 are lower than in 2003, but it is difficult to discern any straightforward link to the deployment as well as enlargement of AMIS. This issue of potential seasonality will be returned to in the analysis.

A visual inspection of the graph in Figure 4.1 does not yield any obvious conclusions as to whether civilian killings are systematic or random, even though the fatality figures are high. To compare whether expected (Poisson) – or baseline – and observed fatality counts are different, and thus whether civilian fatalities may form a systematic pattern, the data are categorized into segments of 25 persons killed per half-month period. Table 4.2 includes the observed distribution across these segments together with the random distribution predicted by the Poisson distribution.

It is clear from data in the table, which is also illustrated in Figure 4.2, that the observed pattern is inconsistent with the Poisson predicted (random) pattern or baseline. The fit between the observed and predicted distributions is not good. Moreover, the variance of the observed distribution is much larger than expected, which means in this case that extreme over-dispersion is evident. Given a half-monthly average of 130.4 civilian fatalities, the Poisson distribution predicts that virtually all half-monthly civilian fatality rates should fall between 100 and 150: if events are isolated and thus independent of one another, and given that the underlying risk of civilian fatalities is constant across

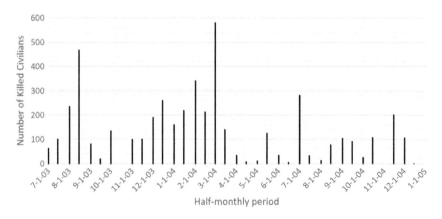

FIGURE 4.1 Civilian conflict-related fatalities in Darfur, July 2003–December 2004

TABLE 4.2 Predicted versus observed number of half-monthly periods for a certain number of fatalities, Darfur July 2003–December 2004

Half-monthly number of civilian fatalities	Predicted (Poisson) number of half-monthly periods	Observed number of half-monthly periods
0–24	0,0	8
25–49	0,0	4
50–74	0,0	1
75–99	0,1	3
100–124	10,9	6
125–149	23,2	3
150–174	1,8	1
175–199	0,0	1
200–224	0,0	3
225–249	0,0	1
250–274	0,0	1
275–299	0,0	1
300–324	0,0	0
325–349	0,0	1
350–374	0,0	0
375–399	0,0	0
400–	0,0	2

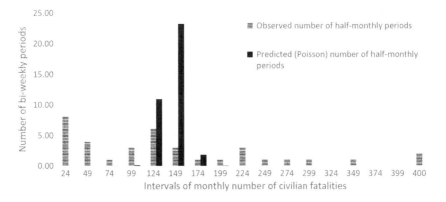

FIGURE 4.2 Predicted versus observed number of half-monthly periods for a certain number of civilian fatalities, Darfur July 2003–December 2004

time, there should ideally not exist half-monthly periods with lower fatality rates, and only one period with a higher fatality rate. However, the observed pattern is very different: there are nine half-monthly periods with the expected number of fatalities, and the remaining periods are distributed across the entire X-axis.

52 Birger Heldt

Applying the standard Pearson Chi-square goodness-of-fit test to assess whether the observed data are Poisson-distributed – that is, whether the observed data fit the predicted data – generates a probability of less than 1 in 1,000,000 that the observed data are drawn from the Poisson distribution. This means that the observed fatality data are not randomly distributed, and, in turn, claims that the civilian fatalities were overall random and isolated instances instead of overall systematic can be rejected with a high degree of certainty. This conclusion applies given that the underlying risk of civilian fatalities is constant across time – that is, there is no material underlying seasonality in the data.

In this case, seasonality may be at hand because of at least two conspicuous factors: the rain period, and the AMIS operation. To reduce the risk for seasonality to undermine inferences, the length of the analysed period was shortened to include only 2004, but the results were the same. The analysis was also rerun after aggregating the data into 18 monthly observations, but the result was the same. Finally, the analysed period was limited to after the 2003 rain period, and up to the ceasefire agreement in April 2004, but the findings were the same: the observed data was heavily over-dispersed, and it deviated from the Poisson predicted observations.

While these results do not prove intent to commit genocide, they constitute strong circumstantial evidence that refutes the UN report's claim that violence against civilians was caused *"primarily" by "counter-insurgency warfare"* and thus did not consist of systematic or inter-connected events. Had the UN report's conclusions been valid, then the observed data of fatalities across time would have been similar to the data predicted by the Poisson distribution. The results meanwhile are supportive of – but strictly speaking do not prove – the United States Secretary of State Colin Powell's claim that a genocide had taken place, although they show beyond reasonable doubt that systematic atrocity crimes had indeed been carried out.

6. Conclusions and the way forward

The outlined approach that focuses on *whether* instead of *where* and *when* involves a narrow and simple task, yet one that is complementary to current early warning and risk assessment methods. This illustrative application may be seen as a first step towards assessing strengths and limitations of the approach that may serve retrospective atrocity crime forensic purposes, as well as prospective atrocity crime early detection purposes. An analysis of data patterns is useful in conjunction with other pieces of direct and indirect evidence (statements, orders, surveys, witness accounts, anecdotes, intelligence, etc.) that in some cases exist in abundance for past as well as ongoing atrocity crimes. The approach can also, for instance, be applied to incident data for attacks of civilians (e.g., destruction of villages), even when the number of civilians killed is unknown. In short, it can be applied to any of the Genocide Convention's dimensions to assess systematic intent, which in conjunction with other pieces of information offers a clearer picture of the character of events. There is thus no inherent need to focus statistical analysis on fatality data alone to unearth systematic features of atrocity crimes. The approach can also be applied to other conflict-related issues, such as to assess whether ceasefire violations in inter- or intra-state conflicts are isolated, accidental, and local events, or whether the events appear to be inter-connected and systematic.

Sometimes, only incident data are available, especially in emerging cases of atrocity crimes. In such emerging cases, this data-driven approach may constitute the only analysis tool available. As stressed earlier, non-randomness of fatality data does not prove intent or genocide, but it does reject claims that patterns of killings are random or accidental as caused by, e.g., crossfire. This, in and by itself, is a useful piece of information, and may in individual cases assist in inducing action by the international community to halt violence, but also to more carefully monitor and collect data on specific cases. Nevertheless, the confounding effects of potential seasonality of data, as well as data quality, need to be carefully considered when carrying out analysis of this type. Hence, as for disease surveillance systems, careful expert assessments of data are crucial to assesses whether and to what extent findings may have been influenced by faulty data, seasonality, or other error sources. That is, the outlined early detection approach should be regarded as a decision support tool.

One feature of the outlined approach is that, in a strict sense, it is not early warning or forecasting, but rather "nowcasting", which means "predicting the present" (Tetlock 2010). Nowcasting is a feature shared with disease surveillance systems that in practice detect outbreaks once they have taken place. However, if systematic atrocity crimes are identified at an early stage, there is still room and time for early action, since historically – with the exception of Rwanda in 1994 – genocides and other systematic atrocity crimes typically develop slowly. Moreover, since the outlined early detection approach builds on actual data and involves nowcasting rather than predictions of atrocity crimes, the findings cannot be dismissed as predictions that may be inaccurate, for the simple reason that the underlying predictive model has insufficient precision and a non-perfect track record.

Another feature is that since the approach does not entail assumptions on triggers or causes – or the *whys* – but only an analysis of fatality data in terms of *whether*, the approach does not offer guidance to the international community on how to prevent, or how to manage, atrocity crimes. A focus on detection sidesteps these important questions. A third feature is that the approach sidesteps the controversial issue of the magnitude of atrocity crimes by examining only one moving part – the pattern of violence – and this means in turn that only very limited amounts of data are required for meaningful analysis. Yet another feature is that the approach is easy to apply, consistent, replicable, and assists in detecting patterns that escape the human eye. As such, the approach appears to be well-aligned with the previously mentioned early warning model criteria in terms of providing "timely, accurate, valid, reliable and verifiable" warnings.

The outlined early detection approach relies on a widely applied and understood statistical distribution and shares features with standard disease surveillance systems. Because of the minimal data requirements, it is a low-cost approach that can in theory be automated in terms of prospective early detection surveillance systems of systematic atrocity crimes at regional or sub-regional levels and rely on real-time and continuously updated fatality data. Such systems could resemble current government-run disease surveillance early warning systems, by adding a layer of expert analysis to assess the veracity of any warnings generated. In that regard, and even though the focus is on fatality distributions instead of fatality volumes, surveillance system templates and lessons learned from the disease surveillance community can be consulted for further technical guidance.

If potential perpetrators are aware of the ability to easily detect systematic patterns of atrocities against civilians, the launch of countrywide early detection systems for countries at risk of genocides or involved in intrastate armed conflicts may serve as a powerful deterrent and restraint against systematic violence against civilians. However, in theory and in a rather far-fetched scenario, a perpetrator of atrocities may then try to be "smart", in that it understands the Poisson distribution and attempts to generate civilian fatalities in a seemingly random pattern across time or space so that the systematic pattern cannot be detected. In practice, such attempts to simulate randomness would require a huge amount of planning, coordination, and communication, which would not only be very difficult or impossible in practice in an organizational context, but also leave other forensic traces behind, such as orders, communication, documents, eyewitness accounts, and so on. It is thus virtually impossible for perpetrators to circumvent a detection system of the outlined character.

Moving from prospective or early detection usage, to retrospective or forensic usage on past instances of atrocity crimes, in some cases there may not exist any other reasonable conclusion from a data analysis than that non-randomness does indeed signal genocide or systematic killings. Whether, as suggested by some scholars, such circumstantial evidence is admissible in court is another question. Yet, given the strength of the outlined method and the few assumptions it entails, there is little reason why a statistical analysis of patterns of killings could not be used in conjunction with other pieces of evidence. Materially, the probabilities and thus indirect evidence obtained from the illustrated analysis of fatality data shares features with probabilities and indirect evidence obtained from DNA analyses of crime scenes, and the latter piece of evidence is admissible in courts.

This chapter has scratched the surface of the complexities of inferring intent and the potential of using detection statistics for such purposes. More research and method development in this direction may be fruitful to identify extensions, limitations, and avenues for further applications of early detection approaches. For instance, potential statistical implications in terms of non-stationary of the underlying risk – as due to, e.g., seasonality in data – for atrocity crimes need to be further considered. However, such concerns can in practice be reduced in forward-looking or prospective analysis if the continuously updated time-periods of interest are short, and also for retrospective or forensic analysis, again if the time-periods are short.

On a final note, the way forward is not confined only to questions of method, as there is also a need for greater clarity of key concepts such as "intent" and "genocide", and how they may manifest themselves in terms of observables. Such an

A statistical approach to early detection **55**

analysis and development of key concepts may assist in more precisely determining what to look for in data patterns, and thus assist in formulating statistical criteria for falsification and rejection of claims of intent and systematic killings. It is likely that a greater interest in data patterns and analysis will spur further development and operationalization of key concepts.

Notes

1 This chapter has benefitted from comments from participants at the Genocide Prevention Advisory Group annual meeting, Israel Academy of Science and Humanities, Jerusalem, 8–10 January, 2017, the editors of this book, and James Finkel.
2 Data are from *UCDP Georeferenced Event Dataset* (GED) Global version 5.0 (2015) and *UCDP One-sided Violence Dataset* version 1.4 (2016). The data cover all countries of the world apart from the ongoing civil war in Syria, and incorporate 128,264 violent episodes of varying length, 749 of which are interstate conflicts. See also Sikkink and Kim (2013) and Kulkarni (2016) for historical data on prosecution of human rights violations, and Fjelde, Hultman, and Sollenberg (2016) for an aggregate descriptive analysis of patterns of violence against civilians in civil wars. Estimates of civilian fatalities are controversial and difficult; for discussion, see Lacina and Gleditsch (2005), Lacina, Gleditsch, and Russett (2006), Spagat et al. (2009), Human Security Report 2010 (2010), Muggah (2011) and Seybolt, Aronson, and Fischoff (2013). As noted by Muggah (2011), there is a distinction between estimates building on incident/event reports, and those building on surveys that are applied as a last resort when incident reports are unavailable. Estimates obtained through the two methods can differ greatly. For a historical overview of efforts and methods to count fatalities in wars, see Jewell, Spagat, and Jewell (2017).
3 This distinction stems from Schmeidl and Jenkins (1998) and Harff (2006, 2009, 2013). See also Butcher et al. (2012). A detailed overview of early warning mechanisms and projects in general can be found in OECD (2009), and an overview of early warning systems within the United Nations can be found in Zenko and Friedman (2011). Neukirch (2015) provides an overview of the early warning system of the Organisation for Security and Co-operation in Europe (OSCE).
4 Harff (2006, 2013), Butcher et al. (2012), and Goldsmith and Butcher (2016). Whereas "genocide" refers to sustained policies and actions intended to destroy groups that share ethnic, religious, or racial traits, "politicide" refers to situations where targeted groups are defined by actual or imagined political beliefs (Harff 2003).
5 See Anderton and Carter (2015) for a comprehensive inventory of cross-national statistical studies and findings. The study also lists, but does not analyze, country or case-specific statistical studies, the findings of which may not be applicable to other countries or cases. Forthcoming cross-national statistical studies focusing on violence against civilians include Raleigh and Choi (2017) and Pospieszna and DeRouen (2017). See also Verdeja (2016), Butcher et al. (2012), and Goldsmith et al. (2013) for overviews of previous statistical studies.
6 Examples of statistical studies that complement slow-moving risk factors with trigger type variables include, *inter alia*, Goldsmith et al. (2013) (variables for political assassination and elections), Wayman and Togo (2010) (variable for military coups), and Wood, Kathman, and Gent (2012) (variable for civilian fatalities incurred by the opposing side in a civil conflict).
7 See Heldt (2012) and Verdeja (2016).
8 See Harff and Gurr (various years) and Goldsmith and Butcher (2016).
9 See Ulfelder (2015) and www.earlywarningproject.com.
10 See Dieng and Welsh (2016) and United Nations (2014).
11 Another study that is often used to illustrate the Poisson distribution was published in 1898 and assessed whether fatalities in the Prussian cavalry caused by horse kicks were

56 Birger Heldt

random events. A simple Google search that combines "horse kick", "data", and "Poisson" will point to many instances of statistics courses at universities in which the classical horse kick study data is used to illustrate the Poisson distribution.

12 Like Richardson, Clarke carried out a standard statistical test to ascertain that the observed data distribution differed in a statistically significant way from the expected (Poisson) data distribution.

13 For detailed discussion of the Genocide Convention, see Ambos (2009), Bauer (2009), Human Rights Watch (2010), and Verdeja (2012, 2013).

14 Information provided by Mr. Ndiaye during a dinner conversation in Budapest, September 2010.

15 The application relies on Uppsala Conflict Data Project data that were originally compiled from incident reports, either directly from the reports themselves (e.g., news reports, radio reports), or indirectly from summary reports from, e.g., NGOs. Numerous reports have been published on the case of Darfur that document atrocities, offer first-hand accounts, and provide a large amount of supplemental information and evidence.

16 For instance, the PRIO GRID covers the entire world and divides it into quadratic grids of roughly 50 x 50 kilometres. See Tollefsen, Strand, and Buhaug (2012) and www.prio.no/CSCW/Datasets/PRIO-Grid/.

17 Data are from UCDP GED version 5.0, 1989–2015, and include battle-related and non-battle-related (e.g., murders and massacres) civilian fatalities. Fatality data used in this application include instances where Government of Sudan and Janjaweed were coded as "side A" and Justice and Equality Movement (JEM) or civilians were coded as "side B" in the dataset. Data for killings of civilians may have errors in terms of size, some violent events may be missing, low-level violent events may be under-reported, and the fatality estimates are conservative. Nevertheless, it is unlikely that large (conspicuous) instances of killings of civilians have been missed. Note that these figures do not include fatalities caused by disease, dislocation, starvation, lack of access to health facilities, or even fatalities caused by injuries sometime after an attack or battle, all of which together are many times higher than the direct fatalities analysed in this chapter. For estimates that take these types of fatalities into account, see Reeves (various years).

18 In a few instances violent events stretched across the half-month periods. In these few instances, the number of civilian fatalities were divided equally across the half-month periods in question.

References

Ambos, K. (2009). "What Does 'Intent to Destroy' in Genocide Mean?". *International Review of the Red Cross*, Vol. 91 (no. 876): 833–858.

Anderton, C. H. and J. R. Carter (2015). "A New Look at Weak State Conditions and Genocide Risk". *Peace Economics, Peace Science and Public Policy*, Vol. 21 (no. 1): 1–36.

Bauer, Y. (2009). "Genocide Prevention in Historical Perspective". *Politorbis*, (no. 47): 25–32.

Butcher, C. E., B. E. Goldsmith, D. Semenovich, and A. Sowmya (2012). *Understanding and Forecasting Political Instability and Genocide for Early Warning*. Sydney: University of Sydney.

Center for Disease Control (2007). Updated Guidelines for Evaluating Public Health Surveillance Systems. Available at www.cdc.gov/mmwr/preview/mmwrhtml/rr5013a1.htm.

Clarke, R. D. (1946). "An Application of the Poisson Distribution". *Journal of the Institute of Actuaries*, Vol. 4 (no. 81): 32.

Dieng, A. and J. Welsh (2016). "Assessing the Risk of Atrocity Crimes". *Genocide Studies and Prevention: An International Journal*, Vol. 9 (no. 3): 4–12.

Fjelde, H., L. Hultman, and M. Sollenberg (2016). "Violence Against Civilians in Civil Wars", pp. 42–49 in D. A. Backer, R. Bhavnani, and P. K. Huth (eds.). *Peace and Conflict 2016*. New York: Routledge.

Gao, P., D. Guo, K. Liao, J. Webb, and S. L. Cutter (2013). "Early Detection of Terrorism Outbreaks Using Prospective Space–Time Scan Statistics". *The Professional Geographer*, Vol. 65 (no. 4): 676–691.

Goldsmith, B. E. and C. Butcher (2016). New Forecasts for 2016–2020 & Evaluation of our Forecasts for 2011–2015. University of Sydney, Atrocity Forecasting Project. Available at http://sydney.edu.au/arts/research/atrocity_forecasting/downloads/docs/AFP_2016_2020.pdf.

Goldsmith, B. E., C. Butcher, D. Semenovich, and A. Sowmya (2013). "Forecasting the Onset of Genocide and Politicide: Annual Out-Of-Sample Forecasts on a Global Dataset, 1988–2003". *Journal of Peace Research*, Vol. 50 (no. 4): 437–452.

Harff, B. (2003). "No Lessons Learned from the Holocaust? Assessing Risks of Genocide and Political Mass Murder since 1955". *American Political Science Review*, Vol. 97 (no. 1): 57–73.

Harff, B. (2006). Risk Assessments and Early Warning of Genocide: Some Guidelines for the Office of the Special Adviser to the UN Secretary-General on the Prevention of Genocide. Unpublished manuscript. Available for download at www.un-ausa.org/atf/cf/%7B49C555AC-20C8-4B43-8483-A2D4C1808E4E%7D/Harff%20January%202006.pdf.

Harff, B. (2009). "How to Use Risk Assessment and Early Warning in the Prevention and De-Escalation of Genocide and Other Mass Atrocities". *Global Responsibility to Protect*, Vol. 1 (no. 4): 506–531.

Harff, B. (2013). "Detection: The History and Politics of Early Warning", pp. 85–110 in A. Lupel and E. Verdeja (eds.), *Responding to Genocide: The Politics of International Action*. Boulder, CO: Lynne Rienner.

Harff, B. and T. R. Gurr (various years). Global Risks. Available at www.gpanet.org/content/global-risks.

Heldt, B. (2012). "Mass Atrocities Early Warning Systems: Data Gathering, Data Verification and Other Challenges", pp. 13–32 in *Guiding Principles of the Emerging Architecture Aiming At the Prevention of Genocide, War Crimes, and Crimes Against Humanity*. Genocide Prevention Advisory Network Conference Report.

Hulth, A., N. Andrews, S. Ethelberg, J. Dreesman, D. Faensen, W. van Pelt, and J. Schnitzler (2010). "Practical Usage of Computer-Supported Outbreak Detection in Five European Countries". *Eurosurveillance*, Vol. 15 (no. 36): 1–6.

Human Rights Watch (2010). Genocide, War Crimes and Crimes Against Humanity: A Digest of the Case Law of the International Criminal Tribunal for Rwanda. Available at www.hrw.org/sites/default/files/reports/ictr0110webwcover.pdf.

Human Security Report Project (2010). "Shrinking Costs of War", Part II in *Human Security Report 2009*. Vancouver: HSRP.

Jewell, N., M. Spagat, and B. Jewell (2017). "Accounting for Civilian Casualties: From the Past to the Future". *Social Science History*, (March).

King, G. (1989a). "Event Count Models for International Relations: Generalizations and Applications". *International Studies Quarterly*, Vol. 33 (no. 2): 123–147.

King, G. (1989b). "Variance Specification in Event Count Models: From Restrictive Assumptions to a Generalized Estimator". *American Journal of Political Science*, Vol. 33 (no. 3): 762–784.

Kulkarni, A. (2016). "Criminal Justice for Conflict-Related Violations – Developments during 2014", pp. 192–209 in D. A. Backer, R. Bhavnani and P. K. Huth (eds.), *Peace and Conflict 2016*. New York: Routledge.

Lacina, B. and N. P. Gleditsch (2005). "Monitoring Trends in Global Combat: A New Dataset of Battle Deaths". *European Journal of Population*, Vol. 21 (no. 2–3): 145–166.

Lacina, B., N. P. Gleditsch, and B. Russett (2006). "The Declining Risk of Death in Battle". *International Studies Quarterly*, Vol. 50 (no. 3): 673–680.

Levy, J. S. (1982). "The Contagion of Great Power War Behavior, 1495–1975". *American Journal of Political Science*, Vol. 26 (no. 3): 562–584.

Mansfield, E. D. (1988). "The Distribution of Wars Over Time". *World Politics*, Vol. 41 (no. 1): 21–51.

Muggah, R. (2011). "Measuring the True Costs of War: Consensus and Controversy". *PLoS Med* Vol. 8 (no. 2): doi:1000417.

Neukirch, C. (2015). "Early Warning and Early Action – Current Developments in OSCE Conflict Prevention Activities" pp. 123–133 in *OSCE Yearbook 2013: Yearbook on the Organization for Security and Co-operation in Europe*. London: Bloomsbury Academic.

OECD (2009). *Preventing Violence, War and State Collapse: The Future of Early Warning and Response*. Paris: OECD.

Park, R. (2011). "Proving Genocidal Intent: International Precedent and ECCC Case 002". *Rutgers Law Review*, Vol. 63 (no. 1): 130–191.

Porta, M. (2014). *A Dictionary of Epidemiology* (6th Edition). Oxford: Oxford University Press.

Pospieszna, P. and K. DeRouen (2017). "Civil War Mediation and Rebel Use of Violence Against Civilians". *Armed Forces & Society*. Online first publication. DOI: doi:10.1177/0095327X16647538.

Raleigh, C. and H. J. Choi (2017). "Conflict Dynamics and Feedback: Explaining Change in Violence against Civilians with Conflicts". *International Interactions*. Online first publication. Doi: doi:10.1080/03050629.2017.1235271.

Reeves, E. (various years). Quantifying Genocide: Dafur Mortality Update. Available at www.sudanreeves.org/.

Richardson, L. F. (1944). "The Distribution of Wars in Time". *Journal of the Royal Statistical Society*, Vol. 107 (no. 3/4): 242–250.

Rosenberg, S. R. (2012). "Genocide Is a Process, Not an Event". *Genocide Studies and Prevention*, Vol. 7 (no. 1): 16–23.

Schmeidl, S. and J. C. Jenkins (1998). "The Early Warning of Humanitarian Disasters". *International Migration Review*, Vol. 32 (no. 2): 471–486.

Seybolt, T. B., J. D. Aronson, and B. Fischoff (eds.) (2013). *Counting Civilian Casualties: An Introduction to Recording and Estimating Nonmilitary Deaths in Conflict*. New York: Oxford University Press.

Sikkink, K. and H. J. Kim (2013). "The Justice Cascade: the Origins and Effectiveness of Prosecutions of Human Rights Violations". *Annual Review of Law and Social Science*, Vol. 9: 269–285.

Spagat, M., A. Mack, T. Cooper, and J. Kreutz (2009). "Estimating War Deaths: An Arena of Contestation". *Journal of Conflict Resolution*, Vol. 53 (no. 6): 934–950.

Sparks, R., C. Okugami, and S. Bolt (2012). "Outbreak Detection of Spatio-Temporally Smoothed Crashes". *Open Journal of Safety Science and Technology*, Vol. 2 (no. 3): 98–107.

Strauss, S. (2016). *Fundamentals of Genocide and Mass Atrocity Prevention*. Washington D.C.: United States Holocaust Memorial Museum.

Tetlock, P. E. (2010). "Second Thoughts About Expert Political Judgment: Reply to The Symposium". *Critical Review: A Journal of Politics and Society*, Vol. 22 (no. 4): 467–488.

Tollefsen, A. F., H. Strand, and H. Buhaug (2012). "PRIO-GRID: A Unified Spatial Data Structure". *Journal of Peace Research*, Vol. 49 (no. 2): 363–374.

Totten, S. (2006). "The US Investigation into the Darfur Crisis and the US Government's Determination of Genocide". *Genocide Studies and Prevention: An International Journal*, Vol. 1 (no. 1): 57–77.

UCDP Georeferenced Event Dataset (GED). Global version 5.0 (2015). Department of Peace and Conflict Research, Uppsala University. Available for download at http://ucdp.uu.se/downloads/.

UCDP One-sided Violence Dataset. Version 1.4 (2016). Department of Peace and Conflict Research, Uppsala University. Available for download at http://ucdp.uu.se/downloads/

Ulfelder, J. (2012). Forecasting Onsets of Mass Killing. Paper prepared for presentation at the Annual Northeast Political Methodology Meeting, a.k.a. NEMP, New York University, May 4, 2012.

Ulfelder, J. (2015). *Promising Initial Results from a New Mass-Atrocities Early Warning System.* Unpublished manuscript.

United Nations (1993). Report by Mr. B.W. Ndiaye. Special Rapporteur, on his mission to Rwanda from 8 to 17 April 1993. UN document E/CN.4/1994/7/Add.1.

United Nations (2005). *Report of the International Commission of Inquiry on Darfur to the United Nations Secretary-General.* New York: United Nations.

United Nations (2014). *Framework of Analysis for Atrocity Crimes.* New York: United Nations.

Unkel, S., F. C. Paddy, P. H. Garthwaite, C. Robertson, and N. Andrews (2012). "Statistical Methods for the Prospective Detection of Infectious Disease Outbreaks: A Review". *Journal of the Royal Statistical Society: Series A*, Vol. 175 (no. 1): 49–82.

Verdeja, E. (2012). "The Political Science of Genocide: Outlines of an Emerging Research Agenda". *Perspectives on Politics*, Vol. 10 (no. 2): 307–321.

Verdeja, E. (2013). "Genocide: Debating Definitions" pp. 21–46 in A. Lupel and E. Verdeja (eds.), *Responding to Genocide: The Politics of International Action.* Boulder, CO: Lynne Rienner.

Verdeja, E. (2016). "Predicting Genocide and Mass Atrocities". *Genocide Studies and Prevention: An International Journal*, Vol. 9 (no. 3): 13–32.

Wayman, F. W. and A. Tago (2010). "Explaining the Onset of Mass Killing, 1949–1987". *Journal of Peace Research*, Vol. 47 (no. 1): 3–13.

Wong, W-K., A. Moore, G. Cooper, and M. Wagner (2005). "What's Strange About Recent Events (WSARE): An Algorithm for the Early Detection of Disease Outbreaks". *Journal of Machine Learning Research*, Vol. 6 (Dec.): 1961–1998.

Wood, R., J. Kathman, and S. Gent (2012). "Armed Intervention and Civilian Victimization in Intrastate Conflict". *Journal of Peace Research*, Vol. 49 (no. 5): 647–660.

Zenko, M. and R. R. Friedman (2011). "UN Early Warning for Preventing Conflict". *International Peacekeeping*, Vol. 18 (no. 1): 21–37.

5

PREVENTING GENOCIDES AND MASS ATROCITIES

Evidence from conflict analysis

Ted Robert Gurr

"Genocide is a process." Adama Dieng, November 11, 2016.

Genocides and mass atrocities: How many? How different?

How different in definition, causes, and character are mass atrocities from genocides and politicides? Barbara Harff reviews their definitions and their standing in international law in Chapter 1. All refer to deliberate, large-scale killing of civilians by government agents. A commonly-used definition for mass atrocities includes genocides, war crimes, and crimes against humanity (Scheffer 2006; Rotberg 2010: 21). Genocide is more narrowly defined in the UN Genocide Convention of 1948 as "acts committed with intent to destroy, in whole or in part, a national, ethnical, racial or religious group, as such" (for a recent discussion, see Verdeja 2013). Genocide is a crime under the 1948 Convention and, in principle, *requires* international humanitarian intervention. A central legal and empirical difference is that genocides and politicides target communal (or political) groups that governments intend to eliminate "in whole or in part." Atrocities target large numbers of civilians, but there is no intent, claimed or inferred, to destroy some larger identity group. Nor is there any obligation in international law to take action against the perpetrators, though they may be prosecuted by international war crimes tribunals.

Between 1955 and 2015, Harff counts 45 genocides and politicides.[1] Politicide, a concept developed and used by Harff (2003), is intentional killing aimed at destroying a group defined by the perpetrators in terms of political affiliation or socioeconomic traits and is regarded by many analysts to be equivalent to genocide, requiring the same international responses. An independent study of mass atrocities by Ulfelder and Valentino (2008) identifies 57 mass atrocities, in addition to the genocides and politicides identified by Harff.[2] They define mass atrocities "as any event in which the actions of state agents result in the intentional deaths of at least 1,000 noncombatants from a discrete group in a period of sustained violence." By "intentional," they mean deliberate killings, as distinct from accidental ones.

Here, I compare and contrast the two datasets, looking for factors that might make it possible to anticipate them and take preventative action. In the next section of this chapter, I analyze the larger universe of civil wars based on the demands of identity groups and review their outcomes, with particular attention to international efforts to contain them.

Both geno/politicides and other mass atrocities share one common antecedent. Without exception, all follow from, or occur in the context of, violent civil conflicts. In some instances, these are civil wars, while others are abrupt and disruptive regime changes that bring to power new elites who are committed to suppressing actual or potential challenges. In Table 5.1, I compare the antecedent conflicts that led to each type of mass atrocities.

Ethnopolitical and separatist wars have been the occasion for more than half of all mass atrocities, including 69% of all genocides and politicides and 49% of other atrocities. Revolutionary wars, in which challengers aim to oust central authorities, were the settings for 23 (22%) of the total 102 episodes of mass killings. Here, there is a substantial difference between seven episodes, or 16% of 45 genocides and politicides, and other mass atrocities numbering 16, or 28%, of 57 other episodes. Repressive regimes, which usually come to power in coups (e.g. the Pinochet regime in Chile in 1973) or successful revolutionary wars (e.g. Cambodia under the Khmer Rouge in 1975), accounted for another 20 of 102 mass atrocities, but less often took the form of geno/politicides rather than others.

What can be inferred from these patterns? Ethnic and regional challengers to governments are more distinct, because of some combination of ethnicity, religion, and locale of residence, and are more readily targeted for annihilation (i.e. genocides and politicides). In the face of revolutionary challenges, regimes are less likely to aim for total destruction of an opposing group, and more likely to stop once repression quells open opposition.

There may be a similar logic in the relative frequency of episodes of deadly but non-genocidal political repression. In Castro's Cuba, for example, between 5,000

TABLE 5.1 Types of internal conflicts leading to geno/politicides and other mass atrocities, 1955–2015[3]

Conflict type	Genocides/politicides n= 45	Other mass atrocities n=57
Ethnopolitical and regional wars[4]	31 (69%)	28 (49%)
Revolutionary wars	7 (16%)	16 (28%)
Regime repression and retaliation	7 (16%)	13 (23%)

and 8335 people died in atrocities from 1956 to 1970. Ulfelder and Valentino's highest case estimate for deaths from any episode of political repression is 85,000 during Saddam Hussein's rule in Iraq from 1963 to 2003, an estimate that does not include separately counted episodes of repression of Shi'a (between 30,000 and 60,000 killed) and genocidal campaigns against Kurds (up to 240,000) (Ulfelder and Valentino 2005: ii, v).

In summary, elites in power after a revolutionary or post-colonial power shift – as in Nicaragua under Somoza 1974–1979, and Malawi after 1964 – are more likely to carry out mass atrocities than genocides. But the differences are not overwhelming. The common principle is that civil wars and revolutionary regime changes are particularly likely to lead to both mass atrocities and geno/politicides. Moreover, as Ulfelder and Valentino show, the mass killings are most likely – in 77% of their cases – to begin in the first year of an instability event, i.e. a civil war or regime upheaval (Ulfelder and Valentino 2008: 10).

The most striking difference between geno/politicides and other mass atrocities is that the former cause far more mass casualties, on average, than the remaining atrocities from the Ulfelder and Valentino roster. The median death toll of the geno/politicides was about 80,000, while the median of other atrocities was less than 10,000. Eight geno/politicides caused civilian deaths estimated at a half million or more each. Using Ulfelder and Valentino's estimated ranges (which are similar to Harff's), they were:

First Sudan civil war 1955–1972: 400,000–600,000
Biafran civil war in Nigeria 1967–1970: 600,000–2,000,000
Bangladesh secession from Pakistan 1971: 300,000–1,000,000
Khmer Rouge killing of "new people" 1975–1979: 1,000,000–2,000,000
Afghan civil wars 1978–1992: 1,000,000–1,800,000
Second Sudan civil war 1993–2005: 1,500,000–2,000,000
Rwandan genocide against Tutsi 1990–1994: 500,000–800,000
Darfur genocide from 2003 to present: 500,000 (estimate from Eric Reeves).

By contrast, only one non-genocidal case of mass atrocities exceeded 100,000 civilian deaths: the Cambodian civil war that began in 1967 and led to the Khmer Rouge seizure of power.

In summary, non-genocidal atrocities differ from geno/politicides mainly in magnitude and intent. They are somewhat more likely to occur in the context of revolutionary wars and in campaigns by post-revolutionary regimes to suppress actual or potential opponents. New and challenged regimes may intend to eliminate all opponents, but intent in these circumstances remains a slippery concept. In effect, the perpetrators in most instances use a strategy of state terror to discourage opposition rather than to eliminate all potential opponents. And in those cases where they do aim at elimination, as in Kampuchea and Darfur, they are guilty of genocide and politicide.

Early prevention of genocide and mass atrocities? Evidence from conflict analysis

Genocides and mass atrocities follow from ongoing and usually long-term conflict processes, as shown in the previous section. But there is nothing inevitable about the sequence. The mantra of both scholars and policymakers is that "early prevention" is better than belated responses after mass killings are underway. James Waller (2016: ch. 4) calls these "upstream prevention strategies." Genocide averted is less costly in human lives and material cost than late responses. This assumes that civil wars can be managed by some combination of long-term political and economic engagement, sometimes accompanied by military intervention. Evidence from conflict analysis is reviewed here.

In the early 1990s, there was an explosion of new civil wars and a parallel surge in international efforts at managing them. From 1993 to 2004, militants began (or renewed) 145 episodes of violent conflict at a low level (25 to 999 conflict deaths per year), of which 35 escalated in the next few years to largescale conflicts (1,000+ deaths annually) (Harbom 2008 cited in Heldt 2009). This illustrates the scope of the global problem of violent civil conflicts, but is too diverse to help us answer our questions about risks and prevention of mass atrocities. What follows is a more manageable and carefully-researched set of relevant cases.

Preventing mass atrocities in ethnopolitical and regional wars

So what do we know about conflict scenarios that culminate in mass violence, or on the good side in conflict management? Mass atrocities, especially on the scale of genocide, almost invariably follow from violent conflict over who holds power, sometimes after a power shift and sometimes as part of the power struggle itself. But this by itself does not allow us to identify points at which a potentially genocidal process might be diverted.

Communal conflicts were the settings for two-thirds of geno/politicides and half of other mass atrocities since 1955, as I showed in Table 5.1 above. So, international efforts at early prevention and mitigation of mass killings should focus especially on these conflicts. They are identity conflicts in which the protagonists – the militants, or rebels – share an identity based in part on a real or fictive homeland. They usually share other bases for identity as well – often ethnicity and religion. Their central objective, that which motivates their challenge to the state, is greater autonomy for that land and control of its resources and their own cultures and destinies. They almost invariably display a group history of autonomous existence before being absorbed by the state(s) that now controls them: for example, Hawaiians in the US, Kurds in the Middle East, Acehnese in Indonesia, and over 100 others (on the crucial role of social identities in violent conflict generally, and genocide specifically, see Waller 2016: 139ff; on the traits that characterize autonomy movements see Gurr 2000: ch. 6).

In 2005, my collaborator Deepa Khosla reported our detailed analysis of the outcomes of all armed conflicts from 1955 to 2004 in which the communal protagonists sought regional autonomy or independence. There were 71 such wars, many of which began in the early 1990s after the breakup of the former Soviet Union and Yugoslavia. In another 77 instances, communal – ethnic and religious – groups sought greater autonomy using conventional or militant politics. Escalation to violence was a risk in some of these cases as well (Gurr 2000: ch. 6; Khosla 2005).

What were the outcomes of the 71 civil wars? By 2005, five groups had gained internationally-recognized independence, by war or negotiation (e.g. East Timor, Eritrea, Croatia). Another 23 groups had negotiated an agreement for greater autonomy within an existing state (e.g. Croats in Bosnia, Mizos in northeast India, Bougainvilleans in Papua New Guinea, Tuaregs in Mali). International actors, including regional states, usually were engaged in the negotiations and guarantees that led to these outcomes. And of course, some "settled" conflicts later flared up again, like the Tuareg rebellion in northern Mali after 2010.

Ten civil wars in 2005 were held in check by peacekeeping forces or ceasefires – "frozen" wars that could easily resume. In six conflicts, the militants had shifted strategies from armed violence to nonviolent politics within existing states. And in 27 cases – nearly four-tenths of the 71 total – violent conflict continued in 2005. As of 2016, serious violence persisted in at least eight of these wars, earning them the sobriquet of "intractable conflicts." Among the protagonists are Palestinians, Muslims in Indian Kashmir, the PKK (Kurds) in Turkey, and Oromo in Ethiopia. Violent opposition also continues at a lower level among Chechens in Russia, the Ijaw and other peoples of the Niger Delta, Darfuri in Sudan, and Uighers in China. It should be noted that most of these intractable conflicts are in strong states that are impervious to international intervention.

With this background, how common were mass atrocities in the course of these 71 civil wars? 11 geno/politicides and 16 other mass atrocities were committed by government-aligned forces in efforts to suppress these rebellions – that is in 27 (38%) of all cases. Yet, massive atrocities often failed to achieve their inferred objectives. South Sudan, whose inhabitants were victimized by two long-term genocidal campaigns, is independent. Genocide against rebel Bangladeshis, Isaaqs in northern Somalia, East Timorese, Bosniaks, and Kosovars did not keep them from gaining independence – usually thanks to international intervention. Other groups gained regional autonomy despite mass atrocities – for example, most Moros in the Philippines (some of whom continue to fight), Acehnese in Indonesia, and Abkhaz in Georgia. On the other side of the atrocities ledger, genocidal Nigerian government policies in Biafra suppressed its war of independence, Pakistan's rebellious Baluch remain firmly under government control, Chechnya is controlled by a pro-Russian regional government, and rebellion in Darfur has largely been suppressed.

No simple accounting is possible, because in a number of instances civil wars continue despite mass atrocities. But by my rough assessment, 27 communal and regional peoples have been targeted by geno/politicide or other mass atrocities since 1955. Of these, 16 subsequently gained either independence or substantial

Evidence from conflict analysis **65**

regional autonomy, while only six were largely or wholly suppressed. And in the eight instances listed above, violent conflict continues in 2017.

Successful international engagement

The broad picture is clear. Many violent conflicts within countries are begun, some rebellions succeed despite mass atrocities, others are contained by political and military actions, and still others persist like bleeding wounds. There may be very good reasons for international engagement in such conflicts, for example to prevent regional instability, minimize damage to trade and economy, limit refugee flows, and so forth. Indeed, such efforts can be very numerous and sometimes successful. There are many instances of wholly or partially successful international management, four of them sketched below. So, early engagement and intervention may deflect genocidal processes, but face multiple limitations.

Croats in Bosnia

Enormous amounts of upstream and midstream international effort may be required to manage violent civil conflicts. In 1992, the Croat minority in newly independent Bosnia began a separatist civil war with the political and military support of the Republic of Croatia. Some hoped for unification between the self-proclaimed but unrecognized Croatian Republic of Herzeg-Bosnia and the newly independent state of Croatia. An alternative solution, proposed by international actors, was a confederal Bosnia state in which the Croatian Republic was one of three constituent entities. This solution was accepted at international conferences in 1994 and 1995, and the civil war ended. Birger Heldt has tabulated initiatives of mediation, offers of good offices, and managed peace talks brought to bear on this conflict by a wide range of international actors including NGO's. They were great in number and feeble in individual effect: for a single year, 1993, he counts 84 peace-making initiatives aimed at ending the civil war (Heldt 2009: 134). Yet, their cumulative effect was an internationally-brokered institutional solution that has held for more than 20 years. It did not end communal hostilities, but channeled them into a democratic political framework.

Albanians in Macedonia

In 2001, Albanian militants in Macedonia began an insurgency. The international – mainly European – response was prompt and diverse. Political and diplomatic pressures persuaded Albanians and Macedonian nationalists to suspend conflict. Incentives – political and economic ones – prompted the Macedonian government to agree to a national pact that gave the Albanians a greater stake in government. European peacekeepers supervised the disarmament of Albanian rebels. When Macedonian nationalists later tried to sabotage constitutional reforms, external pressures were ratcheted up again to keep the peace process on track (Lund 2000 and follow-up research by the author of this chapter).

Central African Republic

In the CAR, early in 2012, a loose alliance of mostly Muslim northerners called Séléka seized power in the capital of Bangui from a grossly ineffective and corrupt government.

> Before and after seizing power its soldiers looted, burned, raped and murdered their way across CAR, terrorizing tens of thousands of civilians, most of them Christians. In response, Christian communities formed a loose network of self-defense groups. Known collectively as the anti-balaka, they attacked Muslim civilians in retaliation for Séléka's crimes. In response, Séléka fighters began explicitly targeting Christians.
>
> *(Brown 2016: 1)*

Technically, this was not a genocide or mass atrocity, as the terms are defined by the authors cited here, because no one claiming authority appears to have authorized the violence. But atrocities they were, and they attracted much concern from human rights and other NGOs. The US government's recently-established Atrocities Prevention Board (see Chapter 9) paid close attention to the situation and advocated US and international action. After nearly a year of bureaucratic wrangling, the US agreed to support UN peacekeeping. Direct US participation was limited to logistical support. The Board is widely credited (by US officials) with spearheading international intervention in a humanitarian crisis. But it did so belatedly, and the response checked, but did not stop, communal massacres. A detailed account of the bureaucratic process and political issues that slowed the response is Brown 2016. It suggests how difficult it is for a major power to develop what is glibly called the "political will" to intervene. In the US case, this was all the more difficult because the US had no political or economic interests in the CAR. The decision was made on humanitarian grounds – against the resistance of a number of US government agencies.

Libya

Libya's civil war of 2011 began as a manifestation of the "Arab Spring." Libyans opposed to Col. Muammar Gadaffi began a campaign of violent protest that prompted the dictator's threat to massacre tens of thousands of his own citizens. Citing UN resolutions regarding threats to regional security, an international coalition led by France, the UK, and the US carried out a decisive air campaign and other interventions in support of the rebels, who won militarily and murdered Gadaffi before the end of the year. The intervention also was justified as an application of the new international doctrine of Responsibility to Protect. In retrospect, the anarchic struggle for power, and the rise of Islamist extremism that followed, illustrate the Law of Unintended Consequences. The fact remains that it was an intervention that aimed to forestall a mass atrocity, and in that limited sense it succeeded.

Toward general assessment of risks

These examples are "for instances" showing that interventions can deflect potential atrocities – after conflict has already begun. But they do not demonstrate general patterns. They are what Waller would call "midstream intervention strategies" (2016: ch. 5). What do we know of upstream interventions, and where? The most promising approach here is to build upon theoretically-grounded empirical studies of past cases to identify contemporary countries at high risk. The most fully-developed effort of this kind is Harff's analysis of "failed states" that are at risk of genocides and politicides. Her pioneering analysis focused on 127 state failures – civil wars or regime collapses – of which 35 included or led to geno/politicides. The research question was: which prior characteristics of the states distinguished those that had such mass atrocities from those that did not? Her results showed that, during the period from 1955 to 2000, geno/politicides were most likely in conflict-ridden countries with these traits: autocratic governance, state-led discrimination against minorities, exclusionary ideologies, and a deep history of genocidal practices (Harff 2003). A current application of this framework, using data through 2015/16, is reported in Chapter 3.

Ulfelder and Valentino (2008) report a similar analysis of the preconditions of their larger universe of mass atrocities through 2005. They find that by far the most important variable is armed conflict – which is treated in the Harff analysis as a necessary precondition of geno/politicides. Their other significant causes are leadership instability (a common trait of autocratic governments), state-led discrimination, nonviolent protest, and infant mortality rate (an indicator of poverty). They also found that an indicator of international economic involvement (membership in the WTO) decreased slightly the risks of atrocities. A similar variable in Harff's analysis also pointed in the same direction. Harff's elite variables were not used in Ulfelder and Valentino's analysis.

These analyses converge on a common explanation. Atrocities and geno/politicides both occur in the context of violent civil conflict. A country's legacy of systematic discrimination increases the likelihood that when ethnopolitical and regional groups resist or rebel, they will be targeted by geno/politicides or other mass atrocities. Such episodes are most likely to occur in politically weak and authoritarian regimes that lack the norms and resources for accommodation. Poverty and weak international connections increase the risks. If there is any one crucial difference in the causal path from conflict to geno/politicide, it is that elites believe in an exclusionary ideology that places the target groups outside what Helen Fein calls the universe of obligation. Armed conflict, and especially resistance by such groups, provides the incentives and cover for campaigns to eliminate them. The relative weakness and instability of challenged regimes make it all the more likely that they will aim for elimination rather than negotiated settlements or reconciliation. Weak regimes seldom have the resources or disposition to respond with reforms.

The first application of these results is to direct international attention to ongoing violent conflicts, and then to focus on countries that exhibit high risk factors.

68 Ted Robert Gurr

Some of the preconditions flagged in these studies are not easily changed, but a long-term focus on alleviating poverty and on stabilizing fragile governments is possible. More immediately, international efforts aimed at reducing minority discrimination and discouraging elites' articulation of exclusionary ideologies are possible. Currently, a civil war between rival ethnies in South Sudan threatens to escalate to genocide, despite international pressures and the presence of peacekeepers, especially because of articulation of hate speech, which is symptomatic of an exclusionary ideology derived from ethnic hatreds. So, empirically-based risk assessments are both a diagnostic tool, when surveying emerging conflicts, and a potential guide to international policies of prevention. Incentives and pressures should focus intensively on conflict situations in countries thus characterized.

Once mass killings are underway, is there any evidence about what might work to contain them? Matthew Krain (1997) has studied the effects of economic, political, and military engagement on year-to-year changes in deaths from ongoing geno/politicides, up to the mid-1990s. He reports that only international military intervention is likely to reduce violence. The finding is not surprising: it implies that, once governments are committed to eliminating opponents, external pressures have little effect. Only force will work.

The Harff template also helps account for genocidal policies by non-state (or non-recognized state) actors such as ISIS. The leadership of the proto-Islamic state is highly authoritarian (10 on the Polity scale), is driven by a Salafist ideology that warrants the elimination of heretics (Shiites, Yazidi, and Christians, among others), and of course discriminates systematically against them. This can be contrasted with quasi-states like Transnistria and Iraqi Kurdistan that are essentially authoritarian but have no exclusionary doctrines or practices, and have committed no atrocities.

In conclusion, international strategies of upstream prevention (again a term from Waller 2016: ch. 4) should focus on emerging violent conflicts in states with several of the risk factors cited above. A secondary focus should be on the co-occurrence of these traits in countries that are not now experiencing civil wars. It is precisely these two types of states that are identified in our current risk analysis in Chapter 3.

Notes

1 See Harff and Gurr 1988 and Harff 2003 for her initial lists of cases. Her last published roster is Harff 2005. She has provided me with revisions and updates through 2015. There are three current cases: the Sudanese government's genocidal campaigns in Darfur and North Khordofan (ck), Syrian killings of civilians suspected of supporting anti-regime rebels, and ISIS killings of Yazids.
2 Prof. Valentino has continued to update the roster of mass atrocities in Ulfelder and Valentino (2008), based on which I have identified and included in this analysis atrocities committed through 2015. My thanks to him for providing the report and current listing.
3 Author's analysis of geno/politicides identified by Harff and other mass atrocities identified by Ulfelder and Valentino. See text for sources and the basis of categorization.
4 Including conflicts with both ethnopolitical and revolutionary objectives, among them four geno/politicides and five other atrocities.

References

Brown, Charles J. (2016) *The Obama Administration and the Struggle to Prevent Atrocities in the Central African Republic December 2012 – September 2014*. Washington, DC: United States Holocaust Memorial Museum.

Gurr, Ted Robert (2000) *Peoples Versus States: Minorities at Risk in the New Century*. Washington, D.C: US Institute of Peace Press (esp ch. 6).

Harbom, Lotta, ed. (2008) *States in Armed Conflict 2006*. Uppsala, Sweden: Department of Peace and Conflict Research, Uppsala University.

Harff, Barbara (2003) "No Lessons Learned from the Holocaust? Assessing Risks of Genocide and Political Mass Murder since 1955." *American Political Science Review* 97, (no. 1) (February), 75–90.

Harff, Barbara (2005) "Assessing Risks of Genocide and Politicide," in Monty G. Marshall and Ted Robert Gurr, *Peace and Conflict 2005: A Global Survey of Armed Conflicts, Self-Determination Movements and Democracy*, College Park, MD: Center for International Development and Conflict Management, University of Maryland, 57.

Heldt, Birger (2009) "Sequencing of Peacemaking in Emerging Conflicts." Ch. 6 in Karen Aggestam and Annika Björkdahl, eds., *War and Peace in Transition: Changing Roles of External Actors*. Lund: Nordic Academic Press.

Khosla, Deepa (2005) "Self Determination Movements and Their Outcomes." Ch. 5 and appendix Tables 11.2 and 3 in Monty G. Marshall and Ted Robert Gurr, *Peace and Conflict 2005*. College Park, MD: Center for International Development and Conflict Management, University of Maryland.

Krain, Matthew (1997) "State-Sponsored Mass Murder: The Onset and Severity of Genocides and Politicides." *Journal of Conflict Resolution* 41, 331–360.

Lund, Michael S. (2000) "Preventive Diplomacy for Macedonia, 1992–1999: From Containment to National Building." Ch. 8 in Bruce W. Jentleson, ed., *Opportunities Missed, Opportunities Seized: Preventive Diplomacy in the Post-Cold War World*. Lantham, MD: Rowman & Littlefield for the Carnegie Commission on Preventing Deadly Conflict.

Marshall, Monty G., and Benjamin R. Cole (2014) *Global Report 2014: Conflict, Governance, and State Fragility*. Vienna, VA: Center for Systemic Peace.

Rotberg, Robert (2010) "Deterring Mass Atrocity Crimes: The Cause of our Era." In Robert Rotberg, ed., *Mass Atrocity Crimes: Preventing Future Outrages*. Washington, DC: Brookings Institution Press.

Scheffer, David. (2006) "Genocide and Atrocity Crimes," *Genocide Studies and Prevention: An International Journal* 1, (no. 3) 229–250.

Ulfelder, Jay, and Benjamin Valentino (2008) "Assessing Risks of State-Sponsored Mass Killings." *Science Applications International Corporation for the U.S. Government's Political Instability Task Force*.

Verdeja, Ernesto (2013) "Genocide: Debating Definitions," pp. 21–46 in Adam Lupel and Ernesto Verdeja, eds., *Responding to Genocide: The Politics of International Action*. Boulder, CO and London: Lynne Rienner Publishers.

Waller, James E. (2016) *Confronting Evil: Engaging Our Responsibility to Prevent Genocide*. New York: Oxford University Press. See esp. chs. 4 and 5.

PART II

Mobilizing International, Regional, and Local Responses

6

ENDING THE SILENCE ON WAR CRIMES

A journalist's perspective

Roy Gutman

For the past seven years, the United States and its allies have watched war crimes unfold in Syria and other places with expressions of anguish coupled with a firm resolve not to intervene.

The world's news media, having provided vivid accounts of regime atrocities in the early years of the Syria conflict, also have largely stopped reporting the travesties occurring in plain view, and NGOs have not done much better.

This combination of inattention and inaction will have consequences, and not just for the victims. The paralysis of the major powers because of deadlock in the U.N. Security Council, the silence of Western political leaders and the absence of a public outcry all contribute to the sense that the world order established at the end of World War II is heading for a breakdown.

To take but one example, governments, the media and NGOs pay little or no attention to the Assad regime's mass expulsions of populations that staged revolts in the towns and cities near the Syrian capital. Where is the outcry over the tactics of "surrender or die," scorched earth and deliberate destruction of health care facilities and camps for the internally displaced?

And where is the drive to put the spotlight on the permanent member of the U. N. Security Council that, through its leading role in the war against civilians, is a principal facilitator of these crimes against humanity? For half a decade, the U.S. ambassador to the United Nations eloquently denounced the atrocities by citing anecdotal evidence, rather than defining them as irrefutable violations of International Humanitarian Law.

My experience in reporting the Balkan wars in the 1990s, convinced me that war crimes are the prelude to crimes against humanity, and these, if they go unchecked, lead to the ultimate crime against humanity, genocide.

I also observed that there are proven tools to halt the descent into barbarism: an internationally agreed legal framework defining what's legal, what's illegal and

74 Roy Gutman

what's criminal in war, and a spectrum of responses ranging from public denunciation to armed intervention. Silence about the crimes sends a signal of its own. Inaction encourages perpetrators to carry on.

The body of law defining crimes of war goes back centuries. The Geneva Conventions of 1949 and the additional protocols of 1977 codified the grave breaches, or war crimes, and crimes against humanity were first defined at the post-World War II Nuremberg Tribunal. The Genocide Convention of 1948 laid out the elements that constitute the crime of genocide. But the law of armed conflict has undergone its most intensive development and refinement in the past quarter century.

The tribunals set up during this period, from Bosnia to Sierra Leone, from Rwanda to Cambodia, along with the judgments they have rendered, have produced definitions, procedures and precedents that add up to a sizable body of case law. The statute establishing the International Criminal Court in 1998 restated what constitutes war crimes, crimes against humanity and genocide.[1]

The creation of these institutions gave some reason for hope that order was emerging. In 2005, members of the U.N. General Assembly agreed unanimously that all states had a Responsibility to Protect citizens from genocide, ethnic cleansing, crimes against humanity and war crimes, and "to take collective action, in a timely and decisive manner, through the Security Council, in accordance with the Charter, including Chapter VII, on a case-by-case basis." The irony is that, just as the laws have become re-codified, tribunals established and the principles of protection universally agreed to, the major powers that had set the process in motion, starting with the United States, opted to drop the language and the demands for observance.

My aim in this chapter is to sketch a path to reawaken public interest in conflict and in the instruments of order defined by humanitarian law. My premise is that public opinion was a major factor in raising demands that governments carry out their obligations under humanitarian law in the 1990s, and that journalism is an essential element in awakening public opinion.

A lot is at stake. "The notion that the postwar world would no longer let leaders indiscriminately kill their own citizens now seems in full retreat," wrote Anne Barnard of *The New York Times*.

> The Syrian government's response to rebellion, continuing year after year, threatens to normalize levels of state brutality not seen in decades. All the while President Bashar al-Assad invokes an excuse increasingly popular among the world's governments since Sept. 11: He is "fighting terror."[2]

By my analysis, the chief factor in the change of focus and the seeming abandonment of humanitarian law – at least in the single worst case of war crimes, Syria – is the rise of terror groups and terror attacks at the end of the 1990s. Statesmen, students of international affairs and reporters largely missed the phenomenon of terror until it landed upon us with the attacks of September 11, 2001. Few understood how terrorist groups with international reach could establish themselves in the first place, rise to international attention and come to dominate the discourse. Few understood the political environment that allows terror groups to take hold or the necessity to address the political causes. The reaction of governments to the rise of terror groups was first complacency, followed by overreaction bordering on panic.

Instead of seeking out allies to defend shared values and forge a common approach with long-term aims, political leaders chose to counter the violent manifestations of terror by bluntly military means. The images of aircraft and drones bombing terror suspects would play well in the evening television news as evidence of resolve, but the military strikes weren't linked to a political outcome, so there was no way they would assure stability and prevent the return of the terror groups.

(I am using an operational definition of terrorism: an action that is intended to cause death or serious bodily harm to civilians or noncombatants with the purpose of intimidating a population or forcing a government to take certain actions in open disregard of the rules of war.[3])

Setting up torture facilities in third world countries where U.S. law does not apply, and "outsourcing" suspects to governments that have neither due process nor a record of respecting human rights, has produced tainted testimonies and made it impossible to hold a fair trial for many suspects. The decision to incarcerate suspects indefinitely in locations such as Guantánamo is an open flouting of the rules of war.

In Afghanistan, where Al Qaida took root in the 1990s, the lesson that should have been learned is that ungoverned spaces provide fertile territory for terror groups, and that we abandon these spaces at our peril.

The Bush administration's intervention in Iraq without a clear political goal and strategy, and its ill-considered decision to dismantle the security forces without an alternative, also created a vacuum that could be filled only at the cost of the lives of American soldiers and Iraqi civilians.

The Obama administration staged a repeat performance. It withdrew U.S. forces from Iraq in 2011 without a solid plan for the security challenges that might arise, and looked away as terror groups exploited the vacuum. In Syria as well, the U.S. refused to develop a policy for the internal conflict following a national uprising. Instead, it provided modest support to moderate rebel forces fighting the Assad regime, and humanitarian aid.

This culminated in the rise of the Islamic State of Iraq and Sham, its conquest of Mosul in June 2014 and its proclamation of a "Caliphate" spanning Iraq and Syria that same month.

I. From Cold War to hot war in Europe

My interest in the norms of international humanitarian law derives from my experience reporting the Cold War from Central Europe and the United States from 1968, its denouement in 1989 and the Balkan conflicts that followed in the 1990s.

My thesis is that the Cold War ended in Europe in a manner that facilitated recognition among political elites that human rights norms could play a vital role in upholding political order. What drove the lesson home was the wilful and flagrant violation of human rights and humanitarian norms during the break-up of Yugoslavia in the immediate post-Cold War era.

I will briefly recount some of the factors that led to rebirth of the independent states in Eastern Europe, the establishment of democratic governance, the reunification of Germany and of Europe and the triumph of human rights ideals and the rule of law.

The world has changed a great deal since 1989, but the factors that led to that historical turning point remain relevant. One aspect of the Cold War is that Western powers united behind a joint threat to use force to deter potential Russian military advances in Europe. Those same powers also united in their response to oppose the Soviet Union's ill-considered invasion of Afghanistan in 1979 by supporting proxy forces that would drive up the cost to Moscow.

Equally important was diplomacy in the form of arms control negotiations to set the limits for the nuclear balance of terror, and political negotiations both to reduce tensions and to expand relations at the human level between East and West. With regional players like West Germany taking the lead, the West accepted Russia's post-World War II division of Europe, and Russia accepted a new protocol for relations based on the free flow of people, goods and ideas.

That process produced a set of norms that inspired drives for human rights and freedoms in the Russian-dominated countries of the east: the so-called Helsinki process. When Russian Communist power collapsed, the way was opened for a peaceful transition to independent, stable democracies.

The prologue to the accord was a series of popular uprisings and reform movements that Russia crushed with tanks and bayonets, mass arrests and severe repression. The Berlin uprising of 1953, Poznan (Poland) in 1956, the Hungarian revolution of 1956 and the Prague Spring of 1968 illustrate the deep antipathy of the populations of these countries to one-party, police state rule, but it was an initiative by Willy Brandt, West Germany's new chancellor in 1970, that opened the way to a dialogue that would allow these oppressed nations to launch their claims to civil and human rights.

Brandt formally dropped Germany's claim to East Prussia, to its historic border in Poland and to a unified Germany in exchange for "détente" with Russia and its satellites. And in 1975, with West Germany again playing a leading role, the United States, the Soviet Union and 33 other countries signed the Helsinki Final Act. Under this accord, all sides pledged to respect the free movement of people, goods and ideas between East and West, and that borders could be changed only by consent, not by force.

The Helsinki Final Act became the unofficial charter for a new Europe. It was a rallying point for political dissidents in the Communist countries, and a platform for Western states to demand more openness in the world of the police states. For 14 years, the Helsinki agreement and the follow-on review mechanism were at the center of the debate over the liberalization of rigid political systems in Europe and the Soviet Union, and they played a critical role in the peaceful transition to multiparty fledgling democracies operating under the rule of law.

Yugoslavia had never been under direct Russian control; it was also a party to the Helsinki Final Act, but had followed a different path. The end of Communist one-party rule in the multi-ethnic state gave way to a multiple-party structure as in Eastern Europe, but with a difference. Parties were formed not along the classic European division of conservatives and social democrats, but on the principle of ethnic identity.

There was a widespread awareness that Yugoslavia would come apart, but the focus of the United States and its Western allies was elsewhere – on the momentous changes in Central Europe, the frontline in the West's confrontation with Russia. History unfolded in multiple theaters simultaneously. Preoccupied with the reunification of Germany and the ouster of Soviet-imposed rulers by pro-Western democrats, Washington paid little attention at first to the political vacuum that the collapse of Communist rule brought about in then-Yugoslavia, and the long-suppressed nationalist rhetoric that came to fill it.

After declaring independence in June 1991, Slovenia, which had militarily prepared for a violent independence struggle, fought a ten-day war that ended with the withdrawal of the Yugoslav army. Its neighbor, Croatia, declared independence the same day but was far less prepared and geographically far more vulnerable to the Serbian-dominated army and its allied militias. It was also at far greater risk demographically because of Serbian population concentrations in several key locations. The war in Croatia lasted until 1995.

In Bosnia–Herzegovina, where Muslim Bosniaks comprised 43 per cent of the population and Serbs 31 per cent, local nationalists led by Radovan Karadzic decided to form a Serb-controlled state that would unite with Serbia. To carry this out, Karadzic devised a plan to force non-Serbs out of municipalities where Serbs could claim a plurality of the population, or which were deemed strategically valuable for Bosnian Serbs.

The Yugoslav army set as its initial strategic goal creating a corridor from western Serbia to Banja Luka, the capital of Karadzic's fledging Republika Srpska. Few outsiders were on hand to witness the "ethnic cleansing" of non-Serbs as it unfolded. Refugees fleeing by the tens of thousands provided the first reports of the atrocities.

I was the European correspondent for *Newsday*, the New York daily, starting in late 1989, and like my colleagues I had my hands full reporting the epochal shifts unfolding in Central Europe. I didn't even visit Yugoslavia until spring of 1991. But I had the advantage of being familiar with the country from my days as Reuters' bureau chief in Belgrade in the mid-1970s, and I quickly saw how the political environment had deteriorated under Serbian strongman Slobodan Milosevic, from one of tolerance and equality to bigotry and ethnic hatred. I expected that war in Bosnia would be far deadlier than in Slovenia and Croatia, because Bosniaks were totally unprepared to fight, and Serbs were set on conquest and destruction.

It was from refugees who had fled to neighboring Croatia that I first heard of the establishment of detention camps where civilians were routinely brutalized and killed. On the day the "corridor" to Banja Luka opened early in July 1992, I was on the first bus convoy to that city. The Yugoslav Army offered to take me to the Manjaca detention camp, where it was in charge, by coincidence on the very day the authorities planned to host the International Committee of the Red Cross.

While in Banja Luka, I sought out Muslim and Croat politicians, and that is where I first heard about Omarska, where non-Serb males were taken at gunpoint, tortured and killed. The Serb military authorities refused me access to Omarska, giving the excuse that they could not "guarantee" my safety, so I became determined to find out what had happened there.

Extensive interviews with refugees who had fled to Zagreb, Croatia, led me to two witnesses, each from a different camp – Omarska in northern Bosnia and Brcko Luka in eastern Bosnia. My report, with input from the International Red Cross, the U.N. High Commission for Refugees, the U.S. government and Serbian officials, was published in *Newsday*.

I recount this story because it is the basis for my conviction that news reports, if timely and accurate, can train the spotlight of international opinion on war crimes in a manner that forces the perpetrators to stop in their tracks.

My story on August 2, 1992, led to the closing of Omarska camp and the saving of thousands of lives.[4] The U.N. immediately organized a fact-finding mission to travel throughout Bosnia, which confirmed the contention in my story that a network of concentration camps existed. The U.S. Congress dispatched investigative teams to interview refugees. Hundreds of other journalists flocked to the region, known as the Bosnian Krajina, and the U.N. even sent peacekeeping troops to Banja Luka.

The spotlight of the media and major governments forced a halt in the "ethnic cleansing" for several months, at least in the Bosnian Krajina region. Reporters were able to move around without limitation, and the Serb authorities had their hands full with them, as well as with foreign political delegations and other visitors. Mass indiscriminate killing also came to a halt after late August 1992 until the fall of Srebrenica in July 1995.

Astute statesmen such as Madeleine Albright, who was to become the U.S. ambassador to the U.N., channeled the international outrage over the abuses into a drive to set up an ad hoc war crimes tribunal for the former Yugoslavia. The same impulse led to a special tribunal for Rwanda after the 1994 genocide there. Later in the decade, the U.N. established an International Criminal Court that could adjudicate war crimes anywhere – or at least in the 124 countries that became states party to the tribunal (the U.S. and Russia are not).

The tribunals have not brought about the full measure of justice and accountability that proponents had hoped they would. They have heard at most a small number of cases, the investigations are costly and slow moving and few countries are prepared to hand over indictees, especially if they are heads of government or state.

An example of the unfulfilled expectations is the Hague Tribunal's verdicts on the mass atrocities in northern Bosnia of May to August 1992 that had prompted the creation of the tribunal in the first place. In their verdict in the trial of Radovan Karadzic 22 years later, the judges ruled that the campaign to expel, torture and kill civilians throughout the region constituted crimes against humanity, not genocide. They ruled the mass executions in Srebrenica in July 1995 a genocide, however. The apparent difference in the two cases was the prosecutors' ability to prove intent in Srebrenica, based on a phone interception in which Karadzic gave the order for execution.[5]

The Karadzic trial exemplifies the slow pace of international justice. Karadzic was in hiding until 2008 and put on trial the following year, but the verdict wasn't pronounced until March 2016. International justice failed to deter war crimes elsewhere, even in the same region. The same Serb-led security forces alleged to have carried out crimes against humanity in Bosnia and Croatia inflicted the same atrocities later in the decade in Kosovo, driving tens of thousands of ethnic Albanians from their homes.

But the trials established a court record based on due process, gave a voice to the victims, laid out the chain of command and responsibility and established the facts for future generations. These actions one day may give pause to politicians hoping to reinvent the past to suit their political needs, and seeking to use force to redress the imagined grievances of the distant past.

Major powers did learn a lesson from the war in Bosnia, and that is the need to intervene promptly at the first sign of potential bloodbath. A U.S.-led NATO intervention indeed prevented that outcome in Kosovo in 1999.

My personal response to the atrocities that I'd reported on was to co-edit a pocket guide to war crimes, which combined vivid journalistic witness accounts of war crimes with legal scholarship to define the actual crimes. The norms of conduct in conflict had been drafted in inaccessible language that few non-lawyers understood. The premise of the book is that a war crime, like any crime, is news, and a journalist should know the rules of war in order to recognize the crime and write about it in real time. Originally conceived for journalists, the book proved to be an accessible guide for the general public as well. The many colleagues who contributed to *Crimes of War* felt as I did that ignorance of what is legal, illegal and criminal in war allowed us to overlook stories that were precursors to the genocide in Bosnia. But a reporter's guide to war crimes can be of value only if there are reporters at the front, as in Bosnia.

In Afghanistan, by comparison, reporters were present in small numbers. They failed to flush out the story of the atrocities that occurred in the late 1990s and to grasp that a terror group, Osama bin Laden's Al Qaida, had set up a state-within-a-state, effectively hijacking the Taliban regime. So, when bin Laden launched his terror assault against the United States of September 11, 2001, there was no journalistic narrative to fall back on that could explain the origins of the attack.

II. The rise of terrorism

The defeat of the Soviet Union in Afghanistan at the hand of U.S. and Saudi-backed Mujahidin was arguably the last nail in the coffin of the Soviet Empire. The Red Army withdrew not only from Afghanistan, but also from East-Central

80 Roy Gutman

Europe, and the ousting of Communist regimes by governments elected in multiparty races brought the Cold War to an end.[6]

Afghanistan thus played a critical role in one of the great turning points of the twentieth century. Twelve years later, at the onset of the twenty-first century, Afghanistan would change the world again when Al Qaida, using Afghanistan as a base, launched terror strikes at the United States, the very country that helped the Afghans free themselves from their Soviet conquerors in the 1980s.

The period between 1989 and 2001 was one of chaos in Afghanistan, arising from the security vacuum that followed the Russian military withdrawal. The United States abandoned the leading role it had played supporting the resistance during the period of Soviet control. As the country passed through a series of internal wars, it generated the world's biggest humanitarian crisis as defined by the outflow of refugees and the displacement of population, and became an ungoverned space. But the United States turned this complex of problems over to the United Nations – that is until 9/11.

The assault that day on the World Trade Center towers and the Pentagon – the intent was to fly one of the hijacked aircraft into the U.S. Capitol or White House in addition – did not constitute an existential threat to the United States. But it provoked the U.S. intervention that overthrew the rule of the Taliban, who had hosted bin Laden.

Historically, the United States had been the leading proponent of the spread of principles of humanitarian law, but as the Bush administration began its "war on terror" against the Afghan state and Al Qaida, it unilaterally began to reinterpret the rules.

The U.S. could claim that mass sweeps and arrests of Al Qaida members and sympathizers constituted a military necessity, but the use of torture and waterboarding on those captives, and the setting up of Guantanamo as an extra-legal detention center beyond the reach of U.S. justice, left no doubt that humanitarian law had been demoted in the hierarchy of American values. The reordering of priorities was frequently affirmed in the dismissive rhetoric of the president and vice-president. As it moved to topple the Taliban government, the Bush administration not only overlooked war crimes that occurred prior to its intervention, but also closed its eyes to crimes carried out by local actors during the U.S. intervention.

A pattern of disregard for the protection of civilians was evident in bombing runs against Taliban targets, and Bush adopted the tactic of reliance on drones to assassinate suspects, which is subject to limited oversight.

One reason Bush could suspend the rules with impunity was that the general public had no idea what had occurred in Afghanistan to produce the rise of Al Qaida and bin Laden's state-within-a-state. Few foreign reporters were present in that country in the 1990s, particularly after the Taliban takeover in 1996. Those who were based in Kabul and covered the Taliban knew little about bin Laden, and those who were able to report on bin Laden – mostly foreign-based reporters invited in on special trips from Pakistan – were not focused on the Taliban or the interaction between the two forces. That realization led me to research and write a book on Afghanistan's internal politics in the 1990s.[7]

In reporting the "war on terror," news media followed the administration's narrative, which centered on delivering a knockout military blow against the Taliban and Al Qaida. But bin Laden's rise was a case of a master provocateur seizing on the political opportunity opened by the collapse of governance and security in Afghanistan.

There were three internal wars in the 1990s. The first pitted different Mujahidin groups against the Russian-supported government forces from 1989 until 1992. The defeat of that government led to a second, internecine war among former Mujahidin forces from 1992 until 1996, when the Taliban took Kabul. The third war pitted the Taliban against the forces led by Ahmed Shah Massoud until 9/11. It was the Taliban's failure to vanquish Massoud that led bin Laden to propose that he set up his training camps and field forces in battle.

The Taliban's first major foray into northern Afghanistan in May 1997 gave Bin Laden his opening. The Taliban had sent forces to Mazar-i-Sharif and, through a series of calamitous bad decisions of their own, lost thousands of fighters, who were captured by warlord Malik Pahlawan, killed and dumped in mass graves.[8] The killers were Uzbeks, and victims were Taliban, but one year later, in August 1998, the Taliban took revenge and carried out a mass slaughter in Mazar-i-Sharif, where the victims were mainly Hazara Shiites.

The Clinton administration had pursued the creation of an ad hoc Tribunal for the former Yugoslavia, and supported the establishment of a permanent International Criminal Court, but it stayed silent on Afghanistan and withheld support for U.N. investigations of either atrocity.[9]

The third slaughter in the very same region occurred after 9/11, when warlord Abdul Rashid Dostum captured thousands of Taliban and Al Qaida fighters and loaded them onto container trucks where most of them suffocated, then dumped the corpses in mass graves in Sheberghan. U.S. troops were in the vicinity, operating as liaisons with Dostum, but this time it was the Bush administration that ignored the travesty, a sign that the United States had at best a passing interest in introducing the rule of law and universal standards of justice in this troubled land.[10]

The U.S. military intervention that brought the war in Bosnia–Herzegovina and Kosovo to a close, and the Dayton Peace Conference that followed, by no means brought a just and stable outcome. Yet, the drive to revive international humanitarian law after the genocide there offered a thin reed of hope that some sort of order would emerge in the post-Cold War world. That order, derived from the lessons of World War II and the Holocaust, set the outer limits for states in conflict, stipulating they could not legally target civilians and other non-combatants.

The story of Afghanistan, which unfolded at the same time as the Balkan wars, encapsulates the opposite pattern. Afghanistan exemplifies the U.S. failure to fashion a policy to deal with the security challenges of the post-Cold War era, uphold the principles agreed to at the end of World War II and observe the norms that developed during the late Cold War.

82 Roy Gutman

A key element was the lack of focus on Afghanistan following a political decision by the Clinton administration to play down the threat from Al Qaida. Its decision not to insist on upholding of the rules of humanitarian law during Afghanistan's internal struggle, nor even to fund U.N.-led investigations, was a case of the selective application of principles.

Afghanistan also provides evidence of what happens in the absence of determined news media reporting, in comparison with Bosnia–Herzegovina. International journalists, with one or two exceptions, failed to pursue the story of the atrocity against the Taliban in 1997 and to uncover the story of the Taliban's slaughter of civilians in 1998. This allowed the Clinton administration to duck its responsibility as the sole remaining superpower, which at the minimum was to support a thoroughgoing investigation.

There would be a price for the failure to seek justice in Afghanistan. The 1997 slaughter provided bin Laden the opportunity to bind himself to the Taliban and start building his state-within-a-state.

"We cannot participate further in your battles. Your commanders are immature. They cannot read the situation correctly. It is very easy for the Uzbeks to cheat them," bin Laden told Mullah Omar. "You give me a commander. We are ready to fight under your commanders," Omar replied.[11]

As bin Laden's influence rose, that of the United States fell. The Taliban refused to begin peace negotiations, despite a visit to Kabul by U.S. envoy Bill Richardson in April 1998, or to expel bin Laden; and they began imposing restrictions on news coverage by foreign reporters.[12]

The container killings of November 2001, which also went uninvestigated, became a recruiting tool for a resurgent Taliban in the decade after it occurred. "Those kinds of things thicken the hatred and cause more people to join," a top U.S. military intelligence official told me.[13]

Journalists failed to expose the atrocities in a timely fashion, to reveal bin Laden's successful hijacking of the state or to explain the context of the stormy decade leading up to 9/11, and that is a major reason that vital lessons went unlearned.

Ungoverned spaces are danger zones in the post-Cold War era and a magnet for non-state actors who take the path of terror. Far from absorbing that lesson, U.S. administrations would repeat the mistake on four more occasions over the next 15 years.

President George W. Bush, for example, went to war in Iraq in March 2003, before bringing security and stability to Afghanistan. He withdrew tactical, language and technical specialists from Afghanistan along with advanced surveillance gear, weapons and thousands of troops. In mid-2005, he even transferred the very capable ambassador, Zalmay Khalilzad, from Kabul to Baghdad.

In Iraq, meanwhile, the Bush administration committed a world-class blunder when Paul Bremer, the top U.S. civilian administrator, dissolved the Iraqi armed forces in May 2003, and closed down the Ministry of Defense, without establishing an alternative source of security. With Bush's acquiescence, the U.S. created the vacuum that allowed terrorists arriving in Iraq from Syria to establish a presence and link up with the newly unemployed officers of Saddam Hussein's military.

After several years of underestimating the threat and then staging a surge of forces to implement a counter-insurgency strategy, the U.S. finally brought stability to Iraq by 2011. That is the year President Barack Obama carried out fitful negotiations culminating in his announcement of the withdrawal of all U.S. military forces from Iraq. The U.S. military had pleaded to retain a relatively small number of troops to keep the country stabilized and to retain political leverage with Prime Minister Nouri al Maliki, a Shiite increasingly at odds with the Sunni minority. Obama never really got involved in the negotiations, and when they failed, he bragged that he had ended the war. Three years later, when Islamic State extremists seized Mosul, the Iraqi army collapsed; troops turned and ran, abandoning their U.S.-supplied weapons.

The final example of the U.S. all but ignoring the political and security vacuum occurred in Syria. When the population rose up to demand a change of government in March 2011, President Bashar al Assad ordered his military to attack them. But officers and soldiers began defecting in significant numbers, and locally garrisoned forces lost control of much of the country.

Although Assad labeled his opponents terrorists, it was he who enlisted militants of three terror groups. Lebanon's Hezbollah militia, under Iranian control, supported Assad from the beginning, and started sending troops in 2012. That same year, he handed over a big swath of northeastern Syria to the Syrian affiliate of the Kurdistan Workers Party or PKK, listed as a terror organization by Turkey, the United States and the EU.

Meanwhile, Assad had released Islamic extremists from his prisons, and when Jabhat al Nusra, the Al Qaida affiliate in Syria, began sending significant numbers of fighters into Syria from Iraq in the spring of 2012, Assad deliberately turned a blind eye. When ISIS took over Raqqa as its capital in April 2013 and set up its headquarters in the governor's offices with a big black flag flying overhead, Assad did not intervene, and the United States took almost no notice.[14]

ISIS's capture of Mosul in June 2014 evoked a minimal U.S. response, and it wasn't until that August that Obama ordered the use of U.S. force to protect the Yazidi minority from a genocide at the hands of ISIS. But late that same month, he announced he had no strategy for dealing with ISIS in Syria.

III. Atrocity crimes in Syria

Syria constitutes an egregious example of mass atrocity crimes, leading to a major humanitarian disaster. What stands out is not only the Assad regime's brazenness, but the indifference of the civilized world to the fate of an entire nation.

Faced with a popular uprising after 40 years of one-family rule, the regime chose to demonize its political opponents as terrorists, then set about fulfilling its prophecy by encouraging veterans of the jihadist insurgency during the U.S. occupation of Iraq to set up operations in Syria. With its ideological message in place, the regime made no effort to resolve the dispute by political means, but resorted to destructive force to punish the civilian population.[15]

The United States became the biggest provider of humanitarian aid as civilian casualties rose and enormous numbers of civilians were displaced; and as defectors from the government security services coalesced into locally organized rebel forces, Washington provided some defensive weapons. But over the course of six years, the Obama administration intentionally avoided devising a policy that would end the war with a stable outcome. Instead, it followed a path that historically has led to failure: pursuing diplomacy without the backup threat of the use of force.

Vacillating between the regime's specious claims and the opposition's often disorganized defense, Washington watched mostly in silence as Assad targeted civilians with offensive weapons, expelled the population and destroyed cities and villages – utilizing foreign forces, including listed terrorist groups, Iran-led militias and the Russian air force, to carry out the job.

The administration felt it had no stake in the fate of this country of 24 million, even after Islamic State extremists captured Mosul, Iraq, proclaimed a "Caliphate," and announced that Raqqa, Syria, would be its capital. Eventually, the administration deployed tactical air in support of a Kurdish militia defending Kurdish Syrians. But its use of Kurds as its proxy force against the Islamic State was an instance of using a known terror force without a clear political goal, targeting Islamist extremists but not addressing the root of the problem, which lay with the Assad regime.

As the regime's crimes unfolded, the U.S. government said little, with the exception of in response to the regime's chemical weapons attack in Eastern Ghouta in August 2013, which killed some 1,429 civilians, according to U.S. figures. Obama announced he was preparing for an armed U.S. intervention, but after the British parliament voted not to take part and the U.S. Congress showed little enthusiasm, he called off the plan.[16]

I began reporting on the war early in 2012, nine months after the uprising began in March 2011. I was the last bureau chief of the McClatchy newspaper chain in Baghdad, closing the office at the end of 2011, and transferred to Istanbul, on the assessment that the Arab Spring was not over, the conflict in Syria was raging and the Assad regime appeared to be carrying out widespread and systematic war crimes. Turkey, which had opened its borders to refugees and was supporting the popular rebellion, seemed to be the best listening post for monitoring the war.

Informed by my research into humanitarian law, and building on my reporting experience in Bosnia-Herzegovina, I made war crimes the primary focus of my reporting. My first encounter with regime practices was on a trip to the border with Turkey in March 2012, where arriving refugees reported that the Syrian military had been planting anti-personnel mines to kill or maim refugees attempting to flee.[17]

By late 2012, the regime was targeting food supplies and destroying agriculture in rebel-held areas, another factor to drive out the civilian population.[18] Town and village authorities had to beg for food deliveries, but the U.N. and all its subordinate agencies, which maintained offices in Damascus, refused to respond, saying they lacked government permission. So, it fell on Turkish charities to sustain the population.[19]

After an investigation of several weeks, I broke the story early in 2013 that the regime had attacked 80 bakeries or breadlines, killing hundreds of civilians, between August and December 2012. The report was missing a key element – a comment from the U.S. government. That was because none was forthcoming. Ten days after publication, the U.S. Agency for International Development issue a statement calling the Syrian regime's actions "unconscionable … simply unacceptable."

On my first trip into rebel-held zones in February 2013, I reported that the regime was attacking whole villages with heavy arms and forcing the population to flee, some taking refuge in caves, and targeting those already displaced from their homes.

Another pattern that I thought would qualify as a crime against humanity was the destruction of hospitals, the arrest and torture of doctors and even a determined drive to eliminate makeshift field hospitals, which medical personnel set up in mobile trailers to treat those wounded in government air attacks.

The U.N.'s special commission on war crimes reported that civilians from rebel areas would be denied treatment at government hospitals. Stephen Rapp, the U.S. ambassador at large for global criminal justice, said the targeting of medical facilities was the greatest seen in modern warfare.

The Assad regime also targeted Sunni mosques. I determined that, on average, a mosque was attacked every other day, or 62 mosques over a 14-week period. In the first 27 months of the war, 1,450 mosques had been attacked and partially damaged and 348 destroyed, according to the Syrian Network for Human Rights. I conducted random checks of SNHR's list and determined that its methodology was sound. The State Department declined comment for my report, however, and took only passing note of SNHR's data in its annual report on religious freedom the next year.[20]

By the summer of 2013, the regime appeared to be running low in its stock of airborne rockets and missiles, and began producing a makeshift weapon of terror. Barrel bombs are improvised explosive devices ranging in size from a lead pipe to a garbage dumpster, filled with shrapnel and primed with an explosive charge that were dropped from helicopters on residential areas. First used in rebel-held Aleppo, they played a growing role in warfare against civilians. I investigated one case, the strategically-located town of Ariha in Idlib province, where the regime targeted the town with wanton firepower until the defenders, their families and townspeople fled en masse.

But, as they fled, regime forces chased them and executed those it caught on the spot. What was so surprising is that, one month after the battle, the U.N. agency that was supposed to keep a tally of IDPs, the Office for the Coordination of Humanitarian Affairs, was unaware that 70,000 people had fled this one town. The U.S. government again had no comment.[21]

It was the latest indication that the U.N. had taken a detached view of IDPs and consistently understated the displacement of civilians and the outflow of refugees. The U.N. High Commission for Refugees had been tasked with assisting the internally displaced, and the U.N. Secretary-General appointed a special rapporteur who was supposed to speak up for the IDPs, but both shirked their responsibilities,

86 Roy Gutman

and no U.N. body argued the cause of the displaced or kept credible tabs on them.[22]

The barrel bombing increased in Aleppo at the start of 2014, driving at least 100,000 civilians to makeshift camps set up on the border with Turkey, but no U.N. agency was able to provide information on their numbers, locations, conditions and what assistance they were receiving. I had to make my own trip into Syria to find out.[23]

An even bigger unknown to the international public was the besieged areas. Even the Syrian Opposition Coalition failed to collect and disseminate the vital data of how many people were living under siege, and the U.S. government and the U.N. once again were of no help. It took me six weeks of digging to report the story.[24]

Four years into the war, in mid-2015, there was still no agreement on the number of people or places under siege. The Syrian–American Medical Society, using a cautious methodology, asserted 640,000 people were living under siege – that is, unable to enter or leave and unable to receive outside support. But local doctors said the real number was more like one million, and Doctors Without Borders estimated an even higher number. Meanwhile, the U.N. OCHA office estimated the number at 212,000, but refused to explain its methodology.

It was only after reports emerged of starvation in the besieged town of Madaya, northwest of Aleppo, that the U.N.'s odd counting system became clear. It was purely and simply a case of political corruption. OHCA handed its estimates on sieges, indeed all its major reports, first to the Assad regime for comment and amendment before publishing them.

Indeed, the Assad regime, which is responsible for over 90 per cent of the deaths of civilians in the seven-year war, also held a veto over the content of U.N. reports. Thus, the annual humanitarian response plan for aid in 2016 omitted any mention of besieged areas.[25]

The U.N. bureaucracy took the blame for allowing the regime to shape U.N. public statements, to downsize U.N. estimates of displaced civilians and change the content of its reports. But everyone knows the U.N. bureaucracy's powers are under the watchful eye of member states, starting with the United States. Governments presumably knew and acquiesced in the opaque methodology used by OCHA to arrive at its statements, and acted only when they were publicly embarrassed.

Throughout the Syrian war, the U.S. government took the route of hand-wringing and anguished rhetoric while failing to call out violations of humanitarian law. Indeed, as it neared the end of its second term, the Obama administration said next to nothing about the siege of east Aleppo from July 2016 until the expulsions of tens of thousands of civilians in mid-December.

Instead, the administration practically gave a green light to Russia and the regime to bombard east Aleppo on the grounds that the main force defending rebel-held east Aleppo was Jabhat al Nusra, an Al Qaida affiliate. Humanitarian aid groups and U.N. officials disputed the assertion, and when I put this to the spokesman for the U.S.-led international coalition, Col. Steve Warren, he acknowledged it was in error. But the State Department continued to use its loose terminology, and there was no outcry, barely even a public protest when the city in fact fell in December.[26]

The Obama administration's posture in Syria seemed to be shaped more by the need to convince the public it was doing something to fight ISIS, than by a strategy to defeat the terror group and deal with the Assad regime, which allowed ISIS to set up a state-within-a-state and operate with impunity.

Starting in autumn 2014, U.S. intervention took the form of airstrikes and modest arms to support the Kurdish People's Protection Force militia, known by its initials YPG, in the north Syrian town of Kobani from attack by ISIS. But with television reporters perched on a hillside just across the border watching ISIS seize more territory by the day, Obama's move inevitably came to be seen as a tactical step to head off adverse news coverage on the eve of midterm congressional elections.

U.S. support for the YPG, the Syrian arm of the banned Kurdistan Workers Party (PKK), evolved into a broad collaboration to oust ISIS from eastern Syria. But the YPG had a lot of baggage. Its affiliation with the PKK made it suspect to U.S. NATO ally Turkey, which had fought a PKK-led insurrection for 40 years. In addition, the YPG had worked closely with Assad's forces in 2013 and 2014, seizing territory from moderate rebel forces in what to appearances was close coordination.[27]

As the YPG captured additional territory in 2015 and 2016, the U.S. government paid little heed to what force would replace ISIS. YPG captured Manbij with U.S. air cover in August 2016. The PKK stepped into the power vacuum and took direct control, while handing over some of its powers to the regime. This raised a question: did the United States intervene in Syria in order to restore key regions to the murderous Assad regime?[28]

IV. Reviving public interest through innovative journalism

The decline in public interest in war crimes stems in part from the decision by world leaders, starting with President Obama, to ignore the horrors of conflict, lest they provoke a public demand for action. This determined indifference undermines international humanitarian law.

The absence of intense journalistic engagement has contributed to the fall off of public concern. The converse also holds true: journalism can play a role in restoring public interest.

Journalism can be a forum for debate, but it can also provoke debate if reporters act as watchdogs of the public interest. Investigative journalism can uncover abuses, and violations of the laws and customs of war by definition constitute news. It is also a proven means to convince the public of the facts through the methodology of finding corroborative sources, seeking the response of the alleged perpetrators and holding them to account.

The hope for the immediate future may be charity, in the form of donations and subsidies by those concerned to fund international coverage in general and investigative reporting in particular, or in vanity investments by well-off financiers who see the long-term potentials of journalism or the costs to society where it is absent.

It is a time for rethinking and for innovation. What I would like to propose is a specific remedy that has the potential to grow into a journalistic institution with the potential to pay its way in a relatively short time.

It was writing about the Syrian regime's conquest of Ariha that got me thinking how reporting is done from war zones where reporters have no access. Here was a town in revolt, besieged by the government for over two weeks from ground and air, including barrel bombs, and, a full month later, the U.N. agency tracking IDPs wasn't aware of its fall, even after its 70,000 inhabitants had been forced to flee.

The international community had lost track of the fate of civilians in the Syrian interior, yet it was possible with the help of its former residents to reconstruct the drama, the pathos and the crimes. It struck me that tapping local residents, some who might be journalists, might hold the key to providing an accurate and engaging report. One might also tap citizen-journalists, educated citizens who agreed to be guided in the journalistic method of seeking out multiple sources and double-checking all facts.[29]

By the time that story was published, in November 2013, Syria was practically off-limits to foreign reporters. Journalists had long been the target of the Assad regime, starting with the deliberate targeting of an opposition media office in February 2012, which led to the death of Marie Colvin, an American reporter for London's *Sunday Times*, and Remi Ochlik, a French photojournalist.[30]

That same month, Anthony Shadid, a highly-experienced staff reporter for the *New York Times*, succumbed to asthma attack as he was departing in February 2012. This rattled editors, starting with the *Times*, which traditionally has set the pace for war coverage. There was also the disappearance of Austin Tice, a freelancer for McClatchy and *Washington Post* who is thought to be in government hands ever since he disappeared as he was departing Damascus in August 2012.

The threat became pronounced with the rise of the Islamic State extremists, who broke away from Jabhat al Nusra, the Al Qaida affiliate, in April 2013. I had traveled to eastern Syria in late July 2013, passing through ISIS checkpoints thanks to a written authorization from ISIS officials in northern Syria. Just days after my trip ended, ISIS issued a warning to journalists not to return.

Those who weren't aware of the message would pay the ultimate price. Steven Satloff, a *Time* magazine freelancer who entered Syria on August 4, just days after I had departed, was captured by ISIS and beheaded in September, 2014. A few days before his barbaric execution, ISIS had beheaded James Foley, an American freelancer who'd been abducted in November, 2012.

Quite why ISIS instituted its policy that month isn't known, but it functioned as an extension of regime policy of banning reporters, except those under its direct control.

In light of such risks in this conflict zone, my idea is to recognize these realities and supplement reportage from crisis zones by tapping local journalists and citizen-journalists. Assisted by a small foundation grant, I've already launched a test of the concept.

My proposal is to develop a non-traditional form of journalism: seeking firsthand accounts from those in the center of the crisis and pairing them with editors operating remotely. Even in the worst places, there are often local journalists or well-educated citizen-journalists. Even if they're living under siege, they have access to communications via the Internet and secure apps.

So, the idea is to commission writers to portray their town or region, first with texts, and at a later stage with still photos and videos.

The letters and articles produced in the first six months of the project tell the human story while providing a reality check on official statements. Both Moscow and Washington portray rebel-controlled Idlib province as being in the grip of a terror movement, the successor to Jabhat al Nusra, the Al Qaida affiliate. But the ground-level view, conveyed in the *Letter from Idlib*, is that Nusra's successor can't even organize its traffic cops, much less force the public to accept its Islamist dress code. And there's no sign of its purported international terror activities.

Russia claimed its evacuation of over 100,000 civilians from East Aleppo was "the biggest humanitarian operation in the world." But it was a deportation at gunpoint, as a Syrian reporter's account demonstrates.

While international news media portrayed "population exchanges" fostered by Iran as a routine activity, the *Letter from Madaya* makes clear that people abandoned their homes only to avert starvation and slaughter.

And the *Letter from Manbij*, a town inaccessible to international reporters, illustrates the aftermath when the U.S. empowers the Kurdish militia affiliated with the Kurdistan Workers Party (PKK) to seize territory from ISIS. Here's what happens: the PKK takes charge, suppresses the Arab population and invites the return of the Assad regime.

And while the Assad regime would often claim that the majority Sunnis were fighting a sectarian war against the minority Alawites, a dissident Alawite in Tartous, Assad's home region, claims it was the regime that deliberately stirred sectarian animosities.[31]

My hope is first to set up a network of citizen journalists throughout Syria, then to expand to other conflict zones that receive little or no in-depth media coverage, such as Yemen, the Egyptian Sinai and northern Nigeria. Later, the network should grow to encompass areas not at war, including Iran, central Asia and sub-Saharan Africa.

This is only one idea, but it could generate journalism that produces a narrative of events that is framed by humanitarian law. It's time to think of other projects and proposals to address the information gap. Not until a situation is defined, either by statesmen or journalists, will it reach the public. Public opinion matters. An informed public is indispensable if humanitarian law is to regain its place in the making of policy.

Conclusion

Throughout this chapter, I have sought to emphasize the centrality of humanitarian law, and a reader might reasonably inquire just why.

In my view, humanitarian law should not be viewed only as a measure of what conduct is acceptable, unacceptable and criminal in war. In setting the outer

90 Roy Gutman

boundaries for conduct in conflict, it provides a guide for humanitarian intervention in the post–Cold War era.

For one thing, the new threats to world order arise from non-state actors and rogue regimes willing to commit massive and systematic breaches of humanitarian law. Rogue actors that carry out these crimes gain their outsize role by exploiting a political and security vacuum that emerges in the absence of interest and involvement by the United States, the sole surviving superpower.

This helps explain the role of Al Qaida in Afghanistan in the chaos of the 1990s and Al Qaida in Iraq after the U.S. dispensed with the Iraqi Army. The U.S. troop withdrawal from Iraq in 2011, and the U.S. refusal to craft a policy to address the vacuum created by the mass uprising of Syrians in 2011, helped open the way for the rise of the Al Qaida spinoff, the Islamic State of Iraq and al-Sham.

But force alone is an insufficient response to the provocations of terror groups. It must be coupled with a strategy to end the political and security vacuum that gave rise to the terror in the first place.

Using force without a clear political goal, even while suspending the application of humanitarian law and ignoring the violations by rogue parties, does not contribute to security; rather, it promotes the breakdown of order. The use of force without a clear purpose undermines the political basis for the use of force, which in a democracy requires the support of the public and Congress.

In Syria in the summer of 2017, the United States was pursuing a contradictory policy, actively supporting a proxy force led by members of a U.S.-listed terror organization, the Kurdish YPG, to capture Raqqa, the self-styled capital of a second listed terror group, the Islamic State. Even as it pledged to turn over control of Raqqa to its rightful inhabitants, the U.S. government was empowering an ethnic minority with terrorist affiliations to dominate the indigenous Arab population. Moreover, the experience in Manbij, conquered in summer 2016, was that the Kurdish militia invited the Assad regime in to take control of key aspects of government.

As for humanitarian law, there was no way an outsider could watchdog observance, for the U.S. military said it had turned over that role to its local Kurdish-led partners. It was a further retreat from transparency.

In an era in which major powers face no existential threat, the primary threat is the destruction of world order through the rampant violation of a key component: international humanitarian law. If states accept their responsibility to uphold order and insist that it be upheld, journalism can hold states to account. If states abandon order, journalism itself is unable to produce anything but snapshots of the chaos that will ensue.

Notes

1 See Part II of the Rome statute. http://legal.un.org/icc/statute/romefra.htm
2 Barnard, Anne, "Syria Changed the World," *New York Times*, April 23, 2017, p. SR 2.
3 Gutman, Roy; Rieff, David; Dworkin, Anthony, *Crimes of War 2.0* (2007). New York: W.W. Norton, p. 396.
4 Gutman, Roy, *A Witness to Genocide* (2003). New York: MacMillan.

A journalist's perspective **91**

5 "All the goods must be placed in the warehouses, before 12 tomorrow," was the instruction. Quoted in http://www.icty.org/x/cases/karadzic/tjug/en/160324_judgem ent_summary.pdf

6 Gutman, *How We Missed the Story*, pp. 7–12.

7 Gutman, ibid.

8 Gutman, ibid., pp. 111–113.

9 Gutman, ibid, pp. 122–125.

10 Gutman, ibid. pp. 279–280.

11 Gutman, ibid, p. 115

12 Gutman, ibid. pp. 127–134

13 Gutman, ibid. p. 337. The official speaking was Gen. Michael Flynn. The first report of the atrocity was Barry, John, Dehghanpisheh, Babak and Gutman, Roy, "The Death Convoy of Afghanistan," *Newsweek*, August 26, 2002.

14 Gutman, Roy, three-part series in *The Daily Beast*, December 1, 2 and 5, 2016. www. thedailybeast.com/articles/2016/12/01/assad-henchman-here-s-how-we-built-isis.html www.thedailybeast.com/articles/2016/12/02/how-assad-staged-al-qaeda-bombings.html www.thedailybeast.com/articles/2016/12/05/how-isis-returned-to-syria.html

15 Gutman, idem.

16 https://obamawhitehouse.archives.gov/the-press-office/2013/08/30/government-a ssessment-syrian-government-s-use-chemical-weapons-august-21

17 www.mcclatchydc.com/2012/03/11/141485/syria-plants-anti-personnel-mines.html

18 www.mcclatchydc.com/2012/12/14/177482/syrians-sounding-alarm-over-growing.html

19 www.mcclatchydc.com/2013/01/07/179069/in-turkish-border-town-charity.html

20 Here are links to stories on war crimes:
www.mcclatchydc.com/2013/01/21/180376/syrian-government-has-pattern.html
www.mcclatchydc.com/2013/02/01/181784/syrian-government-offensive-forces.html
www.mcclatchydc.com/2013/02/01/181784/syrian-government-offensive-forces.html
www.mcclatchydc.com/news/nation-world/world/article24744472.htmlwww.mccla
tchydc.com/2013/02/25/184105/syrian-government-accused-of-targeting.html
www.mcclatchydc.com/2013/06/27/195198/scenes-of-destruction-syrian-mosques.html

21 www.mcclatchydc.com/2013/11/11/207990/battle-for-strategic-syrian-town.html

22 www.mcclatchydc.com/news/nation-world/world/article24745102.htmlhttp://www.
mcclatchydc.com/2012/10/29/172959/experts-divided-on-number-of-syrians.html
http://www.mcclatchydc.com/news/nation-world/world/article24768154.html

23 www.mcclatchydc.com/2014/05/23/228314/fleeing-syrians-find-a-hard-sanctuary.html

24 www.mcclatchydc.com/news/nation-world/world/article24785680.html

25 http://foreignpolicy.com/2016/01/15/u-n-knew-for-months-madaya-was-starving-
syria-assad/
http://foreignpolicy.com/2016/01/27/syria-madaya-starvation-united-nations-humanita
rian-response-plan-assad-edited/

26 http://foreignpolicy.com/2016/05/06/america-is-silent-as-aleppo-is-massacred/

27 Gutman, Roy, two-part series in *The Nation*, February 7 and 13, 2017. www.thenation.
com/article/have-the-syrian-kurds-committed-war-crimes/
www.thenation.com/article/americas-favorite-syrian-militia-rules-with-an-iron-fist/

28 www.thedailybeast.com/articles/2017/05/12/u-s-arms-kurds-who-are-isis-enemies-
turkey-enemies-assad-friends

29 www.mcclatchydc.com/2013/11/11/207990/battle-for-strategic-syrian-town.html

30 http://apps.washingtonpost.com/g/documents/national/lawsuit-charges-assad-milita
ry-killed-american-war-correspondent-marie-colvin/2068/

31 Letters and articles published under the project described in the text:
www.thenation.com/article/letter-from-rebel-controlled-idlib-syria/
http://foreignpolicy.com/2017/01/04/aleppos-survivors-have-nowhere-to-go/
www.thenation.com/article/letter-from-madaya-syria-under-siege-by-the-assad-regime-
for-nearly-two-years/

www.thedailybeast.com/articles/2017/05/12/u-s-arms-kurds-who-are-isis-enemies-turkey-enemies-assad-friends

www.thenation.com/article/in-tartous-syria-women-wear-black-youth-are-in-hiding-and-bitterness-grows/

7

PREVENTING MASS ATROCITIES AT THE LOCAL LEVEL

Using village committees for conflict prevention in Mauritania

Ekkehard Strauss[1]

Introduction

When genocide and other mass atrocities unfold, neighbor turns against neighbor, and long-lasting social and cultural relationships of communities and individuals succumb to the destructive power of identity-based violence. Families, friends, work colleagues, political acquaintances – the whole social fabric of cities, neighborhoods and villages is destroyed and replaced by fear and mistrust.

Since its creation, GPAnet has encouraged its members to promote local data gathering and include the local perspective in discussions on the development of strategies to prevent mass atrocities. The usual discussion on the prevention of mass atrocities considers mainly international, regional and national state actors and only sparingly refers to civil society and victims' organizations, and even less to individuals. More recently, there have been initiatives to include civil society and private business in the implementation of the responsibility to protect and the prevention of genocide. For example, the *Compendium of Practice* compiled by the United Nations Special Adviser on the Prevention of Genocide[2] lists a number of local initiatives to involve civil society more systematically in targeting root causes of mass atrocities, addressing structural challenges and countering identity-based narratives by building on methodologies developed for second-track diplomacy in social conflicts[3] and humanitarian protection.[4]

Research on the motivation of individual perpetrators and participants in genocide provide detailed accounts and analyses that highlight entry points for strategies for prevention at the local level.[5] With increasing knowledge about the character of perpetrators and their motives, it seems consequential for prevention to move from the state level into the realms of local society and the individual. Thus, early-warning and prevention would move towards the immediate perpetrators and victims, and prevention would be understood as a methodological process of responding to a limited

94 Ekkehard Strauss

set of risk factors at the community level, based on a combined qualitative and quantitative approach to data and information gathering.

The following shares our experience of establishing village community committees in Mauritania as a tool to prevent identity-based conflict and violence in regions with a moderate risk of mass atrocities.

General risk factors for identity-based conflict in Mauritania

According to the revised risk assessment of potential state perpetrators of genocide or politicide by Harff, Mauritania is at a medium risk of genocide or politicide, if regime instability occurs.[6]

For Mauritania, there is very little basic socio-economic data and analysis available related to risk factors of identity-based conflict, such as the ethnic composition of the population or the distribution of economic and political power by ethnic, tribal or regional affiliation. This is partly due to the resistance at the national government to gather or publish such data. Part of the international underreporting is caused by the very low absolute number of people affected by past or present events of identity-based conflict, which rarely reached the threshold of international media attention, even though the percentage of the affected population within the total population might have been much higher than in situations currently on the international agenda. However, an identity-based conflict occurring in Mauritania, one that resulted in a dysfunctional or failed state, would affect the security of the Sahel region. Criminal and terrorist movements active in Northern Mali could use the territory increasingly as a safe haven or support structure for carrying out attacks or trafficking in people, drugs or weapons. The lack of attention to the situation from a perspective of preventing identity-based conflict is also concerning with a view to the tribal and clan connections between Mauritania and its neighbors. It has been clearly established that the overall security situation in the Sahel has underlying causes related to inequality and weak governance.[7]

Very limited analysis of the social–political context of Mauritania is provided by national and international NGOs. Their public information is mainly related to the question of slavery and often lacks credibility regarding the substantiation of data and verification of information.[8] The main sources on slavery are national NGOs, which often act in the interest of their broader political agenda related to the revision of prevailing clan, caste and religious power structures.[9]

Mauritania is a multi-ethnic and multi-cultural country with an estimated population of roughly 4 million, 60% of whom live in rural communities[10] with very precarious livelihoods heavily dependent on agriculture and pastoralism. The population can be divided into two groups: the Moors, including the black moors (former slaves, called "Haratins") and the so-called Afro-Mauritanians, including the Peuhl, Soninke, Wolof and Bambara. In the absence of official data on the ethnic composition of the population, this issue has been subject to fierce public discussion. The majority of observers settled on an estimation of 30% Arab-Moors, 40% Haratin and 30% Afro-Mauritanians.[11] According to the findings of UN human rights mechanisms, the majority of stakeholders believe that the Arab-Moors dominate political and economic life, whereas the majority of the population, represented by most of the Haratins and the Afro-Mauritanians, has been de facto systematically excluded. This situation has kept these groups in poverty, fueling frustrations and anger related to the Government's failure to address effectively the root causes of their discrimination and marginalization.[12]

The Haratins are thought to constitute the largest ethnic group and the most politically and economically marginalized in a society deeply stratified by ethnicity, descent and caste. A large majority of dockers, domestic workers and day laborers performing unskilled and low-paid jobs are Haratins, whereas very few Haratins occupy high-ranking civil servant and senior executive positions in the public and private sectors. Haratins also claim that they have been excluded from the business and banking sectors, as commercial enterprises are usually headed by non-Haratins. Similar discriminatory practices affect the Afro-Mauritanian communities. This stratification, which has historical roots, fuels latent tensions and conflicts, which have occasionally turned violent in the past.

During events between 1989 and 1991, summarized as "passif humanitaire", 50,000 Afro-Mauritanians were forcibly expelled to Senegal, and hundreds more were tortured or killed during an undeclared military occupation of the Senegal River valley, where many of the Afro-Mauritanians live. 500 Afro-Mauritanian military officers were reportedly victims of extrajudicial killings. The perpetrators have been granted amnesty by a law adopted in 1993.[13] The victims, who fled to Senegal, returned under a tripartite agreement with UNHCR and while the government declared in 2013 that their return and reintegration was finalized, the so-called "repatriates" claim that they have not been fully restituted into their property, civil status or work.[14] The government rejected repeated demands for a transitional justice process.[15]

In July 2013, violent incidents erupted in Kaedi, the largest city and administrative center of the Gorgol region in the South. The incidents involved individuals from the Moorish and Peulh communities, and left 21 people injured and 15 shops looted, with 29 individuals arrested. Although this was the fourth incident of this kind, there was a much more heightened ethnic dimension than in previous events, reflecting the mounting tensions between the Moors and the Afro-Mauritanian communities during the election process. Reportedly, violence erupted in the city's main market after a young Moorish man assaulted an older Peulh woman, triggering anger among some Peulh people present at the scene, who attempted to retaliate by targeting the Moorish shop holders in the area. Local authorities expressed concern at an increasing instrumentalization of isolated incidents that were then turned into ethnically polarized confrontations. The underlying ethnic discrimination was seen to be evident in the official response, which was to compensate and support the victims from the Moorish communities affected by these incidents only days after the events, while the Afro-Mauritanians who lost assets and profit as a result of the incidents of 1989 received no such help.[16]

More recent incidents of violent conflict involved group identity based on religious orientation, created by false accusations and rumor spread via TV, news pages, Twitter and Facebook. The Internet is accessible through the telephone network, and even remote areas of the country with no access to electricity or state services are illuminated at night by the screens of smartphones charged at small communal solar panels. The general public considers the Internet a reliable source of information and voice messages and video are used to spread information to a largely illiterate people.[17]

In March 2014, hundreds of protesters threw stones and chanted anti-government slogans in Nouakchott after local media reported that copies of the holy Quran were desecrated in a mosque. A young man was killed during the protests after apparently being hit by an exploding tear-gas canister. The violence began minutes after a false rumor was spread that four people dressed in turbans drove to a mosque in the north of the capital and seized copies of the Quran to destroy.[18]

Since January 2014, a young man has been held on charges of alleged apostasy for publishing a critical article on the caste stratification of society, which was perceived by some as blasphemous of the prophet Mohammad. At the end of 2016, while the Supreme Court deliberated on his appeal, a public movement attracted thousands to gather each Friday after the main prayer in cities across the country to demand the execution of the young man. Religious leaders, civil society activists and journalists, who demanded that justice take its independent course, were publicly threatened and attacked, including when a live TV discussion was interrupted by a mob of armed men.[19]

On these occasions, religion has been used to justify threats of violence and public hate speech against so-called "atheists" to defend a particular application of the Sharia, which forms the basis of the legal system in Mauritania.[20] At the same time, these religious identities have ethnic and caste overtones, as particular interpretations of Islam are used to justify the perseverance of the traditional clan and caste structure of society. In addition, religious tolerance among Muslims is decreasing with the increasing competition between the Sufi tradition of Mauritania, upheld by most Afro-Mauritanians and many traditional Moors, and Salafi and Wahabi tendencies, mainly promoted by young Arab-Moors with financial support from the Gulf countries.

Thus, the development of strategies to prevent conflict and violence based on identity has to make pragmatic use of the data and analysis available and adapt its approaches while filling information gaps. In this situation, it appears most effective to work with the immediate potential perpetrators and victims, while addressing the long- and medium-term response strategies with the government and its partners based on a broadening set of information and analysis emanating from the local level.

Preventing identity-based conflict at the local level

The local approach to mass atrocity prevention aims at addressing a limited number of elevated risk factors through the identification of joint local interests beyond group identities and constant data gathering and monitoring of these conflict factors. Where basic socio-economic data for an evidence-based response strategy are either not collected or unavailable, this approach provides a basic set of quantitative and qualitative data that can complement the analysis of national economic and development data for root causes of inequality related to group identities. This approach will help to identify practical options for addressing root causes of conflict at an early stage.

In Mauritania, villages are created on the basis of clan, family and caste structures. With variance among the different ethnic groups and some exceptions, most villages contain members of one or more large families belonging to the same clan, divided by castes. In addition to their identities being based on their affiliation within this structure, people are also defined by vulnerabilities, sometimes acquired ones, such as persons with disabilities, former slaves or women made heads of households by migration or divorce.

Villages may be neighbors to villages of other clans or castes, often created through migration, land allocation or resettlement decisions by the government. Due to climate change, the availability of water, pasture and firewood is increasingly limited. Villages in the same area compete for daily resources and for the allocation of social services, such as health, education, water, additional food supply or electricity by the government and international development actors. In many of the villages away from the paved main roads, people cannot eat more than one meal per day, and visitors bring food and water along in order not to draw on the sparse reserves of their hosts. In areas with nomadic activities, large herds of animals migrate during the vegetation period along traditional routes on both sides of the border with Mali and increase the pressure on food supplies, natural resources and infrastructure during these few crucial weeks.

This situation offers a wide range of risks of day-to-day conflict within or among communities. It also invites government and affiliated tribes and clans to influence the political allegiance, voting habits and political mobilization of large parts of the rural population. Villages composed of former slaves, women heads of household or former nomads, who lost their economic basis due to climate change, perceive that development and humanitarian support has often been conditioned on political allegiances. These allegiances are the basis of political influence of regional tribe and clan notables on the government and within state institutions in Nouakchott.[21]

The tribal structure of the village, with its strict rules of solidarity based on descent, normally leads to the escalation of a conflict within a tribe, which can engage in mediation according to traditional rules. Village community committees seek to create a forum of discussion between families and their members at a lower level, based on a common local interest in preventing the consequences of a conflict following the strict dynamics of tribal involvement. The representation of vulnerable groups within the committees facilitates the creation of alliances based on interests and needs rather than clan or caste affiliation. Religion can play an important role in bringing people together based on joint values similar to those reflected in human rights obligations, and offering concrete solutions in conformity with religious traditions.[22]

The causes of conflict can be expected to intensify to the extent that they are related to climate change and its consequences.[23] Since these developments cannot be halted or reversed, only their consequences can be mitigated. People in rural Mauritania will have to continue competing for fewer natural resources until they finally have to move to other places, mostly cities, where the conflict factors related to ethnicity, clan, family or caste affiliation are retained and often exacerbated under urban living conditions.

Past initiatives by development partners to create village community committees often resulted in multiple committees or contact persons within the same village. Their role as primary interlocutors of the government or international humanitarian or development partners gave these members considerable influence over village affairs. Due to lack of communication among different partners, some villages benefitted from multiple projects, such as the drilling of wells, additional food supplies or the establishment of a school, which were implemented in cooperation with different village committees with sometimes contradictory objectives, while villages in need, in particular those off the tarmac, were neglected by aid organizations. The respective committees normally ceased functioning when the particular project was finished, with no measurable long-term impact. Only when all development partners agree to work with the same village committee created through the same transparent process and representing the most vulnerable, can a critical level of influence on village affairs be created to provide the members with sustainable conflict-mitigating authority. This approach also needs to involve local authorities. It is important that state structures do not perceive the village committees as competition. They can persuade reluctant families within a village, provide basic security through the police and gendarmerie and promote the role of the committees *vis-á-vis* national and international development partners.

This empowerment through participation in the development and implementation phases of village projects also helps the committees to counter the potential influence of armed groups on the relationship of host populations with Malian refugees in the Southeast of the country. While not directly involved in the conflicts between refugees and villagers, the presence of members of armed groups, visible inter alia through the recruitment of child soldiers from villages close to the border or in the refugee camp in M'bera,[24] can change the balance of mediation due to the mere possibility of their involvement in the dispute.

The regions with the highest risk of identity-based conflict are at the same time the poorest rural areas of the country. However, the rural depopulation concentrates conflict factors related to inequality in the main urban centers, because rural people move to family and friends from the same area, thus creating urban districts characterized by largely homogenous social and ethnic identities. There is a moderate international interest in providing humanitarian and development assistance to Mauritania within broader security interests in the Sahel region, but, with regard to the root causes of discrimination and poverty,[25] there is very little attention to the impact of strategies and projects on identity-based conflicts, particularly those related to systemic human rights violations.

The creation of village community committees

Identification of priority locations

The process of creating village community committees required, first, the identification of priority locations where conflict prevention was most needed. Through a desk review, project staff sought to establish an inventory of existing local mechanisms of prevention and management of conflict, gathered public data on the socio-economic situation of the different regions, analyzed reports of past projects and interviewed humanitarian and development actors, local authorities (including police and gendarmerie) and national and international NGOs. The main generic conflict factors identified include ethnic and clan composition, past instances of violence, including the "passif humanitaire", the presence of nomadic cattle herders during the year, development and humanitarian support from the state or international partners, accessibility ("beyond the tarmac") and the presence of refugees from the M'bera camp. This review led to identification of the South-East region of Hodh El Chargui and three wilayas in the South as general priority areas.

On this basis, project staff visited particular villages in order to map any existing committees or other mechanisms, and to evaluate their operational capacity and functioning with regard to the challenges faced by the respective communities. During the visits, village meetings following social tradition were organized – i.e., in groups with the participation of existing self-organization structures such as the village head, women and youth representatives. Specific requests were made for the presence of people with disabilities, IDPs, refugees, women heads of household, members of minority ethnic groups, clans or castes and former slaves. The range of the village population is between ten and 30 households with multiple members. Project staff sought to establish the human rights violations, which are perceived as related to distinguishable identities. Group interviews were based on a questionnaire on human rights violations regarding discrimination in accessing social and economic rights, sex and gender-based violence (including child marriage), migration and trafficking, access to justice, health and education, political participation, past human rights violations and related issues. The group interviews were followed by in-depth interviews of a sub-set of individuals selected on the basis of self-identification during the group interviews.

Based on the analysis of quantitative and qualitative data gathered, 26 priority villages were identified within the host communities of the Malian refugee camp in M'bera and 30 in the other priority areas in the country.

As the presentation of the detailed analysis would go beyond the objective of this chapter, the following will be limited to the villages of communities hosting the camp of Malian refugees since 2012, which has been among the poorest areas of Mauritania.

It was established that the main concerns of the villagers as related to group identity included the management of water points, which are under stress by the livestock of different sedentary and nomadic groups, including the animals brought

100 Ekkehard Strauss

along from Mali by the refugees. Villagers also often intercept carts carrying firewood for sale in the camp, which caused violent friction within the villages and between villagers and refugees, according to local administrative and security authorities. The pressure on pasture land, which is increasingly rare due to a lack of seasonal rain, is also perceived as a cause for identity-based conflict among villagers and between the villages and the refugees. In addition, host communities have highlighted the problem of cattle rustling by nomads and refugees from the camp. The perceived inactivity of local authorities when alerted to such cases created frustration among the affected villagers, who expect immediate compensation according to local custom. According to reports, confirmed by the police and gendarmerie, women in the villages around the M'bera camp were repeatedly victims of violence by men from the camp. In addition, several thousand Mauritanian beneficiaries from neighboring villages were deregistered from the refugee camp, which caused frustration among those villagers, who had once benefitted from the humanitarian assistance and often shared their rations with their village, but now imposed additional burdens. Also, the partial introduction of cash transfer instead of food deliveries is another potential factor of tension with the host population. People from the host community perceive an inflation of prices for basic food items in the local markets and feel discriminated against compared with the refugees, who are provided with pecuniary means of subsistence.

The mapping and evaluation process is continuing, including in other regions of the country, taking into account the developments of insecurity in Northern Mali and its impact on Mauritania. A number of villages requested the mediated creation of committees. In addition to gathering data and analyses related to human rights violations, the process allows the establishment of contacts for exchange and data gathering on an ongoing basis. This makes it possible to identify trends and patterns of violations and to prioritize the implementation of humanitarian and development activities in villages with an elevated risk, including by government and by international governmental and non-governmental actors. The data and analysis are shared with humanitarian and development actors to address common underlying causes of poverty and conflict, based on an agreement of all stakeholders to work with the same committees.

Establishment of representative village community committees

The establishment of village community committees in the 26 priority locations in the South-East involved the following steps: (1) the organization of village gatherings, with an emphasis on the representation of vulnerable and minority groups, to discuss the situation in the village, past incidents of conflict and the joint priority interests and needs; (2) the explanation of the basic functions of the committees – i.e., to represent all interests in the village, mitigate conflict within the village and with neighboring or nomad communities, contribute to effective humanitarian protection through upholding the basic principles of participation and assist in early warning of human rights violations and other incidents; (3) the election of the committee members upon proposal by the village gathering; (4) public pledges of the newly-elected committee members to the village population, including the frequency of meetings and priority interests and needs to address and related deadlines.

This process takes from a few hours to a number of days or even weeks, depending on existing friction and conflict within the community. The support of local authorities has been important in finding compromises and arriving at a representative composition of the committee, in particular if different clans are present and one group risks losing its domination.

Project staff provided two initial, very basic, trainings on conflict prevention and protection mainstreaming to the newly-elected committees, based on slides and role-plays built around the concrete conflict situations faced by the respective village. The mostly illiterate members of the committees were encouraged in discussions of pictures to gather more targeted information and to develop practical options to address conflict factors.

In addition, committees were encouraged to immediately start working on village development plans and agreements on the use of joint resources. The aim was to connect different groups to a village identity on the basis of joint interests towards local authorities and humanitarian and development actors.

Preliminary conclusions

In order to detect relevant developments regarding mass atrocities in a country with considerable difficulties in accessing rural locations and gathering data, it is important to limit the data collection according to the local context. While human rights violations have been recognized as general warning signs of future identity-based conflict, existing early warning approaches require the collection of data along too many variables, which are often not available,[26] or concentrate on developments at the national level, where discrimination patterns may be difficult to detect.[27] In order to narrow the data, there is a need to filter information on human rights violations by its connection to perceived or real group relationships, taking into account multiple identities.

Pre-existing group identities can be based on a past history of violence, sociopolitical affiliation along ethnic or tribal lines, religious orientation or ethnicity. New group identities or perceptions thereof can form around recent events, and require a qualitative analysis at the local level. Complex processes of identity formation take place on the basis of rumor and conspiracy theories, which only subsequently may be attributed to pre-existing group identities. The evaluation of the local impact of new identities perceived or created at the central level also offers an opportunity to respond at the impact level rather than the causation level, which has been difficult to attain in most mass atrocity situations in the past.[28] In fact, there are a limited number of events that could be exploited for identity-based conflict, because of the realities on the ground. In Mauritania, potential conflict between, e.g., Malian refugees and host communities could break out over access to water, pasture, firewood, cattle rustling and harassment of women.

The onset of genocide has changed over time from the implementation of an extermination plan carried out by systematically indoctrinated, highly-developed state institutions, to mere violent civil unrest based on identity. Concerned governments are often weakened by shifting and informal power structures, unleashing large-scale violence against certain groups with a tacit understanding of impunity for these acts. Village community committees allow the identification of key actors at the central and local level, including a deterrent use of individual criminal responsibility.

Collective or group rights are little developed in human rights law. The Genocide Convention is, in fact, the only human rights instrument protecting a group as such, apart from the Declaration on National Minorities and the Declaration on the Rights of Indigenous Peoples, which are not legally binding.[29] At the same time, historically – e.g., during the French Revolution, the American War of Independence or the fall of communism – individual human rights were used collectively to demand changes in group relationships and group-based power structures. The democratic system, as the most favorable environment for the realization of individual rights and freedoms, is based on the principle of institutionalized majority decision, which includes the possibility of changing majorities based on shifting interests and identities, combined with protections for minorities. This mechanism, however, does not necessarily function in societies based on tribalism and a strict caste system. New challenges create new interests and, thus, new identities with a demand to reform or replace altogether institutions servicing the old identity-based power structures. Village communities can contribute to stability by absorbing violent change through joint decision-making and compromise. At the local level, individual rights need to be reformulated into group interests based on multiple identities. The UN would be best placed to help develop and formulate standards for different identities according to international human rights obligations.

Experience with the increasing use of Internet-based mass communication for identity-based radicalization shows that rumors and perceptions have become more influential than facts, which resembles the experience in Rwanda and Bosnia regarding conventional mass media. However, today, incitement to hatred and violence is more easily generated by popular forces within the society, and then taken on by politicians for election purposes. Even moderate parties may feel forced to follow popular demands, thus elevating minority radical positions to the political mainstream. From this perspective, the Internet has replaced the street or marketplace in political disputation, so the messages have to be countered at the level of the addressees rather than the senders. One possibility is the attempt to define common interest at the local level, which counters the impact of radical messages related to ethnic, racial or religious identity. Knowledge of local capacities to counter radical messages is important for the evaluation of sources of incitement, monitoring their impact and identifying main actors.

Depending on the resources available and the degree of coordination between different actors, community-based humanitarian and development action can

Conflict prevention in Mauritania **103**

contribute a range of elements to information gathering and data analysis for purposes of mass atrocity prevention, if the main risk factors are agreed upon and the relevant communities are targeted. This would mean a considerable shift of prevention from the institutional to the community level, taking advantage of our increasing knowledge about the causes and accelerators of mass atrocities.

Notes

1 The views expressed herein are those of the author and do not necessarily reflect the views of the United Nations.
2 *United Nations Office on the Prevention of Genocide and the Responsibility to Protect, Compendium of Practice. Implementation of the Responsibility to Protect 2005–2016*, www.un.org/en/genocideprevention/documents/RtoP%20Compendium%20of%20Practice%20(Provisional%20Pre-Publication%20Version)%20FINAL%2020%20March%202017.pdf
3 See, e.g., Louis Kriesberg/Bruce W. Dayton, *Constructive Conflicts: From Escalation to Resolution*, 4th edition, Lanham, MD: Rowman & Littlefield Publishers, 2012.
4 See, e.g., Gezim Visoka, National NGOs, in: Roger MacGinty/Jenny H. Peterson (eds.), *The Routledge Companion to Humanitarian Action*, London and New York: Routledge, 2015, p. 267 et seq.
5 See, e.g., Paul R. Bartop, *Encountering Genocide: Personal Accounts from Victims, Perpetrators, and Witnesses*, Santa Barbara, CA: ABC-CLIO, 2015.
6 The risk assessment analyses the variables of (1) state-led discrimination against any ethnic or religious minority; (2) exclusionary ideology held by a ruling elite, minority elite or contention over elite ethnicity; (3) the type of polity, i.e. autocracy versus democracy; and (4) the past use of genocidal policies. See Risk Assessments 2015: Potential State Perpetrators of Genocide and Politicide, www.gpanet.org/node/567. See also the 2017 update, Chapter 3 in this book.
7 Report of the Secretary-General on the situation in the Sahel region, S/2013/354 of 14 June 2013, paras. 5 et seq.
8 The Special Rapporteur on Slavery recommended in 2010 that the government undertake a comprehensive study of the history and nature of slavery in Mauritania: *Report of the Special Rapporteur on Contemporary Forms of Slavery, Including Its Causes and Consequences, Gulnara Shahinian. Mission to Mauritania*, A/HRC/15/20/Add.2 of 16 August 2010, para. 103. A similar recommendation from Canada during Mauritania's second-cycle UPR was not supported by the government: *Report of the Working Group on the Universal Periodic Review. Mauritania*, A/HRC/31/6 of 23 December 2015, para. 129.34.
9 See, e.g., Walk Free Foundation, *Global Slavery Index 2016*, p. 122 et seq., www.globalslaveryindex.org/index/#; Society of Threatened People, "Slavery in Mauritania. Written Statement, Human Rights Council 18th Session, 24 August 2011", www.gfbv.de/fileadmin/redaktion/UN-statements/2011/Mauretanien_Sklaverei_Item_3_Contemporary_slavery_The_case_of_Mauritania.pdf
10 http://data.worldbank.org/country/mauritania
11 *Report of the Special Rapporteur on Extreme Poverty and Human Rights on His Mission to Mauritania*, A/HRC/35/26/Add.1 of 8 March 2017, para. 27.
12 *Report of the Special Rapporteur on Contemporary Forms of Racism, Racial Discrimination, Xenophobia and Related Intolerance, Mutuma Ruteere. Mission to Mauritania*, A/HRC/26/49/Add.1 of 8 May 2014, paras. 5–10.
13 See for more details Human Rights Watch, *Mauritania's Campaign of Terror. State-Sponsored Repression of Black Africans*. New York: Human Rights Watch, 1994. https://www.hrw.org/sites/default/files/reports/MAURITAN944.PDF
14 *Accord Tripartite entre le gouvernement de la République Islamique de Mauritanie, le gouvernement de la République du Senegal et le Haut-Commissariat des Nations Unies pour les réfugiés*

pour le rapatriement volontaire des réfugiés Mauritaniens au Senegal, November 2007. www.ihrda.org/wp-content/uploads/2010/10/ACCORD-TRIPARTITE.pdf

15 See for an early demand e.g. FIDH, Mauritanie: "Une Instance vérité réconciliation doit contribuer au règlement du passif humanitaire", Communique, 10 December 2007.

16 *Report of the Special Rapporteur on Contemporary Forms of Racism, Racial Discrimination, Xenophobia and Related Intolerance, Mutuma Ruteere, Mission to Mauritania*, A/HRC/26/49/Add.1, 7 May 2014, paras. 5 et seq.

17 According to UNICEF, the youth (15–24 years) literacy rate (%) in 2008–2012 for males was 71.6 and for females 66.2. The number of mobile phones per 100 population was 111.1 in 2012. See www.unicef.org/infobycountry/mauritania_statistics.html

18 See www.aljazeera.com/news/africa/2014/03/protests-mauritania-over-quran-desecration-20143474732393880.html$

19 See heu.org/iheu-briefing-on-mohamed-cheikh-ould-mkheitir-case/

20 The preamble of the Constitution of 1994 defines the country as an Islamic Republic and recognizes Islam as the sole religion of its citizens and the state. The Sharia provides legal principles upon which the law and legal procedures are based. See www.constituteproject.org/constitution/Mauritania_2012.pdf

21 Mariella Villasante Cervello, From the Disappearance of "Tribes" to Reawakening of the Tribal Feeling: Strategies of State among the Formerly Nomadic Bidan (Arabophone) of Mauritania, in: Dawn Chatty (ed.), *Nomadic Societies in the Middle East and North Africa. Entering the 21st Century*, Leiden and Boston, MA: Brill, 2006, pp. 144–171.

22 Philippe Marchesin, *Tribus, ethnies et pouvoir en Mauritanie*, Paris: Karthala, 2010.

23 *Report of the Office of the United Nations High Commissioner for Human Rights on the Relationship between Climate Change and Human Rights*, A/HRC/10/61, 15 January 2009.

24 See "Mauritania, M'berra camp: Islamist groups recruit child soldiers among Malian refugees", *Dune Voices*, 17 March 2015, http://dune-voices.info/public/index.php/en/border-issues-mauritania-eng/item/458-mauritania,-m%E2%80%99berra-camp-islamist-groups-recruit-child-soldiers-among-malian-refugees. The majority of the more than 50,000 refugees in the M'bera camp arrived from Northern Mali in 2012–2013. In 2016, UNHCR registered more than 5,000 additional arrivals. Many refugees are nomads, who arrived at the camp with thousands of livestock in constant need of water and fodder. The total population of the district of Bassikounou prior to the arrival of the refugees was estimated at 45,000. See UNHCR, Mauritania Factsheet April 2017, http://reporting.unhcr.org/sites/default/files/UNHCR%20Mauritania%20Factsheet%20-%20March%202017.pdf

25 "End-of-mission statement on Mauritania", by Professor Philip Alston, United Nations Human Rights Council Special Rapporteur on extreme poverty and human rights, Nouakchott, 11 May 2016, www.ohchr.org/EN/NewsEvents/Pages/DisplayNews.aspx?NewsID=19948&LangID=E#sthash.c54WXQ4p.dpuf

26 Office of the Special Adviser on the Prevention of Genocide, *Framework of Analysis for Atrocity Crimes. A Tool for Prevention*, United Nations, 2014.

27 Barbara Harff, Assessing Risks of Genocide and Politicide, in: Monty G. Marshall and Ted Robert Gurr (eds.), *Peace and Conflict 2005. A Global Survey of Armed Conflicts, Self-Determination Movements, and Democracy*. College Park, MD: University of Maryland, 2005, p. 57 et seq.

28 Mark Kielsgard, *Responding to Modern Genocide. At the Confluence of Law and Politics*, London and New York: Routledge, 2016, p. 96 et seq.

29 Corsin Bisaz, *The Concept of Group Rights in International Law. Groups as Contested Right-Holders, Subjects and Legal Persons*, Leiden and Boston, MA: Martinus Nijhoff Publishers, 2012, p. 104 et seq.

8

IN THE ABSENCE OF WILL

Could genocide in Darfur have been halted or mitigated?

Eric Reeves

Let me frame my analysis here with two remarkable statements. The first is a memo from August 2004 in Misteriya, North Darfur—headquarters of Musa Hilal, the most notorious of the *Janjaweed* leaders—and almost certainly authored by Hilal himself. It is brief but comprehensive:

> "Change the demography of Darfur; empty it of African tribes."[1]

The second comes from a Human Rights Watch report of 2015, 11 years later, examining the emergence of the "new *Janjaweed*," the Rapid Response Forces (RSF). While training in North Darfur in December 2014 for the 2015 campaign, "Ahmed," a 35-year-old defecting RSF member, told Human Rights Watch investigators that regime Second Vice President Hassabo Mohammed Abdel Rahman had addressed him and his fellow fighters before they began their enormously destructive assault:

> Ahmed said that a few days prior to leaving for East Jebel Marra, Sudanese Vice President Hassabo Mohammed Abdel Rahman directly addressed several hundred army and RSF soldiers: "Hassabo told us to clear the area east of Jebel Marra. To kill any male. He said we want to clear the area of insects … He said East Jebel Marra is the kingdom of the rebels. We don't want anyone there to be alive."[2]

Skepticism about whether Darfur is the site of genocide would seem to be thoroughly untenable, given the clear intent evident in countless thousands of violent actions directed specifically against the non-Arab or African tribal populations of Darfur, and by such high-level military instructions.

The actions of the National Islamic Front/National Congress Party regime, which came to power by military coup almost 30 years ago (June 30, 1989), should have commanded serious international attention from the beginning of its brutal and tyrannical rule. Focus was indeed given to issues of terrorism, particularly since Osama bin Laden was welcomed by the regime from 1992–1996, formative years for Al Qaida; but little attention was paid to the genocide in the Nuba Mountains, ongoing for most of the 1990s. The "oil wars" in what was then Western Upper Nile (now mainly Unity State) in South Sudan had become the occasion for Khartoum's regular and militia forces to engage in a massive campaign of ethnically-targeted destruction and displacement from oil concession areas. But as late as 1999, very few paid any attention to any part of what now must be referred to as "greater Sudan" (Sudan and the recently independent South Sudan).

The least attention was paid to Darfur, although it suffered the same marginalization and abuse at the hands of those in Khartoum, men who have been consistently guided by a viciously Arabist and Islamist agenda. Even students of Sudan for the most part knew little and wrote less about the region.

This changed dramatically with the outbreak of war in Darfur in 2003, and in particular with Khartoum's shift to a policy of genocidal counter-insurgency after the humiliating defeat of regular armed forces by the Darfuri rebels at el-Fasher air base in April 2003. Following this, it became clear that the destruction of the perceived base of civilian support for the rebels—primarily the non-Arab/African Fur, Zaghawa, and Massalit—was the primary military strategy. It has remained so, *mutatis mutandis*, for more than 13 years. The Darfur genocide is the longest-lasting of the past century.

Could this have been forestalled? Were there moments in these terrible years during which actions by international actors of consequence could have halted the violence and civilian destruction? I suggest there were in fact six such moments:

[1] The NIF/NCP should have been under much greater scrutiny by the international community, as well as economic and diplomatic pressure, from the moment it seized power. Its radical, ideologically-driven Islamist and Arabizing agenda was well-known, as was its opposition to the peace agreement with rebels in South Sudan—an agreement that was aborted by the NIF/NCP coup. Ignoring these features of the regime had consequences almost immediately, particularly for its waging of war in the peripheral regions of what was then the largest country in Africa. If the regime had been convinced early on that it was understood for what it was, actions such as genocide in the Nuba Mountains, the extreme violence of the oil wars (1997–2002), and even the Darfur genocide would likely have been seen as diplomatically and economically costly enterprises by a regime that has always been exceptionally canny in assessing the strength and credibility of international responses and pressures. Instead, the world—guided by a wide range of self-interested motives—simply looked away, and Khartoum's *génocidaires* came to understand full well that they were not going to face serious pressure. U.S. economic sanctions imposed in the 1990s were mainly for Khartoum's perceived support of international terrorism; they were unrelated to domestic atrocity crimes.

[2] Reports from a wide range of organizations (human rights and humanitarian), from the UN, and from journalists, made clear well before the end of 2003

that genocide was underway. The situation cried out for humanitarian intervention with the primary goal of protecting the civilian population of Darfur. As I argued in a February 2004 op/ed in the *Washington Post* (published well after the piece had been originally drafted and submitted):

> Khartoum has so far refused to rein in its Arab militias; has refused to enter into meaningful peace talks with the insurgency groups; and most disturbingly, refuses to grant unfettered humanitarian access. The international community has been slow to react to Darfur's catastrophe and has yet to move with sufficient urgency and commitment. A credible peace forum must rapidly be created. Immediate plans for humanitarian intervention should begin. The alternative is to allow tens of thousands of civilians to die in the weeks and months ahead in what will be continuing genocidal destruction.[3]

The situation has changed painfully little in the intervening 13 years, and the worst civilian destruction may well lie ahead. And in fact, it is not "tens of thousands of civilians" who have died in genocidal destruction, but hundreds of thousands. I believe the data suggest an estimate of 500,000.[4] The constantly cited "UN figure" of 300,000 is essentially a crude extrapolation made by the head of UN humanitarian operations during a press conference in April 2008. It is nine years old, and reflects none of the later data or research.

Others would also take up the call for intervention, including senior officials for African policy in the Clinton administration (Susan Rice and Gayle Smith). Nicholas Kristof of the *New York Times* reported repeatedly on the genocide-in-progress, as did many others. A broad-based American civil society movement took up the cause of Sudan passionately from 2004 through 2008. In the wake of the U.S. invasion of Iraq, however, there was little international inclination to engage in any sort of "humanitarian intervention," no matter how great the risk to millions of lives.

[3] The Abuja (Nigeria) peace talks yielded the deeply flawed, indeed failed "Darfur Peace Agreement" (DPA) in May 2006, the culmination of talks that had been proceeding off and on since 2005. It was bound to fail because there were no guarantors for the various pledges and promises that Khartoum made, knowing full well it would be able to renege whenever it wished. The agreement also split the rebels: only one rebel leader, Minni Minawi, would sign, and other rebel leaders have subsequently been permanently at odds with Minawi, as well as each other. The agreement was a classic example of Khartoum's "divide and conquer" military and diplomatic strategy. Robert Zoellick, the U.S. special envoy at the talks, engaged in an impatient version of "shotgun diplomacy," and this led to much of the disastrous outcome.[5] Supposed experts involved in the talks, such as Alex de Waal, contributed to the disaster by touting the DPA as something it would and could never be. This was the last time peace could be truly negotiated.

[4] Throughout much of summer 2006, the UN's Department of Peacekeeping Operations worked on a plan for a peace support operation in Darfur with a

108 Eric Reeves

primary mandate to protect civilians, who were still being slaughtered and displaced. Camps for the displaced grew increasingly dangerous (and continue to be so to this day). In August 2006, a UN Security Council Resolution authorized some 22,000 UN peacekeepers to deploy to Darfur under Chapter 7 auspices. The force may well have been able to staunch a great deal of the violence, but China effectively vetoed the resolution with a demand that language be included, requiring Khartoum to *accept* this UN "invitation" to deploy. Khartoum of course contemptuously declined, and in early September the UN Secretary-General's primary representative for Darfur, Jan Pronk, essentially acquiesced to Khartoum's adamant refusal, thereby destroying any leverage the resolution might have created in the negotiations that followed.

[5] Throughout 2007, negotiations continued in Addis Ababa on what sort of peacekeeping force Khartoum would accept in Darfur. Out of these negotiations came the disastrous notion of a "hybrid" force: comprising AU and UN forces, but with UN forces predominantly African. This predictably came to mean *exclusively* African, and the AU Peace and Security Council—only a few years old at the time—was presented with a task that was daunting even for UN DPKO and impossible for the resourceless AU. The Security Council vote to authorize the UN/African Union Mission in Darfur (UNAMID) came in July 2007—the month before the Olympic Games began in Beijing (China was stinging from the rapidly-accelerating "Genocide Olympics?" campaign, and wanted to be seen as doing something positive for Darfur).

The Mission has been a disastrous failure from the beginning, and in countless ways: ill-equipped and ill-trained troops deployed simply for the UN monetary stipend to troop-contributing countries; a terrible deficit in transportation and communications equipment, especially helicopters; poor leadership and an absence of what military planners call "inter-operability"—the list goes on. AU support for the Mission is currently driven mainly by financial benefits and fear of the "optics of failure."

One measure of how disastrous a response this was to Darfur's violent realities is the number of people newly displaced since UNAMID officially took up its mandate (January 1, 2008): the figure is well over 2 million.[6] And, since displacement has correlated very highly with violence since the beginning of the conflict, this becomes an all-too-meaningful measure of the levels of continuing violence.

[6] In March 2009, following the indictment of President al-Bashir for crimes against humanity by the ICC, the regime expelled 13 distinguished international relief organizations representing roughly half the total humanitarian capacity in Darfur. There was some international bluster, but in the end the reaction was essentially acquiescent—even after Khartoum's massive extortion of funds and equipment from the expelled organizations.

This should have been the galvanizing moment for the international community. These expulsions, as well as the closing of three key Sudanese NGOs, ensured that the risk to civilians would increase dramatically—and in fact this increasing risk has defined the past eight years for Darfur, even if the UN and African Union refuse to acknowledge these realities in anything approaching adequate terms.

Khartoum, seeing that even such drastic action would not provoke meaningful international action, has slowly ratcheted up the violence in Darfur, as well as the humanitarian deficit (including more expulsions and an outrageous suspension of the International Committee of the Red Cross in January 2015). Current violence is as extreme as that of the early, most violent years of the genocide, and retains a fully genocidal character.

Conditions throughout Darfur are appalling, worse in all likelihood than at any previous point in the genocide, and more dangerous. The UN and UNAMID have been intimidated into silence about humanitarian conditions, and most of what can be learned comes from a single source: Radio Dabanga (run by Darfuri expatriates in The Netherlands, with myriad sources inside Darfur). One telling example: it has been some five years since the UN humanitarian leadership has released figures for Darfur for either Global Acute Malnutrition or Severe Acute Malnutrition (SAM). These are by far the most important humanitarian indicators within a distressed population, and yet although a great body of data has been collected, the data have not been collated and published—at Khartoum's behest. Khartoum also refuses to allow credible data on mortality to be reported—or on the number of rapes, even as tens of thousands of girls and women have been sexually assaulted, and often gang-raped or abducted. UN Secretary-General Ban Ki-moon was often disgracefully silent about sexual violence, even though it is an integral feature of genocidal war.

The UN World Food Program has a drastically short supply of "implementing partners"—those who actually distribute food in the camps and to needy populations. In fact, WFP has taken to using "food brokers," essentially businessmen who take a healthy cut of any food they actually distribute. It is only the most telling reflection of the lack of humanitarian capacity.

The humanitarian infrastructure is collapsing; UNAMID has failed; and all INGOs will withdraw if the fig-leaf of protection provided by UNAMID is withdrawn, or if insecurity grows. Only 3 percent of those working for relief organizations in Darfur are expatriates. A total collapse of protection in the camps and humanitarian services looms closer by the month, and the international community in early 2018 had no palatable options.

[7] In the fall of 2010, the Obama administration decided that it could deal with only two key issues in greater Sudan: the self-determination referendum in the South, and finding a way to continue counter-terrorism cooperation with the Khartoum regime. Darfur did not fit into these primary policy concerns and was, extraordinarily, "de-coupled" from the primary bilateral issues between Washington and Khartoum. The word "de-coupled" was actually used by a senior administration official speaking on the record; a State Department briefing, which does not provide the name of the official, gives a verbatim transcript and general description of the speaker.[7]

It was clear—to the Europeans, to the AU and UN, and to other countries concerned about halting and preventing genocide—that the U.S. was not going to take the lead on Darfur. But instead of stepping up, countries backed away, and in the process allowed an ambitious and expedient Qatar to take the lead in providing diplomatic auspices in Doha. This would lead to the signing of the Doha Document for Peace in Darfur (DDPD, July 2011), another diplomatic disaster. There were no meaningful Darfuri signatories, only representatives from the so-called "Liberation and Justice Movement" (LJM), a group of very small or factitious splinter factions cobbled together by Libya's Muamar Gadhafi and the hopelessly incompetent and inexperienced U.S. special envoy for Sudan, Major-General (retired) Scott Gration.

The process was entirely unrepresentative, and both the DDPD and the LJM have been overwhelmingly rejected by Darfuri civil society as well as by the largest and most consequential rebel groups. For its part, Khartoum was happy to sign and receive credit for diplomatic "cooperation." Unsurprisingly, Khartoum has done almost nothing to fulfil the terms of the DDPD, while the international community has been prepared to declare that the DDPD is the basis for all future negotiations on peace in Darfur. A diplomatic "dead letter"—one that no Western government truly believed in and which had no support from the key Darfuri constituencies—was used until very recently to avoid the difficult task of real negotiations, with real demands made of Khartoum. Such negotiations would require meaningful pressure—especially from the Europeans—in the event of stalling or reneging. Given the perverse efforts of several European countries to engage in a significant *rapprochement* with the Khartoum regime, the EU hardly seems like a source of help in such negotiations.

The situation in 2017

The opportunities to forestall or mitigate genocide in Darfur have been many; we've had no lack of information about Khartoum's ambitions. But despite the promulgation of "R2P" in the September 2005 UN World Summit "Outcome Document" (para. 138, 139), there has been in the past no willingness to take advantage of what opportunities have existed. A greater willingness in the future—given the massive chaos presently defining Darfur—seems extremely unlikely. What has long been classed as "genocide by attrition," or as Human Rights Watch has put it, "Chaos by Design," will continue indefinitely.[8]

Moreover, the lust for counter-terrorism has badly skewed U.S. policy toward Khartoum. In December 2011, as renewed genocide was well underway in the Nuba Mountains and Blue Nile state, U.S. special envoy Princeton Lyman, speaking to the Arabic news outlet *Asharq al-Awsat* about Sudan and the "Arab Spring," declared: "Frankly, we do not want to see the ouster of the [Sudanese] regime, nor regime change. We want to see the regime carrying out reform via constitutional democratic measures."[9]

So long as such preposterous assessments prevail—suggesting that somehow the current genocidal regime might begin "carrying out reform via constitutional democratic measures"—there will be no end to the genocide. The military offensives during the dry seasons of 2013–2016 in East Jebel Marra (North Darfur) and the Jebel Marra massif itself (Central Darfur) have all the earmarks of earlier geno-cidal violence, entailing comprehensive village destruction, mass murder and rape, looting of livestock, and destruction of food stocks and water points. The Rapid Support Forces, which have replaced the vaguely designated *Janjaweed*, are better armed, better trained, and cooperate even more closely with Khartoum's regular military forces—and they are openly embraced by the regime, as the *Janjaweed* never were.

Explaining continuing inaction

The UN is in the midst of significant changes in leadership, with a new Secretary-General and a new head of the UN's Department of Peacekeeping Operations; there are no signs of real commitment to improving human security in Darfur. Disastrously, the UN Security Council slashed UNAMID in its re-authorization vote on June 30, 2017, cutting critical military personnel by 44 percent. This is likely to be followed by further cuts when re-authorization again comes before the Security Council in June 2018. Khartoum has made no secret of its fervid desire to see UNAMID gone, and it has powerful veto-wielding allies on the Security Council in Russia and China. The African Union is immobilized by its deference to Khartoum, despite understanding that UNAMID has failed badly. Europe has expanded its ties to Khartoum as interest in halting the flow of African migrants to the European continent intensifies. Germany has agreed to build what are essen-tially "concentration camps," overseen by Khartoum's intelligence services and armed with high-tech European surveillance and registration equipment.

The U.S. under the Trump administration seems woefully incapable of responding with either intelligence or compassion to the complex challenges posed by Darfur, especially given the U.S. intelligence community's continuing lust for whatever counter-terrorism intelligence the Khartoum regime may be willing to provide.

Khartoum denies all meaningful access to Darfur by journalists and human rights reporters. This effort to turn it into a "black box" will be complete with the inevitable full withdrawal of UNAMID and the accelerating withdrawal of huma-nitarian organizations. The success of these efforts has left us with stark and deeply dismaying lessons to be drawn: the Khartoum regime—which retains its monopoly on national wealth and power, including the army and massive security apparatus—now has a fully tested strategy for genocidal insurgency warfare, one that has been deployed in South Kordofan and Blue Nile States since summer 2011. The regime—to prevent was it sees as "another Darfur"—has imposed a humanitarian blockade on all rebel-controlled areas within the two states. This has created a large refugee flow out of Sudan and is destroying the agricultural economies of the two areas. Malnutrition rates, established on the basis of hit-and-run assessments and reports from the ground, are terrifying. But Khartoum, looking at Darfur, knows all too well that there will be no meaningful international response, merely inter-national posturing and disingenuous comments of the sort we have seen for more

112 Eric Reeves

than five years. (For areas of greatest current ethnically-targeted violence, see highlighted map below.)

The future of Darfur itself is unspeakably bleak. The failure to intervene in Darfur, failure to muster the political will to end a catastrophe that continues because most international actors have simply tired of it or have more pressing business with Khartoum, ensures that what is already the longest genocide in well over a century will continue—and may well become the most successful.

Notes

1 Julie Flint and Alex de Waal, *Darfur: A Short History of a Long War* (New York & London: Zed, 2005), 39.
2 Human Rights Watch, "Men with No Mercy: Rapid Support Forces Attacks on Civilians in Darfur, Sudan," September 2005, non-paginated PDF, www.hrw.org/report/2015/09/09/men-no-mercy/rapid-support-forces-attacks-against-civilians-darfur-sudan.
3 Eric Reeves, "Unnoticed Genocide," *Washington Post*, A14, February 25, 2004.
4 My own survey of data and analyses of the mortality in Darfur remains the most recent and comprehensive: "Quantifying Genocide: Darfur Mortality Update, 6 August 2010," (updated November 2016), http://wp.me/p45rOG-AB.
5 Zoellick impatiently imposed an unreasonable timeframe for completion of the agreement, ensuring that no meaningful security guarantees could be negotiated. Pressure on the rebel leaders was extreme and finally counter-productive, leading to a split among these leaders at the very moment when unity was essential. Moreover, Zoellick made no adequate provision for the representation of Darfuri civil society, believing—mistakenly—that an agreement between belligerents was sufficient to bring peace to Darfur.
6 Eric Reeves, "UN Displacement Figures for Darfur: Assessment, Confused Guesses, or Dissimulation?" *Sudan Tribune*, December 20, 2015, www.sudantribune.com/spip.php?article57442.
7 State Department press release, "Senior Administration Officials on Developments in Sudan," November 9, 2011, http://geneva.usmission.gov/2010/11/09/senior-administration-officials-on-developments-in-sudan/.
8 Human Rights Watch, "Darfur 2007: Chaos by Design: Peacekeeping Challenges for AMIS and UNAMID," September 19, 2007, non-paginated PDF, www.hrw.org/report/2007/09/19/darfur-2007-chaos-design/peacekeeping-challenges-amis-and-unamid.
9 Interview with Princeton Lyman, *Asharq al-Awsat*, December 3, 2011, http://english.aawsat.com/2011/12/article55244147/asharq-al-awsat-talks-to-us-special-envoy-to-sudan-princeton-lyman.

9

ATROCITY PREVENTION FROM OBAMA TO TRUMP[1]

James P. Finkel

In our increasingly globalized world, genocide and mass atrocities in places far removed from the United States can have serious implications for US interests and security, including mass flows of refugees that overburden and destabilize bordering states, the development of ungoverned spaces that harbor and incubate terrorist groups, or disruption of oil supplies and other key resources. The recent spillover of conflict from Syria to Iraq, and concerns about further potential spillover to Turkey, Jordan, and Lebanon, provide just the latest cause for sober reflection.

Too often, the US only reacts to these situations when the threats to its interests are already present. At that point, the options for influencing events on the ground are limited and costly – in the case of military intervention, often unacceptably costly to the American public. Ever since the disastrous failures to stop ethnic cleansing and genocide in Bosnia and Rwanda in the 1990s, professionals inside and outside government who deal with the consequences of such events have sought to determine whether it is possible to prevent these events before they gain momentum and spiral out of control, or, failing that, at least to find a way to mitigate the damage.

The past two decades have seen considerable progress in Washington's ability to identify situations that threaten to escalate into mass atrocities and its theoretical understanding of how to respond to these situations, but considerable work remains. The United States has various tools at its disposal – diplomatic, security, economic, and judicial, to name just a few – to help societies manage conflict without resorting to collective violence, and deter those who would use violence to secure their interests. Until recently, the departments and agencies responsible for deciding how to use these tools frequently failed to do so in close coordination with one another, and coordinated even more rarely for the purpose of preventing atrocities in at-risk countries. As outlined below, the Obama Administration, through efforts like President Obama's Atrocity Prevention Board (APB), worked to develop a more consistent government-wide and multilateral approach to preventing and stopping mass atrocities, and to draw up a menu of prevention tools and approaches to apply as individual situations warranted. Those who follow prevention issues closely are anxious to see whether the Trump Administration will continue those advances, cast them aside, or develop a completely different approach.

President Obama's choice of the US Holocaust Memorial Museum as the venue for his August 2011 launch of Presidential Study 10 (PSD 10) – aimed at finding more effective ways for the US government to prevent or, failing prevention, to respond to atrocities beyond our borders – was deliberate. Indeed, the former President went so far in that initial speech as to declare the prevention of genocides and mass atrocities a core national security interest and a core moral responsibility of the United States, placing these issues for the first time squarely at the center of an administration's agenda. He returned to the Museum some eight months later in April 2012 to declare that the study had been completed, that he had accepted all of its recommendations (PSD 10 included over 100 recommendations), and that he was instructing his National Security Council to establish an Atrocity Prevention Board whose job would be to further flesh out the study's findings, put them into practice, and ensure that Washington's efforts to prevent genocides and other forms of mass atrocity would hereafter have real bite. The Board was to consist of representatives from some nine departments and agencies at the Assistant Secretary level or above, people theoretically with broad enough control to move personnel and other resources to potential trouble spots whenever and wherever they were needed. It initially would be chaired by NSC Senior Director for Multilateral Affairs and Human Rights Samantha Power, a strong atrocity prevention advocate and close Obama associate. Power would later go on to serve as Ambassador to the UN during President Obama's second administration.

Highlights of the APB announcement

President Obama announced the establishment of the APB in a speech at the US Holocaust Memorial Museum on April 23, 2012. According to the White House press release accompanying the speech, the APB was to:

- Include representatives from the Departments of State, Defense, Treasury, Justice, and Homeland Security, the Joint Staff, the US Agency for International Development, the US Mission to the United Nations, the Office of the Director of National Intelligence, the Central Intelligence Agency, and the Office of the Vice President, who were:
    - at the Assistant Secretary level or higher;
    - appointed by name by their respective Agency heads.
- Be chaired by the NSC Senior Director for Multilateral Affairs and Human Rights;
- Meet at least monthly and additionally as urgent situations arise;

- "Oversee the development and implementation of atrocity prevention and response policy";
- Submit an annual report on its work to the President and have its work reviewed:

  - at least twice a year by the Deputies;
  - at least once a year by the Principals.

After six months of operations, the APB chair was to draft an Executive Order that would "set forth the structure, functions, priorities, and objectives of the Board, provide further direction for its work, and include further measures for strengthening atrocity prevention and response capabilities as identified in the course of the Board's work."[2]

After five years of activity, many past and recent Board members would concede that the APB's record at the end of President Obama's tenure remained mixed. The Board played a significant role in focusing policy attention on the plight of Burma's Rohingya and, the situation in Burundi: contributed to discussions aimed at reducing the risk of violence during Kenya's previous and most recent parliamentary elections; helped orchestrate Washington's response to the political and humanitarian crisis in the Central African Republic (CAR);[3] and launched an effort aimed at better understanding the potential drivers of atrocities elsewhere in Africa and to mitigate those risks by working with US officials, both those posted in-country and others.

The Board's engagement with the conflict in Syria, by contrast, has been contentious. The conflict was already underway when the Board was first unveiled and convened. Although individual Board members were outspoken throughout the Obama Administration's intensive discussions of the continuing civil strife in Syria and Iraq, their arguments gained far less traction than might have been hoped. Scholars have only recently begun to dig more deeply into the Board's work on CAR and South Sudan. Although the press and some APB participants have generally applauded Washington's role in the initial international response to recent events in CAR, others close to that process and some NGOs have questioned why, in light of the early and prolonged attention that CAR had received from the APB, Washington failed to engage earlier.[4] If part of the answer to the questions raised by CAR can be traced to the fact that a permanent US diplomatic presence in Bangui was absent between December 2012 and September 2014, as some have argued, and that CAR has been viewed in Washington as a country where Paris traditionally takes the lead, the same could not be said of South Sudan, where the US has had a large diplomatic and development presence since independence and where Washington played a key role in the country's birth.

Despite its mixed record, I continue to see strong merit in retaining some form of structure akin to the Atrocity Prevention Board, if not the current Board itself. Indeed, based on my time in government working on these issues, I believe that, should the Trump administration decide to disband the Board, events beyond our

116 James P. Finkel

borders will eventually force more thoughtful members of the administration to conclude that they need an alternative.

It is important to remember that each of the country situations cited above is complex, some have frustrated several administrations, and each has been the subject of an ongoing deliberation within separate interagency policy coordinating bodies. The APB's first challenge was to find appropriate bureaucratic space where it could contribute meaningfully to those groups' deliberations without slowing them down or otherwise disrupting them. I believe the APB offered the opportunity to enhance those deliberations in two ways. First, it provided a structured, functional process for identifying emerging atrocity situations at a much earlier stage and proposing steps to try to mitigate them. For example, the Atrocity Prevention Board's efforts to raise Burundi's profile within US government circles came some two years before Burundi's political and security situation began to deteriorate dangerously, and provides an excellent example of the Board's utility. Second, the Board was able to identify and mobilize expertise and tools that previously had been overlooked or ignored by the regional-based policy coordinating forums.

Earlier attempts

The Atrocity Prevention Board was not the first time the US has attempted to organize high-level attention to the problem of atrocity prevention, although PSD 10 was the Washington bureaucracy's most intensive and comprehensive recent effort that I am aware of. Former Ambassador-at-Large for War Crime Issues David Scheffer, midway through the second Clinton Administration, was authorized to organize an earlier Atrocities Prevention Interagency Working Group. That group, which functioned between 1998 and 2000, met once a month. Its participants primarily included a number of bureaus and offices at the Department of State,[5] the Agency for International Development's (USAID) Deputy Administrator, and various offices from across the Intelligence Community.

The format for those meetings resembled what generally took place in the Obama APB: each meeting began with an all-source intelligence briefing drawn from a variety of materials ranging from the most highly classified to open source press and scholarly articles followed by a question and answer session, and then a policy discussion. The quality of those meetings varied. When they worked best, they consisted of the following: an intelligence presentation that was solid, well-sourced, and unambiguous; substantive give-and-take between the analysts and the policy officials; serious discussion of policy options by officials who, though they might disagree on details, all agreed on the value of atrocity prevention; and a final summing-up by Scheffer of the consensus reached. A memo summarizing the group's recommendations was then jointly forwarded to the Secretary of State for further deliberation among senior State Department and interagency staff that could set action in motion.

After considerable discussion, the newly-elected George W. Bush Administration decided to retain an Office of the Ambassador-at-Large for War Crimes, and appointed Pierre Prosper – a former Justice Department attorney, Rwanda

Tribunal prosecutor, and aide to Scheffer – to head it. The office's work became more circumscribed, however, with its modest number of officers initially pre-occupied with the everyday operations of the various international tribunals, and having little time for atrocity prevention. One former senior official noted that the incoming administration felt it made more sense organizationally to leave genocide and atrocity issues primarily to the requisite NSC-led regional policy coordinating bodies (IPCs). Politics and ideology may have played a role as well. Primarily through his work on the negotiations leading up to the Rome Statute and the International Criminal Court, Scheffer had become something of a lightning rod within conservative political circles. Some of the Bush administration's incoming officials felt strongly that the type of international judicial activism and focus on war crime and atrocity issues with which Scheffer had become closely associated should be sharply curtailed.

Like the Clinton administrations that preceded them, and the Obama administrations that followed them, the George W. Bush administrations certainly included senior officials who were passionately concerned about – and continue to advocate for – the prevention of genocide and atrocities. They were fewer in number, however, and, especially following 9/11, found it harder to make their voices heard. And as the wars in Afghanistan and Iraq got underway, the small interagency cadre who supported Scheffer's Interagency Atrocities Prevention Working Group was redirected to a variety of other war-related tasks.

It took ten years from the end of the second Clinton Administration (the two Administrations of President George W. Bush and the first two years of President Obama's initial term) for Washington to resurrect a more systematic approach to atrocity prevention.[6] Atrocity prevention issues during the George W. Bush Administration were placed under the Regional Interagency Policy Committees, and the attention given to these issues more often than not depended on the background, temperament, and bureaucratic situation of the individual chairpersons. Even in those instances where the Regional IPC chairperson was inclined to take a more inclusive and holistic approach to the country in question, personnel turnover and the press of business made that approach difficult to sustain.[7]

Greater uncertainty

Although the actual form that the Trump administration will take is far from settled as I write, and several key positions are likely to remain unfilled in the months ahead, early signs suggest that the White House once again will seek to simplify government structure. When the views about foreign policy that the President and several of those close to him have expressed during the election campaign and the first months of his administration are taken into account, there still appears a good chance that the APB will eventually suffer the same fate as Ambassador Scheffer's Interagency Group. But, while it is generally accepted that each administration will want to undertake some bureaucratic restructuring and will reprioritize issues, the Atrocity Prevention Board, its approaches to deliberations, and the assessment instruments and policy tools it has developed deserve serious consideration from the Trump people. To do otherwise would be again to throw the baby out with the bath water.

A new administration normally offers an opportunity to reconsider what has worked well, what hasn't, and how to improve policy performance. One would hope that Secretary Pompeo, for example, can still find a way to reverse the downward spiral that has gripped the State Department since the presidential inauguration.

In particular, one would hope that the Secretary might help the White House and his senior counterparts understand how a broad range of US interests are advanced by the leadership role that Washington has assumed in the international system throughout the post-World War II period. That discussion presumably would include a recognition that the broad categories of human rights concerns – the kinds of issues that the APB has struggled with – rather than being ephemeral, provide important indicators of the direction of events abroad, and may presage developments that can seriously harm US interests over time. Although mass atrocities by and large take place in out-of-the-way places where we and our key allies usually have a limited diplomatic presence and fewer traditional interests, it remains important to consider the potential secondary and tertiary implications those situations pose for the US. The refugee flow from Syria offers no better example. The effects of that movement have reverberated politically and socially through Turkey, Jordan, and the EU, key US allies all, and their ramifications will not be clear for some time. The continuum of violence in failed, failing, or fragile states, which all too frequently moves from accelerating human rights violations to full-blown, systematic atrocities, can give rise to ungoverned spaces that, in turn, become breeding grounds for terrorist and other groups who eventually may pose threats directly to the US, or to our friends and key trading partners. These same circumstances can give rise to pandemics and other forms of deadly disease that in today's interconnected world can easily jump the US's Atlantic and Pacific moats.

A proposal

Assuming that the current crop of senior policymakers can be persuaded that the issues and situations giving rise to atrocities really are of core concern to long-term national US interest, rather than "niche" or "boutique" issues as some have dismissed them in the past, what might the basic elements of an ideal prevention process look like? I would argue strongly for the following:

- It would be based on a continuing consensus that the US plays a unique role in the international system and that it is still in the US interest to help pursue a world where Departments of State pursue peace at home and abroad.

- It would be characterized by inclusive, seamless cooperation between and within Washington-based departments and agencies and our diplomatic missions abroad. It would be orchestrated either by a Senior Director at the NSC or an Under Secretary at the Department of State.
- Technology would be used to bring representatives from the field into Washington conference rooms for important deliberations and to bring additional Washington expertise into country team discussions.

- Participants in the process would agree that policies aimed at atrocity prevention have the best chance of succeeding and can be pursued most cost-effectively when they are undertaken further "upstream," "when an accurate understanding of the risk factors that place a society at peril for violent or genocidal conflict" first begin to come into focus.[8]

- There would be common understanding among senior officials that when they talk about "upstream prevention" they are talking about both security and development in a broad sense and that that discussion should extend, for example, to: professionalization and appropriate equipping of military and police forces, counterterrorism, economic development, governance, rule of law, healthcare, education, food security, identity, and related issues. Moreover, Washington would be prepared to work with like-minded states and international organizations to pursue legal and proportionate military responses to protect at-risk legitimate states and civilian populations when all other options fail.

They would also agree that:

- Policies aimed at prevention further upstream have a better chance of success if they are pursued as part of a broader program rather than in isolation.
- Better understanding of conflict, need, language, and political culture at the local level and beyond the confines of a country's capital are essential to articulating sound prevention policies.
- Initiatives that originate from the bottom up and at the local level, rather than top down and internationally, have a better chance of success over the long term.
- There will be times when, despite their best intentions and their very best efforts, unforeseen factors will come into play and the "magic" won't work.

Serious hurdles

From the start, the Obama APB faced three major hurdles that impacted its performance: 1) a lack of dedicated resources to fund its work; 2) making its voice heard in the midst of competing interests and competencies within the federal bureaucracy; and 3) managing the expectations – good and bad – naturally attendant upon a body that recommends US actions in foreign countries.

The Albright-Cohen Genocide Prevention Task Force Report (GPTF) originally envisaged an atrocity prevention process modeled after Washington's counter-terrorism and counter-proliferation processes, and the report emphasized up front that additional resources would be necessary.[9] Yet, Ambassador Power had made clear from the beginning of the PSD 10 discussions that the Atrocity Prevention Board would have to be a resource-neutral undertaking, given the cuts already taking place to longstanding programs in many departments and agencies. The effort required sufficient manpower to accurately assess the many countries at risk of atrocity and to positively impact the situation on the ground. But Congress has followed a pattern of reducing funds for programs aimed at improving governance and reducing graft and corruption overseas, seriously weakening some of the most important tools in Washington's prevention toolbox.

The Board's status as an unfunded program only heightened the hurdles it had to overcome, as the newcomer to turf that was already rife with competing interests. Washington's national security bureaucracy, regardless of department, tends to be divided into both regional and functional bureaus, issues, or offices. Regional bureaus generally focus on a geographic area such as Africa, while functional bureaus focus on crosscutting issues, as in the case of the State Department's Bureau of Conflict and Stabilization Operations (CSO). There is a long history of rivalry and tension between these regional and functional entities. The APB's mission to weigh in on both countries and issues for which other parts of the bureaucracy had responsibility caused it to be viewed with skepticism and sometimes outright hostility in some quarters whose cooperation was necessary to carry out its recommendations.

Part of this reaction can be traced to mundane bureaucratic considerations: the more players that are added to a policy discussion, the more bureaucratically complex a problem becomes. Hubris or simple turf considerations may also rear their heads, with some participants taking the position that "This is my sandbox, I know it best, and you're not going to play in it." Personal relations between key players in different offices can often make or break initiatives. All too often, situations have been ignored simply because one official "couldn't stand" another, and either didn't want to listen to the message that person was conveying or, having heard it, didn't want to do anything that might give that individual's office, agency, or department a leg up in the broader bureaucratic game, regardless of the potential consequences.[10] Barring a situation where US interests are clearly threatened, or intervention by a more senior leader who directs the two sides to put their differences aside, the chances of events taking a negative turn will be immense.

The Genocide Prevention Task Force report assumed that to make itself heard in interagency policy debates and to win the cooperation it needed, an APB-like body would require a strong departmental-level champion to push its cause. The report took as a basic premise that the Department of State should be in the lead when it comes to genocide and atrocity prevention, and suggested that the Bureau of Democracy, Human Rights, and Labor (DRL), as the

State Department's largest genocide and prevention stakeholder, should play a special role.[11] But State has had great difficulty coming together on genocide and atrocity issues since the end of the second Clinton administration and the disbanding of Scheffer's original Interagency Working Group. Each subsequent administration seems to have begun with several organizations within State – the Bureau of Democracy, Human Rights, and Labor, the Office of Global Criminal Justice (CGJ), USAID, and, more recently, the Bureau of Conflict and Stabilization Operations (CSO) – all making a claim to leadership on these questions, at least until the first big prevention test has arisen. At that point, they have found themselves stymied by bureaucratic politics and forced to subordinate themselves to the appropriate regional bureau, which, depending on the circumstances and personal relations between the various State Department entities' senior leaders, may or may not have accepted the advice of the functional-prevention bureaus and offices.

The creation of the State Department's Undersecretary for Civilian Security, Democracy, and Human Rights (known in the State Department by the acronym "J") – which became the parent bureau of DRL, GCJ, and CSO, among others prompted mixed reactions throughout the Department. Bureaus and offices quietly began calculating how J and the reforms outlined in the initial Quadrennial Diplomatic and Development Report (QDDR) more broadly might impact their bureaucratic spheres of control. PSD 10 and APB supporters within State on the whole were initially enthusiastic, and looked to J as a way to strengthen their collective voice. That enthusiasm waned over time, as supporters felt J was not making sufficient headway winning active, long-term support from the Secretary, the Undersecretary for Political Affairs, and more importantly State's Regional Assistant Secretaries. One former State Department official opined that, like the individual bureaus and offices cited earlier, "J wanted to take the lead on these questions, but at the same time, it didn't want to take the lead." Taking the lead meant engaging in a lot of intra-State Department arguments, and J understood that, as in any bureaucracy, it also needed those same bureaus' and offices' cooperation to get things done. The initial State Department Task Force put together by J to support PSD 10 and the APB fell into disarray over time as senior participants drifted off to other issues, and as J's reluctance to weigh in more strongly with counterparts grew. Moreover, the Task Force meetings devolved into information-sharing and note-taking exercises, rather than serving as opportunities to actively deliberate over atrocity prevention issues under discussion at the APB and sub-APB levels with the various offices within the department.

Given the lofty goal expressed in its title and the complex and controversial issues it deals with, the APB naturally invited outsized expectations and suspicions. Although Ambassador Power repeatedly cautioned that the "P" in APB didn't stand for "panacea," some expected the APB would spearhead an aggressive US policy to stop atrocities in places like Syria, South Sudan, and CAR. Meanwhile, others, skeptical of the benefits of foreign involvements following the prolonged

122 James P. Finkel

wars in Afghanistan and Iraq, worried that the APB was a formula for expanding US commitments and expenditure of personnel and materiel from conflict to conflict.

Stumbling over Syria, South Sudan, and CAR

Syria, South Sudan, and CAR all merit close scrutiny to determine what actually transpired behind Washington's closed doors, and those who inherit the atrocity prevention portfolio under President Trump would benefit from reflection on these and other atrocity events. Syria, in my view, at least at the beginning, was a victim first and foremost of timing. With so much else going on in the midst of Arab Spring and, in particular, the upheaval in Egypt, which was viewed as central to the future of the entire region, Syria commanded less attention from the bureaucracy's overstretched Middle East hands and the Obama Administration's senior policymakers, who were already running on very little sleep. Initial assessments pointed towards a different situation than Libya, for example, which had by comparison produced a fairly large refugee flow more quickly. Syria had what was viewed as a sophisticated military – with a particularly complex air-defense system – and a history of quickly cracking down on and crushing dissent. Thus, as the senior policy community wrestled with its Arab Spring triage, Syria tended to receive less attention. When Syria finally began to move up the priority list, President Obama's well-known reluctance to employ additional force in the region strongly influenced Washington's deliberations. The originally small community of Syria watchers eventually evolved into a much larger group, but each time its efforts pointed towards an important decision, most of the key options were judged too risky, or, for diplomatic, resource, legal, or military reasons, too difficult to carry out. Policymakers also frequently stumbled over the "what comes next" question. Each time they went back to the drawing board, the situation and deliberations became more difficult. The APB, formed long after the Syria decision mechanism was well-established, was ill-positioned both collectively and as individuals to influence that process, especially in light of President Obama's strongly held views on the use of military force.

The APB was better established in the summer of 2014 when the case of South Sudan came to the fore. Unlike CAR, South Sudan was a country in which the Obama Administration was highly invested. Washington has poured millions of dollars into South Sudan since its independence. Indeed, Washington was intimately involved in South Sudan's creation, and the many hours and careful attention that Ambassador Power and others spent trying to anticipate and stave off possible problems as the transition in Sudan unfolded not only formed one of the most detailed and deliberate efforts of its kind, but also provided a standout foreign policy moment for the first Obama Administration.

Unlike the case in Bangui, the US had a large diplomatic presence in Juba, South Sudan's capital. The Atrocity Prevention Board and others had devoted considerable time over the months preceding the political breakdown to the potential threat of atrocities in South Sudan, but had focused on Jongley State and other places that were experiencing inter-ethnic violence rather than on Juba itself.

Somehow, that large US presence in Juba failed to assess correctly the dangerous dynamic that was developing. One former US official who watched the situation unfold has noted privately that our embassy was paying close attention to relations between President Kiir and Vice President Machar, but had seen them pull back from the brink just a few months before. They originally assumed that this would happen once again. But the same official also pointed toward an underlying situation among senior US officials that somewhat resembled the situation Peter Uvin described in his study of aid agencies' attitudes towards Rwanda prior to the genocide: they were so vested in the success of their efforts in South Sudan that they were either unable or unwilling to recognize and confront the fact that Kiir and Machar's relations had reached a breaking point. Thus, even if the APB had had a sense that the Juba arrangement was about to come undone, it would have faced strong headwinds pressing its case with those more directly responsible for South Sudan.[12]

In the case of the Central African Republic, Charles Brown, in his recent excellent study of US policy, suggests that once the tactical situation on the ground became clear in summer 2013, members of the sub-APB, in particular, acted along with Ambassador Power's successor at the NSC, Senior Director Steve Pomper, and Ambassador Power herself to push for prevention measures at the UN, as well as for humanitarian aid and US logistical support to the French and African peacekeeping force in Bangui. Brown credits the APB "process" as having played a significant role in raising CAR's profile within senior government circles, but Brown's study also raises serious questions about why it took so long for that process to become engaged, and argues that most senior members of the Board itself played only a modest role. Brown also argues that the Board contributed less to the discussion of how best to proceed in the aftermath of the initial crisis than might have been expected.

It would be difficult to find a single cause for the failure of the APB to engage earlier. Surely Washington's traditional lack of attention to CAR, strong reluctance on the part of the State Department's senior management in the wake of Benghazi to keep the Embassy open in Bangui, turnover of key diplomatic personnel, genuine disagreement between the Intelligence Community and the Policy Community over the level of atrocity risk, and reluctance to employ more resources at that stage all played a role. But Brown's description of the eventual APB response resting primarily with Ambassador Power, her NSC successor, and select members of the sub-APB, while laudatory, is in some respects disturbing, as it suggests a step back to previous practice where a small group of dedicated mid-level officials would rally around a committed senior on an ad-hoc basis to accomplish what needs to be done and then settle back into standard operating procedure. Although Brown gives strong credit to

124 James P. Finkel

the APB "process," what he describes, at least during the initial and subsequent phases, would appear to fall short of the structured, sustained deliberation and action envisaged during the PSD 10 discussions.

BOX 9.1 CALCULATED DECISIONS RATHER THAN LACK OF POLITICAL WILL

President Obama may have intended to signal a new approach when he characterized the prevention of atrocities as a core national security interest and moral responsibility of the US, but bureaucracies don't adjust longstanding policies and practices easily. Alexander George and Jane Holl point out in their article "The Warning-Response Problem and Missed Opportunities in Preventive Diplomacy" that most policymakers traditionally have tended to view issues like ethnic conflict or gross patterns of human rights violations as less of a threat to US interests, and often have been less inclined to demand early warning on these questions or to take those warnings seriously and respond to them.[13]

George and Holl argue that warning often forces policymakers to confront difficult or unpalatable decisions that most people would prefer to avoid, or at least put off as long as possible, in the hope that the worst simply won't come to pass. Thus, they observe, "even if a leader expects a situation to deteriorate, additional warning to this effect may not prompt preventive action."[14]

Decisions to respond to these types of contingencies, even at their early stages, may require complicated decisions about expending financial resources, if not deploying military or other personnel. It would be rare for this type of decision to be taken outside an interagency context and, rather than resulting from a "lack of political will," a conclusion to stand aside most likely would be based on a hard-nosed calculation among senior personnel after weighing the potential costs and rewards both at home and abroad of taking some type of action.[15]

Squaring the circle

There is strong consensus among those who have served on the APB and the sub-APB that turnover within both bodies presented a serious test of the Board's effectiveness and durability. It would be especially hard to find anyone associated with the APB who would argue that Ambassador Power's move to the UN in 2013 didn't have a strong impact on the Board. On one hand, the move initially was seen as potentially advantageous for advancing the APB's work, since Power theoretically would be better positioned to roll out diplomatic strategy and help synchronize the APB's efforts with those of various UN bodies and key like-minded allies. However, Ambassador Power's long personal relationship with the President, combined with her scholarship on atrocity questions, clearly strengthened her hand during White House scrums. It had fallen primarily to Ambassador

Power and her staff at the NSC to ensure that the information and views shared within the APB about various countries made their way into the White House-led deliberations of the many Interagency Policy Committees. Although Ambassador Power continued to work closely with her former office at the NSC and with the APB in her new position at the UN, it was probably inevitable that her successor at the NSC would face a tougher slog as he attempted to coordinate and push APB positions through a White House increasingly preoccupied with other issues.

Asked what, in retrospect, they would want to do differently if the APB were being launched today, one former senior official suggested that it probably would have been useful the first time the Board met to go through the Genocide Prevention Task Force recommendations together to ensure that everyone was on the same page. That suggestion may be even more valid for incoming members of the Trump Administration who might find these issues part of their portfolio. I would also recommend adding a summary of the US Army's MARO and MAPRO[16] handbooks, a list of all of the requirements contained in the PSD 10 report, the December 2010 Senate Concurrent Resolution 71, and the November 2016 Final Report of the Experts Committee on Preventing Mass Violence, "A Necessary Good: U.S. Leadership on Preventing Mass Atrocities," issued by the Friends Committee on National Legislation Education Fund on behalf of the Prevention and Protection Working Group.

Assuming that there will continue to be a place for considering steps to prevent large-scale and systematic atrocities in the new Administration's agenda, it will be especially important to ensure that those responsible for these questions have a common understanding of what they really mean by prevention. I strongly suspect that various players will have very different notions about what prevention should and can accomplish. It might be useful for members of whatever structure assumes the responsibilities of the APB in the new Administration, and the working-level people that have made up the sub-APB, to program an annual retreat to discuss these issues and review the APB process' strengths and weaknesses. Such a meeting might also provide an opportunity to include other key NSC Senior Directors and various Regional Assistant Secretaries.[17]

Early prevention requires early warning. The combination of social science statistical modeling and more traditional analytic approaches has reached the point where analysts within government and civil society can provide a fairly accurate strategic projection of which countries are at greatest risk of experiencing large-scale atrocity events over the next two to three years.[18] I believe that anyone who has sat in the APB's monthly meetings, heard the briefings, and read the accompanying materials and the original National Intelligence Estimate on the Global Risk of Atrocities and any updates would be hard-pressed to argue that strategic early warning has been missing. The greater challenge, as Ambassador Power has noted on a number of occasions, is to heed that warning, find the resources, and orchestrate a whole of government prevention approach at an early enough stage.

Successful early prevention requires a robust intra-governmental coordination effort, which the APB can be credited with having helped to advance, but it will take some time before this type of approach becomes second nature to broad swaths of our civil servants. Unfortunately, at the end of the day, the press of business, budget cycles, and bureaucratic rivalries simply make it much easier for individual departments and agencies to consider policies and actions in isolation from one another. This ad-hoc, uncoordinated approach is often far less effective and much more expensive.

BOX 9.2 WATCH LISTS

A cursory glance across the many warning and watch lists prepared by the scholarly community and NGO world covering a variety of issues stretching from fragility to atrocities, terrorism, corruption, peace, etc., reveals at least one startling fact: the same 20 or 30 countries are frequently found at the top/worst position on many of these lists, albeit in different relative positions. Although the particularities of each of these countries' internal situations differ, many of the underlying structural issues contributing to their high risks are similar. The length of these lists traditionally has caused considerable angst in some government quarters, with both analysts and policymakers frequently insisting that available time and resources preclude so broad a focus. The debate has flared on and off over time. The most recent iteration has found those supporters of the Atrocity Prevention Board charged with actually articulating and implementing prevention policies generally favoring a narrower, more focused approach. Others, who believe prevention requires a broader rethinking of Washington's efforts – and hope to infuse prevention into the State Department's DNA – argue that focusing more narrowly will only reinforce the status quo.[19]

Step by step

Clearly some sort of annual assessment from the Intelligence Community (IC) needs to be central to the atrocity prevention process, and some members of the GPTF felt strongly that the Intelligence Community should produce a formal National Intelligence Estimate (NIE) on the Global Risk of Mass Atrocities each year. But full-blown NIEs are complex, time-consuming undertakings, and very few are undertaken on an annual basis. In fact, the IC has a number of alternative assessment art forms available that are similar to an NIE. Indeed, as Presidential Study Document 10 participants were completing the draft of their report in November 2011, members of the IC were already at work on a broad assessment of the global risk of atrocities that was being prepared in anticipation of an initial meeting of the APB. While some might view the final product as failing to carry the weight of an NIE, in substantive terms there seems to be no particular reason why this type of assessment could not substitute for a formal NIE during most years.

This ought especially to be the case if the IC continues its initial practice of providing the Board or a successor entity detailed monthly updates on each country that appears in its annual assessment along with a context assessment of a country singled out each month for deeper study. The format of the IC's monthly briefing packages was flexible enough that it allowed the Intelligence Community to bring to the Board's attention situations that might not have been factored into its annual assessment, but were subsequently showing worrisome signs. One question the new Administration will need to decide is when during the year the Board would like to receive the IC's annual atrocity risk assessment, which presumably ought to signal the start of the Board's or its successor's work program for the next twelve months.

Recommendation 1: Organize annual off-site meetings

Under the best of circumstances, completion of the annual IC atrocity risk assessment would be followed soon after by the annual assessment suggested above, bringing together, at a minimum, members of the APB or its successor entity, those who immediately support it, Regional Assistant Secretaries, and senior NSC regional directors. The centerpiece of that meeting would be a presentation by the IC of that assessment, followed by a broad discussion among the assembled policymakers of the report's implications. The meeting would also provide attendees with an opportunity to compare the IC's atrocity risk list with other governmental and non-governmental lists focused on such issues as political instability/fragility, terrorism, corruption, human rights, proliferation, complex humanitarian emergencies, drugs, human trafficking, and so on. The goal of the meeting would be not only to try to help narrow the gap between the functionalists and regionalists on a range of atrocity prevention-related issues, but also to begin breaking down bureaucratic barriers at a senior level and focusing on common structural drivers and potential policy responses.

The meeting would also offer an opportunity on an annual basis to revisit the question more holistically at a fairly senior level of what prevention is supposed to mean and what recent experience might be telling us about what is working and what isn't. It would likewise allow for a discussion of what type of atrocity prevention (or combination of prevention) – pre-conflict, conflict, or post-conflict – might be most appropriate for each country the IC has highlighted.

Recommendation 2: Alert country missions

The Bureau of Conflict and Stabilization Operations, as the State Department's designated secretariat for atrocity prevention matters, would seem the logical candidate to plan and organize the off-site meeting. CSO would also have responsibility for keeping the meeting's minutes, from which a special reporting message would be prepared for those diplomatic missions in the top 20 or more countries that appear on the IC's atrocity risk list.

- That message would formally alert the Chief of Mission that his or her country was on the IC's list, explain the reasons behind its inclusion, and summarize the discussion about their country that had taken place.
- It would also instruct the Chief of Mission to designate a senior coordinator for atrocity prevention who, depending on the size and makeup of the Mission, might be the Deputy Chief of Mission, the Political Counselor, or the Senior AID Administrator.
- Copies of those messages would also be transmitted simultaneously through military and intelligence channels to appropriate Regional Combatant Commanders, Senior Defense Attaches, Chiefs of Station, and Treasury representatives, and would put them on notice that they are to support the Mission's prevention efforts.

Recommendation 3: Initiate horizontal and vertical dialogues

Designation of an atrocity prevention coordinator at each relevant Diplomatic Mission should set in motion two related discussions. The first, within the Mission country team itself, would consider the feedback from the annual Washington off-site meeting, organize a preliminary Mission assessment, review the Mission's existing programs that contribute to atrocity prevention, and begin the process of identifying key gaps. The second discussion would be between the Mission country team, the APB or its successor body, and the appropriate regional Interagency Policy Committee.

Recommendation 4: Carry out conflict/atrocity assessment

As part of that latter discussion, those bodies would jointly agree to organize and schedule a multi-agency, multidisciplinary conflict and atrocity assessment with CSO and AID as co-leads. Although AID and CSO have done pioneering work aimed at adopting conflict/atrocity assessments within the US government, their methods have still to gain broad acceptance. Good conflict/atrocity assessments cover a broad range of topics and are labor intensive. All too often, Chiefs of Mission are less familiar with the practice and wary of having Washington play in their sandbox – especially if the outcome could be a report that conveys bad news, or at least a storyline that deviates from the picture that the mission heretofore has been conveying.

Past members of the APB have marveled at some of the obstacles that have been raised by missions and home bureaus following proposals from the APB that they host a conflict/atrocity study team. From the APB's perspective, it was offering an opportunity to bring additional resources to bear on what were often small, out-of-the-way missions that, under sequestration, likely found themselves even more resource-strained than usual. The APB saw the studies as an initial step to try to get ahead of problems and to gain better understanding of conflict and potential atrocity at the local level. A given conflict/atrocity assessment rarely, if ever, provides the last word. Instead, it renders a snapshot of where things stand at a given moment. The scholarly literature suggests that they can be most effective as part of an ongoing process. In those instances where Chiefs of Mission have been open to hosting these study teams, even on a onetime basis, the results, according to most accounts, have been very positive. For Washington, when missions have been on board, the challenge has been to find the appropriate personnel and funds to respond to the demand.

Recommendation 5: Seek out like-minded allies

Similar dialogues should also be initiated or strengthened where they already exist with like-minded partners in mission states, in Washington, and in other capitals. Seeking the views of civil society, the NGO community, other bilateral missions, key international organizations like the UN, and international financial institutions, especially at a local level, will be key to better understanding individual situations within countries and orchestrating more effective initiatives. Regular sharing of information and coordination of different programs locally have proved invaluable in a variety of situations. But US policy would also benefit from a more regular, structured discussion about the risk of atrocities with a variety of like-minded partners in Washington, with UN offices in New York, including the office of the Special Advisors on Genocide and R2P, DPKO, and the Peace Building Commission, among others, and appropriate offices within the EU, OSCE, OAS, ASEAN, and the AU, including the latter's subordinate regional organizations. Each of these elements has had its own experience wrestling with prevention, and both they and Washington could benefit from a regular exchange of views encompassing both theory and practice. One means of helping to facilitate those interactions might be to reinstitute and expand the Annual Genocide Prevention Conference that Washington hosted for five consecutive years from 2002–2007. Organized at the working level, these meetings brought together representatives from some 14 governments, civil society, and leading members of the scholarly community for frank, unclassified, off-the-record discussions of methodologies for determining risk, evolving norms, links between prevention and development, and a variety of other related topics. On a more day-to-day basis, it will be up to whoever ultimately chairs Washington's atrocity prevention effort, working in conjunction primarily with the Department of State, to decide at the end of each interagency atrocity prevention coordinating meeting which partners might be usefully engaged and whether Washington or a specific bilateral mission is best suited to do it, and then check systematically to ensure that those contacts actually take place.

Recommendation 6: Create country task forces

As the country conflict/atrocity assessments are completed, the APB or its successor should:

- Task the Department of State to establish a series of intra-Departmental, inter-Agency, country-specific, multi-disciplinary atrocity prevention task forces to consider the assessments' findings.

- Take into account information that has been gleaned from other partners and, in conjunction with the Mission Country Team, make specific policy recommendations to the interagency atrocity prevention coordinating group and the appropriate regional IPC.
- The Task Forces would also share the information they have gathered and their recommendations with the Regional Commands' contingency planning cells and other appropriate government planning bodies.
- Once those recommendations are approved by the coordinating group and regional IPC, and any necessary higher approvals are obtained, the appropriate parts of the Washington foreign policy community and especially the Mission Country Team would implement them.
- The task forces should continue to monitor progress on a regular basis and to undertake additional formal assessments at agreed intervals.

Looking ahead

From the parochial view of someone who was charged with ensuring that a broad range of senior policymakers were regularly kept abreast of the risk of atrocities and other events as they unfolded, the fact that the APB held regular meetings that brought together a large number of high-level intelligence consumers to hear and discuss the same presentation was an enormous improvement from the fractured situation of past administrations. The prospects for misunderstanding and the time gaps between policy feedback and additional tasking of intelligence collection were considerably reduced. Steps taken by the Intelligence Community to preview its single country briefings to the sub-APB helped further ensure that APB members arrived for Board meetings with a fuller understanding of the situation within the country under discussion. These factors, along with department and agency participation on the Board, the familiarity it facilitated between members, all contributed significantly to what Charles Brown might characterize as some of the benefits of the APB "process."

Although some members of the sub-APB, in particular, have worked very hard to close the gap, what has still been lacking, in my view, is a comparable, systematic presentation from the policy community outlining the programs and policies already in play in the various at-risk countries, along with the current gaps. A comprehensive companion policy briefing, prepared for senior members of the Board, or whatever structure might be chosen to follow it, and pre-briefed to the rest of its future support structure, should help to further improve prescriptive deliberations on these issues.

Steve Pomper, Ambassador Power's successor as the NSC's Senior Director for Multilateral Affairs and Human Rights, a consummate professional who shouldered much of the burden of making the Board work since its inception in 2012, and others tried a variety of initiatives to advance collaboration between the APB and the various country IPCs, and went so far in some instances as to hold joint meetings.

APB and sub-APB alumni have characterized the results of those efforts as mixed, with some regional NSC Directors, for example, generally welcoming help from the APB, and others still preferring to keep the APB at arm's length. Efficiently bridging the functionalist/regionalist divide on atrocity prevention issues government-wide will remain, after the resource issue, one of the toughest challenges to effective atrocity prevention. It has reared its head at one time or another in all of the Departments and Agencies that have participated in the APB.

It will be some time before judgment can be reached as to whether the Department of State under Secretary Pompeo will succeed at bridging its own regional/functional divide and take up the leadership role in atrocity prevention that the GPTF report envisioned for it. When former Undersecretary Sewell assumed her duties at J in 2014, after the post was vacant for nearly a year, the State Department's PSD 10/APB supporters looked to her for strong leadership, and she received high marks from many quarters. Sewell stressed the inter-relationships between the different Bureaus and Offices that make up J, and stressed the need to incorporate prevention – and atrocity prevention in parti-cular – into the State Department's approaches to policymaking. Her designation of the Bureau of Reconstruction and Stabilization as the State Department's secretariat for atrocity prevention and advocacy for additional resources for the Bureau helped to reinvigorate the State Department's efforts to arrive at coor-dinated positions. She likewise emerged as a strong advocate for the Atrocity Prevention Board in meetings with civil society, highlighting, for example, the Board's role in elevating Burundi's profile some two years in advance of the current crisis.

Some have postulated that the most effective way to narrow the State Depart-ment's regional/functional divide is simply to dismantle the J group and disburse sections of its constituent Bureaus and Offices to strengthened, more contained Regional Bureaus. CIA's experience with its centers may be instructive on that score. Although the Agency seems to be having considerable success building its new regional-based Centers, progress in those individual units has turned on the quality of their individual leadership and, in particular, the ability of those unit heads to visua-lize how their centers' component parts must and can work cohesively.

But CIA also chose to retain several of its existing functional Centers. CIA would have been hard-pressed to provide sufficient people with the requisite expertise to fulfil the functional needs of each new regional-based Center. Each of those Centers would then have had to take on the added burden of continuing to build and maintain those officers' expertise and connectivity to other key parts of the bureaucracy.

The State Department might benefit from attaching some additional small units that mirror J to its Regional Bureaus, but completely dismantling their present functional bureaus would either require the hiring of considerable numbers of additional personnel with comparable expertise or weaken their future effective-ness. Dismantling J would also deprive its constituent bureaus and offices of a

Eyes on the White House

The path to preventing atrocities in the future is likely to lie less in big theoretical breakthroughs, and more in the direction of better coordination and integration of policy approaches, both without our own government and with key like-minded partners. Perhaps the single most important factor that will determine whether progress continues to be made in fulfilling the Obama Administration's PSD 10 recommendations and an atrocity prevention program into the new Trump Administration will be the level of commitment from the White House. While it is still early in the Trump Administration, the initial signs do not evoke great optimism. Bureaucracies are especially adept at parsing senior leaders' formal pronouncements, zeroing in on what is said as well as what is not said, and adjusting accordingly. Washington's atrocity prevention community is certain to continue to struggle in the months ahead to press its case in the face of an "America First" narrative.

The atrocity prevention community would benefit from a further public explanation of how the prevention of atrocities is closely linked to other US foreign policy goals, including counterterrorism, economic growth and development, reducing poverty, and strengthening rule of law, among other dimensions. Atrocity prevention currently stands at an important turning point. If the effort advanced under President Obama is to fulfil its potential in the years ahead, it will need additional resources, continued strong leadership within the Department of State, closer coordination among key Departments and Agencies as well as with key allies and civil society, along with a workforce better prepared to wrestle with this toughest of twenty-first-century challenges. It will also need the endorsement and support of President Trump and key members of his cabinet.

Notes

1 An earlier version of this essay was first prepared by James P. Finkel under the auspices of the United States Holocaust Museum's Simon-Skodt Center, which hosted Mr. Finkel as its 2013–2014 Leonard and Sophie Davis Genocide Prevention Fellow. That version may be accessed at www.ushmm.org/m/pdfs/20140904-finkel-atrocity-prevention-report.pdf. A second essay, which drew considerably from that initial research, appeared in the *Journal of Genocide Studies and Prevention*, 9:2, pp. 138–147, 2015 and can be found at http://dx.doi.org/10.5038/1911-9933.9.2.1361144.

Mr. Finkel left federal service in May 2013 after almost 35 years, the last 20 of which provided him a bird's eye view of US policy towards the prevention of genocide and mass atrocities. He was a participant in President Obama's PSD 10 study and was a frequent attendee during the first year of Atrocity Prevention Board meetings. This essay is drawn primarily from his personal recollections and discussions with long-time observers of US policy towards atrocities. The conclusions reached in the essay are strictly his own, however, and do not necessarily represent the views of his former agency, other federal departments or agencies, the Center for the Prevention of Genocide, or the US

Holocaust Memorial Museum. Information as of February 2017 was used in the preparation of this essay.

2 See White House, *"Fact Sheet" A Comprehensive Strategy and New Tools to Prevent and Respond to Atrocities*, accessed August 25, 2015, http://m.whitehouse.gov/the-press-office/2012/04/23/fact-sheet-comprehensive-strategy-and-new-tools-prevent-and-respond-atro. The drafting of the Executive Order proved far more controversial than anticipated, with strong opposition from those who feared that issuing an Executive Order would prompt further criticism of the Obama Administration's policy towards Syria. Those concerns began to soften as the Administration entered its final year and APB supporters both within and outside government began to search for ways to strengthen the case for retaining the APB into whatever Administration might follow. An Executive Order was finally issued by the Obama White House in May 2016. The Order emphasized that the APB would be retained, although some of its provisions were weaker than those originally put forward in PSD 10. The text of President Obama's Executive Order can be found at https://obamawhitehouse.archives.gov/the-press-office/2016/05/18/executive-order-comprehensive-approach-atrocity-prevention-and-response. As of this writing, it is unclear whether President Trump plans to revoke President Obama's Executive Order.

3 For an extensive study of US policy towards the recent crisis in the Central African Republic, see Charles J. Brown, "Had We Known Enough… The Obama Administration and the Struggle to Prevent Atrocities in the Central African Republic, December 2012–September 2014," www.ushmm.org/m/pdfs/20161116-Charlie-Brown-CAR-Report.pdf.

4 Rebecca Hamilton, "Samantha Power in Practice," *Foreign Affairs*, February 3, 2014, accessed August 25, 2014, www.foreignaffairs.com/articles/140709/rebecca-hamilton/samantha-power-in-practice.

5 The Working Group participants from the State Department included: the Office of War Crime Issues (SWICI) – now the Office of Global Criminal Justice (J-GCJ); Policy Planning; the Bureau of Democracy, Human Rights and Labor (DRL); and the appropriate regional Assistant Secretaries.

6 For a more detailed discussion of the evolution of the Atrocity Prevention Board, see James P. Finkel, "Atrocity Prevention at the Crossroads: Assessing the President's Atrocity Prevention Board after Two Years," www.ushmm.org/m/pdfs/20140904-finkel-atrocity-prevention-report.pdf; and Charles Brown, "The Obama Administration and the Struggle to Prevent Atrocities in the Central African Republic, December 2012–September 2014," www.ushmm.org/m/pdfs/20161116-Charlie-Brown-CAR-Report.pdf.

7 The Regional IPC's have tended to vary in size, department and agency participation, and duration. They are most likely to be formed, or called back into session, in response to a more immediate crisis. Few have been organized with the intent of performing the type of horizon-scanning and broader calculus role that the Atrocity Prevention Board has played.

8 James Waller, *Confronting Evil, Engaging Our Responsibility to Prevent Genocide*, Oxford, UK: Oxford University Press, 2016, p. 147. See Chapter 4 for an excellent discussion of upstream prevention.

9 *Preventing Genocide: A Blueprint for U.S. Policymakers*, Madeleine K. Albright and William S. Cohen, Co-Chairs, Genocide Prevention Task Force, 2008, The United States Holocaust Memorial Museum, The American Academy of Diplomacy, and the Endowment of the United States Institute of Peace, pp. xvii and 11. Hereafter cited as GPTF Report.

10 Having sat through some of the earliest APB discussions about CAR and having been present during some of the corridor chatter that took place afterwards, it is hard to avoid the conclusion that turf and personal relations factored significantly.

11 GPTF Report, p. 9.

12 Peter Uvin, *Aiding Violence: The Development Enterprise in Rwanda*. West Hartford, CT: Kumarian Press, 1998.

13 Alexander L. George and Jane E. Holl, *The Warning-Response Problem and Missed Opportunities in Preventive Diplomacy*, in Bruce W. Jentleson, ed. *Opportunities Missed, Opportunities Seized*. Lanham, MD: Rowan and Littlefield, 2000, p. 22.

14 Ibid. p. 24.

15 Ibid. p. 25.

16 *The Mass Atrocity Response Operations Military Planning (MARO) Handbook* was published in May 2010. As the PSD 10 discussions got underway, the Army Peacekeeping and Stability Operations Institute began work on a companion informal white paper for the *MARO Handbook* aimed at policymakers concerned with mass atrocity and response. That publication, *The Mass Atrocity Prevention and Response Options (MAPRO) Handbook*, was published in March 2012.

17 For a further elaboration of this and other recommendations for improving the effectiveness of the Atrocity Prevention Board, see Finkel, "Moving Beyond The Crossroads: Strengthening the Atrocity Prevention Board," *Journal of Genocide Studies and Prevention*, 9:2 (2015), http://dx.doi.org/10.5038/1911-9933.9.2.1361144 and *A Necessary Good: U.S Leadership on Preventing Mass Atrocities, Final Report of the Experts Committee on Preventing Mass Violence*, November 2016, the Friends Committee on National Legislation Education Fund on behalf of the Prevention and Protection Working Group.

18 The most important pioneering work aimed at attempting to systematically model the widespread and systematic risk of atrocities was carried out by this volume's editors, Barbara Harff and Ted Gurr, under the auspices of the US Government's Political Instability Task Force. While the Task Force and its models have evolved over time, at its core, its work on genocides and politicides continues to rely on Harff's earlier work. For further information on the Political Instability Task Force, see Wikipedia: https://en.wikipedia.org/wiki/Political_Instability_Task_Force.

19 Finkel, "Moving Beyond the Crossroads: Strengthening the Atrocity Prevention Board," *Journal of Genocide Studies and Prevention*, 9:2 (2015), http://dx.doi.org/10.5038/1911-9933.9.2.1361144.

10

PREVENTION THROUGH POLITICAL AGREEMENTS

The community of Sant'Egidio and the Central African Republic

Andrea Bartoli and Mauro Garofalo

Any political agreement is a fragile construct, and violence – especially the kind that can kill masses – seems too strong to be contained by political methods. Yet, without a political agreement that creates the foundational framework for coexistence, no effort to prevent mass atrocities can truly take hold. Stability is the product of an alignment of collective intentions and political institutions. At times, these agreements become possible through the services of international actors such as the Community of Sant'Egidio. The Community first became known internationally in the early '90s for its role in the peace process in Mozambique. It has been involved in many cases since then, and most recently facilitated important initiatives in the Central African Republic. This brief account analyzes the principles and practices by which Sant'Egidio gains the confidence of those who agree to meet, discuss, and sometimes negotiate a settlement. Peacemaking is a difficult challenge, and it is important to convey a sense of how and when the process works, while stressing that peace processes are never truly finalized. In a country that has known a long period of French colonialism and the egregious imperial experiment of Colonel Jean-Bédel Bokassa (the self-appointed Emperor Bokassa I), as well as a series of military coups, patience will be required to witness the emergence of a political culture open to democratic values and practices, attentive to the rule of law and human rights, and capable of institution-building adequate to the task of successfully controlling powerful armed groups that confront each other violently.

At the moment of the meeting of the Security Council dedicated to the Central African Republic (June 12, 2017), the situation in CAR remained fragile. As UN Secretary-General Guterres noted, this year, 2017:

> was marked by uneven progress in the political process. Intensified clashes between armed groups in central and eastern prefectures marred peace and

recovery efforts, causing a deterioration of the humanitarian situation. In contrast, a period of sustained calm in Bangui created the conditions for key institutions to address the multiple stabilization and recovery challenges.[1]

While the transition led to peaceful conduct of elections and the nomination of Faustin Archange Touadéra in 2016, 70% of the territory was still outside government control. Armed groups still control territories that are key to the development of the country, such as border and mining areas. President Touadéra promoted a national dialogue, but the process of disarmament, demobilization, reintegration, and repatriation (DDRR), as agreed during the Forum of Bangui in 2015, was still rejected by the main armed groups.

The security situation is still worrying. The former allies of Seleka are now fighting each other in the northern part of the country. The conflict pits the Coalition, made up of the Front Populaire pour la Renaissance de la Centrafrique (FPRC) of Noureddine Adam, the Mouvement Patriotique pour la Centrafrique (MPC), and the Rassemblement pour la Réconciliation des Centrafricains (RPRC), against the Union pour la Paix en Centrafrique (UPC) of Ali Darrass. The infighting between former Seleka groups also heightens ethnic tensions in the country. The Coalition comprises Arabs, Goula, Kara, and Ronga ethnic groups from the center of the country. The UPC is considered a foreign group, not only because it is led by a foreigner, but also because it is formed by nomadic and cross-border shepherds, especially Pewl. This ethnic drift is also felt in Bangui. The Muslim community, composed mainly of young people, is also beginning to experience ethnic division. This ethnic turn in the conflict might lead to a protracted war.

As stressed by the UN Secretary-General and his Special Representative, Parfait Onanga-Anyanga, the process of further stabilizing the government of CAR is crucial, and disarmament and reconciliation are key components. It is of paramount importance to counter the isolation of the armed groups scattered throughout the country, to find a way to disarm the combatants, and to agree the conditions for reintegration.

Involvement of the Community of Sant'Egidio

Well-known and widely respected in the CAR, the Community of Sant'Egidio began its activities in the early 2000s under President Ange-Félix Patassé. Founded in Rome, Italy in 1968, the Community of Sant'Egidio is an international subject recognized in many countries. The Holy See has recognized it as a Public Lay Association. As an NGO, the Community of Sant'Egidio has consultative status with the UN-ECOSOC. On June 9, 2017, it signed a letter of intent with the UN Department of Political Affairs.

The President of the transition, Michel Djotodia, contacted Sant'Egidio to facilitate dialogue and reconciliation in 2013. Since then, the Community of Sant'Egidio has worked with political parties, armed groups, representatives of religious communities, and civil society to reinforce national initiatives and to lay the ground for peaceful elections and reconciliation.

This mediation work led to the signing of the "Pacte Républicain" in November 2013 by President Michel Djotodia, Prime Minister Nicolas Ntiangaye, and the President of the National Transitional Council, Alexandre Ferdinand Nguendet. This agreement, a true "code of conduct" for the political world of CAR, negotiated under the mediation of Sant'Egidio, is mentioned in very positive terms in the UN Security Council Resolution 2127 (2013) of 5 December 2013.

In February 2015, leading personalities, including four former Prime Ministers, signed a pre-election agreement declaring their intention not to resort to violence and to respect electoral results. In collaboration with the Gendarmerie of the Holy Sea, the Community of Sant'Egidio facilitated a truce between the Anti-Balaka and former Seleka fighters in Bangui ahead of Pope Francis's visit to the country in November 2015. This visit, especially in Muslim PK5, has had positive effects on the political life of the country.

President Faustin Archange Touadéra campaigned as a peacemaker who could bridge the religious divide. He has known the Community of Sant'Egidio for a long time. In November 2016, during a confidential talk with the President, the Community was given the mandate to explore ways to involve all the armed groups in the DDRR process. In December 2016, a delegation of Sant'Egidio went to CAR for a mission of rapprochement with these armed groups. The same month, a delegation of Anti-Balaka came to Rome. In February and March 2017, Sant'Egidio successively held four confidential meetings with delegations of politico-military groups at its headquarters in Rome. These talks were intended to encourage a frank discussion in a climate of trust, to restore the political and social role of armed groups, to listen to their requests, and to assess hurdles on the way to the implementation of the DDRR process. Such a path could lead to significant steps towards pacification of the country and full recognition of its institutions.

The Community worked to meet the remaining armed groups active in CAR to complete the *tour de table*, create a framework of concrete proposals and solutions to rebuild a lasting coexistence, and imagine an effective DDRR process. In preparation for the meetings in Rome, a delegation of Sant'Egidio briefed the UN Security Council on the situation in CAR and suggested some steps for further dialogue. The following week in Rome, at the headquarters of the Community of Sant'Egidio, the delegates of Faustin A. Touadéra, Président of the Républic Head of State and of the Government of the Central African Republic, met with the representatives of politico-military groups hailing from all regions and representing the great diversity of the CAR landscape. The meeting was facilitated by the Community of Sant'Egidio in the presence of UN Secretary-General Special Representative, Parfait Onanga-Anyanga. At the conclusion of the meeting, the document *Entente de Sant'Egidio Accord Politique pour la paix en République Centrafricaine* was signed (see Appendix).

How was it possible to reach such an agreement? What are the principles and practices by which Sant'Egidio gains the confidence of those who agree to meet, discuss, and sometimes negotiate a settlement?

War is in many ways an effort to secure a non-negotiated outcome. Unconditional surrender of the enemy is the maximum goal of victorious armies. Unfortunately for the war advocates, clear-cut victories are not common, and, in addition to the high costs of war, uncertainty of results and the need for long-term political stability move human systems in the direction of constructive dialogue.

Peace processes (like any human endeavor) are always unique, yet successful engagements generally exhibit common characteristics or drivers:

- An intense investment in personal relationships involving deep, prolonged listening and accurate feedback;
- A significant attentiveness to the consequences of words, to the requests shared, to the promises made;
- A willingness to explore what is possible beyond the constraints of the current conditions (the first limitation to peace is believing that it is impossible);
- Sincerity from facilitators who have no agenda other than the emergence of peace;
- The careful management of relationships with a multiplicity of actors;
- The commitment to institutions as the conduit for the management of contradictions, tensions, and divergent patterns, and as the manifestation of the collective will across space and time.

It took more than eight months for the team of the Community of Sant'Egidio to establish the conditions for a fruitful meeting of all relevant actors. The personal engagement of each, together with considerable patience, were indispensable elements of the relationship-building phase. Each potential participant was approached individually and institutionally, ensuring that, in addition to the capacity to represent a group, there was the basis for a genuine human connection, indispensable to properly "read" statements, situations, and suggestions.

The six drivers allow for an interesting blend of approaches that scholars of political science might be inclined to define as "realist", "liberal", and "constructivist." The Community of Sant'Egidio understands itself as an international subject operating in a context in which history is not a vestige of the past but is constantly remade. History is the result of collective responsibility; it is the product of human choosing. Humans created the conflicts that they experience; humans can find the way out of those conflicts if they attend to actual data attentively and respond properly. Yet, this capacity is one of the first and most enduring casualties of any violent conflict. All information is distorted. Frequently, events are manipulated in ways that make it difficult (if not impossible) to ascertain what truly happened. Meaning is clouded by the political and military interests of the day. Knowledge is power and is confined, contained, and controlled in an effort to maximize the chances for victory, for the desired outcome, for the preferred solution.

Sant'Egidio believes that it is always possible for parties in conflict to explore options for peace, but, for that to happen successfully, the participants' security must come first. Repeatedly, the Community of Sant'Egidio has enabled peace negotiations among leaders actively committed to military victories by suggesting, accepting, or designing security arrangements that would guarantee the life and welfare of the participants. Security concerns should never be underestimated, and the guarantees to address them must be effective, even if this may mean putting the life of the negotiators at risk. While military protection is an option, key questions are: who is trusted to provide it, and what security calculations are at stake? In the case of the negotiations prior to the visit of Pope Francis to Central African Republic, there was no doubt that the visit could have been perceived as dangerous and even provocative. The Gendarmerie of the Holy See has no real military capacity, and the only way to overcome UN concerns about the security of the Pope was to ensure a truce between the Anti-Balaka and former Seleka fighters in Bangui. The very conception of the truce recognized that security was to be offered by the parties rather than imposed by external actors. Thanks to these negotiations, Pope Francis's visit to the country in November 2015 was a success, and the presence of the Pope, especially in Muslim PK5, has had long-lasting positive effects on the political life of the country.

Yet, the question remains: what if the Pope had been shot? What if there were riots while he was visiting? What would have happened if, instead of a peaceful welcome, the armed factions had decided to use the occasion to score military and political points, perhaps through covert operations that sought to displace blame onto others? Such hypothetical reasoning is always part of the Sant'Egidio negotiators' concerns. Experience and scholarly research tend to reveal that open communication, self-correcting processes, and intentional verification heighten security. Paradoxically, because Sant'Egidio as the Gendarmerie of the Holy See has no military capacity and cannot deter any actors by forcing them to behave in a way that would guarantee security, it can lead all actors into considering cooperative security arrangements that are fundamentally pragmatic, encouraging them to:

- recognize forces on the ground as they are;
- accept the self-organization of groups and the self-identification of leadership;
- assume the capacity of leadership to negotiate in good faith and implement agreements;
- assume that the leadership has the capacity to control internal dynamics including dissidents and threatening actors.

When a preventive security agreement is successful, as in the visit of Pope Francis to Bangui, it has significant political implications. First, armed forces are politically recognized as relevant actors. Second, if dangerous security issues can be resolved, other agreements might be possible. Third, the direct communication channel utilized for the successful security agreement can serve the parties in a new round of negotiations.

This pragmatism, together with the commitment to more peaceful political processes, explains why all relevant actors of the government as well as those "representing all the politico-military groups of the country, coming from all the

140 Andrea Bartoli and Mauro Garofalo

regions, representing all its components in their diversity" gathered "in Rome under the mediation of the Community of Sant'Egidio, which has been engaged relentlessly for years for peace in the Central African Republic."[2] Who was invited? Those who – by the very parties themselves – hold some relevant role in the political and military areas. The very list of invitees was the product of a relational acknowledgment that a given group was indeed relevant in determining the future of the country as a whole.

Beyond the strategic choice of who should participate, peace processes accumulate wisdom through the time spent together by the participants. It becomes possible to share the history of the country, and an understanding of why "things are the way they are". The preliminary relation-building phase allows for a delicate tune-in process in which even difficult steps and conversations generate further understanding. De facto, participants recognize each other as relevant actors for the current situation and the future of the country. The participants are in charge of suggesting and vetting others. This process does not happen in a vacuum, but is rather the expression of previous relational investments by the members of the Community of Sant'Egidio. It is carefully calibrated in relation to the commitments of the international community.

The issue of inclusion and the risk of impunity have been raised several times in the context of ongoing peace processes as serious concerns. They will be addressed systematically in another text, but it is essential to stress how positions that are excessively ideological and dogmatic might reduce the international debate on the Central African Republic to a false dichotomy between amnesty or no-amnesty. For the participants in the Rome process, the issue revolved more around agency. In any peace process, there are questions such as: shouldn't the peace process be open only to actors who did not engage in destructive behavior? Or: should actors who have chosen violence contribute to peace negotiations? For some, these questions should not be asked at all. For those who participated in the *Entente de Sant'Egidio*, there was the painful recognition that the horrors of violence must be addressed, but that political and judiciary institutions must be established first.

The discipline of mutual recognition has offered a meaningful reference point in navigating the treacherous waters of negotiations with violent actors. These discussions must be free from violence and the threat of violence, which is why physical location and security arrangements are so crucial, especially when parties are negotiating with active enemies without a consolidated ceasefire. It is exactly because violence is still occurring that the talks must be preserved from any form and threat of violence. In many ways, the talks become an experiment in the political give-and-take that might take hold if the proper institutional environment were created. The Community of Sant'Egidio doesn't believe that powerful actors can impose a stable peace from the outside. Rather, peace is the expression of a cost-benefit calculation, constantly recalibrated by the parties themselves. Peace is stable when those who are contributing to it find it preferable to violent alternatives. Correctly understanding the cost- benefit calculation of each actor is part of the preparatory work of the Community of Sant'Egidio's team. This approach assumes that actors within a conflict are capable of making strategic choices and exploring alternatives. In the case of the Central African Republic, the alternatives that the Community of Sant'Egidio's team has encouraged have a constitutional quality; they aim at creating a political environment in which diversity is expected and allowed, distribution of power is by design, and the exercise of power allows for checks and balances. The historic task at hand is not only to reach a ceasefire agreement; it is actually to contribute to the formation of the state as a stable political platform for the proper representation of all citizens and groups.

The Central African Republic is a country in the making. Its history has been marked by significant oppression, and, as Tatiana Carayannis and Louisa Lombard (2015) have noted:

> democracy, in any kind of a meaningful sense, has eluded the country. Since the mid-1990s, army mutinies and serial rebellion in CAR have resulted in two major successful coups. Over the course of these upheavals, the country has become a laboratory for peacebuilding initiatives, hosting a two-decade-long succession of UN and regional peacekeeping, peacebuilding and special political missions.

The next period is crucial for CAR and the international community.

The Community of Sant'Egidio firmly believes that the first and most important actors in determining the fate of the Central African Republic are its leaders and citizens. Working for peace is working for an institutional framework through which these responsibilities can be effectively exercised. A country is built through the alignment of its constitutive narrative with its political institutions. At the moment, no one in Central African Republic has full control of the territory: not the government, and not any other armed or political actor, including the United Nations. This inability to exert meaningful control requires the involvement of those who could contribute to the establishment of such a framework. This is why it is essential to recognize the effort of the Community of Sant'Egidio to strengthen institutions. The opening of the *Entente de Sant'Egidio, the Political Agreement for Peace in Central African Republic* signed in Rome June 20, 2017, appropriately declares:

> We, the representatives of HE Mr. Faustin A. Touadera, President of the Republic Head of State, and the Government of the Central African Republic,
>
> Representatives of all the politico-military groups of the country, coming from all the regions, representing all its components in their diversity,
>
> Gathered in Rome under the mediation of the Community of Sant'Egidio, which has been engaged relentlessly for years for peace in the Central African Republic,

142 Andrea Bartoli and Mauro Garofalo

In the presence of Central African delegations representing the National Assembly and the political class …

Words do count. A country stays together not only because of the effectiveness of some in exercising power, but because its *raison d'être* is spelled out in a convincing way. Central African Republic is rebuilding itself as a country where the prevention of violence is inscribed in political agreements institutionalized through a culture that can self-correct by means of political engagement. This hopeful trend is extremely fragile, and must be pursued with great care. The role of the United Nations, and especially of the UN Secretary-General Special Representative, Parfait Onanga-Anyanga, is crucial. States do not fail alone. States such as the Central African Republic must find international support in a form that does not impose solutions, but strengthens the determination of those within CAR to build effective institutions. The *Entente de Sant'Egidio* is an important step in this direction.

Notes

1 Report of the Secretary-General on the Central African Republic S/2017/473.
2 See *Entente de Sant'Egidio*.

References

Bartoli, A. (2005) "Learning from the Mozambique Peace Process: The Role of the Community of Sant'Egidio." In R. J. Fisher (ed.), *Paving the Way: Contributions of Interactive Conflict Resolution to Peacemaking*, pp. 79–104. Lexington, MA: Lexington.

Boutros-Ghali, B. (1992) An Agenda for Peace: Preventive Diplomacy, Peacemaking and Peace-Keeping, *Report of the Secretary-General Pursuant to the Statement Adopted by the Summit Meeting of the Security Council on 31 January 1992*. New York: United Nations.

Carayannis, T., and L. Lombard (eds.) (2015) *Making Sense of the Central African Republic*. London: Zed Books, www.zedbooks.co.uk/paperback/making-sense-of-the-central-africanrepublic

Collier, P. (2003)*Breaking the Conflict Trap: Civil War and Development Policy*. Washington, DC: World Bank.

Crocker, C. A., F. O. Hampson, and P. Aall (eds.) (1999) *Herding Cats: Multiparty Mediation in a Complex World*. Washington, DC: United States Institute of Peace Press.

Dieng, A. and J. Welsh (2016) "Assessing the Risk of Atrocity Crimes." *Genocide Studies and Prevention: An International Journal* 9(3).

International Commission on Intervention and State Sovereignty (2001) The Responsibility to Protect. *International Commission on Intervention and State Sovereignty*.

Kumar, C. (2011) "Building National 'Infrastructures for Peace': UN Assistance for Internally Negotiated Solutions to Violent Conflict." In A. Bartoli, S. Allen Nan and Z. Mampilly (eds.), *Peacemaking: From Practice to Theory*, pp. 384–399. Santa Barbara, CA: Praeger Publishers.

Riccardi, A. (1997) *Sant'Egidio, Rome and the World*, Cinisello Balsamo, Italy: San Paolo Edizioni.

Saulnier, P. (1997) "Le Centrafrique: Entre mythe et réalité." *Études africaines*. Paris: L'Harmattan.

United Nations (2005) *World Summit Outcome*. A/RES/60/1.
United Nations (2009) *Implementing the Responsibility to Protect*. A/63/677.
United Nations (2015) *A Vital and Enduring Commitment: Implementing the Responsibility to Protect*. A/69/981–S/2015/500.
Woodfork, J. (2006) *Culture and Customs of the Central African Republic*. Westport, CT: Greenwood.

11

AN AFRICAN REGIONAL PERSPECTIVE ON PREVENTION

Experiences from the Great Lakes region

Ambassador Liberata Mulamula and Ashad Sentongo

Introduction

The Great Lakes region is marked by the fragility of each of its member states.[1] Various scholars attribute this situation to self-interested elites,[2] while others point to undemocratic forces in the region. A number of states and communities have experienced deadly conflicts; indeed, until recently, little was known about this region other than wars, mass atrocities and Rwanda's genocide of 1994. At one time, the countries of the Great Lakes region produced more refugees, internally displaced persons and war orphans than any other region in the world.[3]

Tarrow has argued that political opportunities that constrain social actors who lack resources of their own create a collective challenge, common purpose, solidarity and collective identity that fuels violence.[4] Similarly, member states of the Great Lakes region are marked by contentious political processes during state formation, where groups often organized along ethnic or religious lines persistently claim to be denied access to power and other opportunities. Such grievances and claims of deprivation, discrimination, oppression, injustice and domination account for the enduring cycles of violence perpetrated to redress persistent disparities. The grievances are often explained along ethnic lines to differentiate between insiders and outsiders, and this tends to make inter-ethnic compromises difficult (Horowitz 1985). These group identities are often of critical concern to in-group pride and self-esteem.[5] Ethnicity thus presents special difficulties that perpetuate cycles of violent conflicts and continue to pose uncharacteristic challenges for democratic politics in the region.

Recognizing how enduring cycles of violent conflicts affect the social, political and economic destinies of states and communities, especially after the 1994 genocide in Rwanda, heads of state and governments from the Great Lakes region, under the joint auspices of the UN and the then-OAU, signed a legally binding

Pact on Security, Stability and Development in the Great Lakes, in Nairobi, Kenya in December 2006. The Pact established the International Conference on the Great Lakes Region (ICGLR), an intergovernmental body that holds enormous potential for sustainably transforming legacies and cycles of violent conflict and genocide and promoting greater coexistence between communities and states in the region. In this way, it is an important milestone in the search for peace and stability in the region. It remains a well-crafted consensus that seeks to move beyond the quagmire of the region's most recent conflict-ridden history.[6]

Morada states that perpetrators of violent crimes "often seek to split international consensus and actively exploit mechanisms and processes that best place them to pursue their objectives, a fact which makes consistent and effective coordination even more critical."[7] This paper examines experiences from the ICGLR with respect to regional coordination and practices regarding genocide and mass atrocity prevention. Existing initiatives and numerous efforts to effective implementation of the protocol are discussed, including recommendations to build and institutionalize synergies between regional and national mechanisms for prevention to promote regional peace and stability.

Prevention as a practice

The practice of preventing violent conflicts, genocide and mass atrocities involves a commitment to preserve the human family. It is a struggle to pursue collective learning regarding the underlying causes and process in their unique environments, for example, as tribes, communities, organizations or sovereign states. As a practice, prevention involves linking available knowledge about causes, processes and manifestations with policies, practices and programs that may be implemented at different levels to respond, deescalate or terminate hostile conditions and situations. Reychler makes a distinction between "proactive conflict" prevention (before conflict escalates) and "reactive conflict prevention" (preventing conflict that has occurred from escalating).[8]

Fisher states that "management and resolution of conflicts work to increase cooperative aspects, while recognizing that competitive elements will require a firm and yet conciliatory combination of strategies."[9] In the Great Lakes region, historical and contemporary experiences suggest that prevention and management of conflicts involves engineering a fundamental reorientation in approaches to social, political, economic and institutional conditions that breed negative perceptions, hostilities and violence. The fact that violence and mass atrocities continue in the Democratic Republic of Congo, Burundi, South Sudan and Central Africa Republic clearly indicates that little or no learning has occurred in the wake of the tragic experiences in Rwanda in 1994 or Uganda from 1980–1986. For this reason, violence remains the preferred language to settle grievances, and its consequences remain evident everywhere.

Ould-Abdallah has argued that "preventive diplomacy must dig deep to be able to understand the current problems in light of broader historical, geographical, economic, demographic, religious, and ethnic issues."[10] Similarly, in the case of the Great Lakes region, prevention should involve re-engaging with processes of nation-building. In particular, this requires recognizing the sub-national character of tribal communities that the post-independence state is struggling to manage under unitary governments. Citizenship versus ethnicity, and modern versus traditional forms of governance, seem to be permanent contests, the consequences of which remain inconsistent with the demands of either democracy or globalization. In this case, therefore, effective prevention occurs when state and communal initiatives implement tailored interventions to manage these contests to redress manifestations of colonial legacies, economic disparities and deprivation of opportunities to access power.

Prevention of genocide and mass atrocities in the Great Lakes region

The Protocol on Prevention and the Punishment of the Crime of Genocide, War Crimes and Crimes against Humanity and All Forms of Discrimination is one of the ten protocols that constitute an integral part of the ICGLR Pact on Security, Stability and Development (2006). Signing of the Pact demonstrated the strong political will of states to build structures and expand the scope of responsibility for prevention beyond governments to include civil society actors. The Protocol also mandates roles and responsibilities for states and other stakeholders aimed at prevention at the political and operational levels.

In the context of prevention, all ten protocols in the pact are considered important because of the confluence of the various causes for violent conflicts and the issues the various protocols seek to address. Examples include: 1) The Protocol on the Prevention and Suppression of Sexual Violence Against Women and Children, 2) the Protocol Against the Illegal Exploitation of Natural Resources and 3) the Protocol of Non-aggression and Mutual Defense in the Great Lakes region, which is in line with the United Nations Charter and the Constitutive Act of the African Union. Thus, while there is a protocol with a specific focus on prevention as a regional aspiration, the protocols focus on related causes and drivers of violent conflicts in the region. For example, the history of grave human rights abuses, the illegal exploitation of natural resources, the influx of refugees and insecurity along common borders, etc., create favorable conditions for transnational crimes and intrastate and inter-state hostilities.

From this perspective, ICGLR was conceived with clear acknowledgement of a range of bottlenecks to prevention, most importantly political divisions across communities and between states, and how the violent past in the region would limit the capacity of each state to effectively respond to conflicts. These concerns notwithstanding, the regional approach to addressing this range of issues was seen as the most viable framework. Thus, the structure and composition of ICGLR mechanisms reflect a multi-level and multi-dimensional approach to implementing the protocol on prevention of genocide and mass atrocities.

The ICGLR genocide and mass atrocity prevention mechanism

The then-UN Special Advisor on Prevention of Genocide, Mr. Francis Deng (2010), noted that, at a regional level, states have common concerns, and learn more easily from each other which kinds of solutions and best practices work for them. These views underscore the spirit and functions of the region's prevention mechanisms for genocide and mass atrocity, which include the Regional and National Committees dedicated to this task.

As Dukes has further argued, the mechanism seeks to deal with problems of disintegration of community, public alienation from governmental institutions and an inability to resolve public problems and conflicts peacefully.[11] In this case, prevention occurs when transformation approaches involve nurturing and sustaining an engaged community, a responsive government and building public capacity for conflict resolution and problem-solving. The prevention mechanism under the ICGLR is not only multi-level and largely hierarchical, but also multi-disciplinary in a way that underscores its potential to become more effective in generating associated policies and programs, especially at country and community levels.

The heads of state from the region constitute the Summit, which is the inter-governmental policy-making organ of the conference. It is supported by the Regional Inter-Ministerial Committee (RIMC), composed of members from Ministries of Foreign Affairs from all Member States, and the National Coordinating and Collaboration Mechanisms in each of the 12 member states. The Executive Secretariat, established in 2007, with its headquarters in Bujumbura, Burundi, is the technical arm and coordinating body of the ICGLR, which facilitates the implementation of the Pact and its ten protocols by all member states.

The ICGLR's regional security mechanism consists of the following: the Joint Intelligence Fusion Centre (JIFC) based in Goma, eastern DRC, and charged with collating and sharing intelligence on negative forces; and the Expanded Joint Verification Mechanism (EJVM), also based in Goma and charged with verifying claims and counter-claims by neighboring states regarding support for each other's destructive forces, as well as to patrol the common border between the DRC, Rwanda, Burundi and Uganda. The mechanism also includes the ICGLR Committee of Ministers of Defence, the Committee of Chiefs of Defence Staff and the Committee of Chiefs of Intelligence Services.

Similarly, heads of state in the Great Lakes region recognized the effects the conflicts in Member States had on all countries and communities in the region. The leaders signed and committed to the Pact and its protocols to demonstrate their political will to prevent escalation of hostilities. The Pact is based on the recognition that political instability and conflicts in these countries have a considerable regional dimension that requires a concerted effort of all stakeholders across sectors in order to promote sustainable peace and development. For example, in 1994, no country remained immune to the effects of the genocide in Rwanda. Instead, it became a regional problem. This brought to the fore the realization that each state has a role to play in bringing peace in the region for sustainable development of individual countries and the region as a whole.

In the same way, the first war in DRC 1996–1998, along with the eastern DRC crisis of 2008–2009 and 2012 involving the CNDP and M23 rebel groups respectively, adversely impacted the region as a whole. The Summit and the Secretariat accordingly invoked ICGLR instruments to call relevant actors and parties to the negotiating table. It is in this context that the ICGLR initiated a series of talks between the belligerent parties, the M23[12] and the government of the Democratic Republic of Congo. The peace negotiations between the DRC Government and the M23 began following the ICGLR Summit Declaration of 24 November 2012 in Kampala, Uganda, which directed the M23 to withdraw from Goma and cease all war activities and threats to overthrow the democratically-elected government of the DRC.[13] The Summit further requested that the DRC Government listen to the legitimate grievances of the M23, and mandated the Chairperson of the ICGLR, H.E. Yoweri Museveni, to mediate the process. The protracted negotiations, coupled with pressure by the international community, and the weakened state of the M23 led eventually to the signing of the peace agreement that resulted in the cessation of hostilities and a period of relative peace in the eastern DRC.[14]

However, arguably,[15] operational capacity to respond within the ICGLR mechanism has been limited in Burundi since 2009, as demonstrated by the current political crisis of 2015–2016. The constitutional amendment that allowed Burundi's incumbent President, Pierre Nkurunziza, to seek re-election for a third term resulted in post-election violence. It is further argued that, unfortunately, the conflicts in eastern DRC monopolize most of the ICGLR's resources, as was evident in the place of the M23 rebellion in several extraordinary ministerial and heads of state meetings in which the situation in the DRC was the sole item on the agenda. This limitation is attributed, among other factors, to conflicts and growing tensions between Rwanda and Burundi, as well as between Heads of Sates of Rwanda and Tanzania, and divergent interests in the Burundian crisis that have impacted the will and consensus decisions of the ICGLR to seek a solution to the crisis and thus prevent mass violence.[16]

Implementation of the ICGLR protocol

Concerning implementation of the ICGLR Protocol on Prevention and Punishment of Genocide and Mass Atrocities, a Regional Committee was formed in September 2010, composed of one representative from each member state. The mandated functions of the committee include regularly reviewing country situations in member states by collecting and analyzing relevant information and alerting the Summit of the Conference to respond in a timely way to identified threats. The Regional Committee can also suggest measures for states to take against impunity, implement regional and country programs to raise awareness, educate citizens about prevention, peace and reconciliation, make policy recommendations and take other initiatives to encourage governments to protect and guarantee the rights of victims, including gender-sensitive measures.

A number of positive steps have been taken at a country level to increase consciousness and awareness about prevention, while also promoting consensus around the causes of violence, genocide and mass atrocities in the region.[17] Foremost is the establishment of National Committees, which began in 2012 with the launching of the Tanzania National Committee for Genocide and Mass Atrocity Prevention. This was followed by Kenya, Uganda, South Sudan and DRC, and is soon to be joined by Zambia. The process has been slow in some states, for example Sudan, Angola, The Republic of Congo and Rwanda.

The composition of National Committees is equally multi-disciplinary and uniquely structured to allow representation and involvement of critical actors in the prevention architecture of each country. For example, the Ugandan National Committee is composed of 15 representatives from key Government Ministries, including the Office of the Prime Minister, civil society groups and human rights organizations.[18] The National Committee also formed a bureau composed of a Chair from the Ministry of Justice and Constitutional Affairs, a Vice-Chair from the Ministry of Foreign Affairs and a Rapporteur from the Uganda Human Rights Commission.

As Fisher emphasizes, processes that seek to respond to conflicts are "participative and collaborative, leading to de-escalation and reconciliation toward a sustainable future, and to outcomes that are mutually beneficial and supported by relationship qualities of trust and respect."[19] This type of composition of national committees in each country in the region, as explained above, continues to stand out as a unique space where various stakeholders interact to imagine the future of countries and communities through prevention. In the same way, a network of state, academic and civil society actors is slowly emerging in the region, devoted to preventing the occurrence or escalation of hostilities to genocidal levels in each state.

Local and international partnerships have also contributed greatly, giving the Regional and National Committees an identity and character that enable them to function with technical and financial support. The United Nations High Commissioner for Human Rights (UNHCHR), the UN Office of the Special Advisor on Genocide Prevention, the Auschwitz Institute for Peace and Reconciliation,[20] Swiss Peace, George Mason University, Global Action Against Mass Atrocities (GAMAAC) and other partner institutions have conducted various programs and provided technical and financial support towards capacity building, research, planning and the management of projects for preventing atrocities and achieving sustainable peace and security.

Training seminars to promote capacity building at regional and country levels have focused on various topics considered critical to the work of the committees, including early warning and early response, prevention of land and electoral conflicts, prevention of gender-based violence and other inter-communal conflicts and so on. The partnerships have increased collaboration among international, regional, national and local actors to transform legacies of mass crimes, civil war and genocide and promote peace and stability in the member states.

At the country level, National Committees have already taken practical steps towards prevention. The Tanzania National Committee is currently developing a Regional Early Warning Center and has established Community Peace Forums composed of leaders from religious communities, traditional institutions and the civil society. The Kenya National Committee has started the process of developing a Never Again Museum in Nairobi, while the Uganda National Committee[21] has developed a draft Bill of prevention of genocide and mass atrocities awaiting Parliamentary approval as a way of domesticating the ICGLR Protocol.

The AIPR has also developed an online resource manual for genocide and mass-atrocity prevention in the Great Lakes region, to facilitate training and general capacity building of constituent leaders and other regional actors. The resources further guide development and implementation of tailored national and communal projects, for example working with women and youth, traditional and political leaders, and also contain legal, analytical and early-warning and response mechanisms.

A manual of best practices for the establishment and management of National Mechanisms for Mass Atrocity Prevention is being developed by the African Working Group in the context of the GAAMAC and under the coordination of the Ugandan National Committee. It is still a work in progress, but with potential prospects to find home-grown solutions to local problems.

Through these efforts, the region is making tremendous progress in terms of building, strengthening and ultimately institutionalizing a regional mechanism of state and civil society leaders focused on raising awareness and implementing national and regional policies, projects and programs. Leaders at state and civil society levels, and from academia, who are members of National Committees, along with those who participate in associated programs, are increasingly standing up for prevention. Many continue to affirm new relationships within and between ICGLR member states and their respective communities to support prevention work at the local level. These developments are necessary to terminate the cycles of mass atrocities and promote resistance to them in the future.

Collective responsibility and learning

Preventing genocide, war crimes, crimes against humanity and all forms of discrimination is a collective enterprise, as declared by the UN Secretary General in his address to mark the 15th Anniversary of Genocide in Rwanda (2010).

The experiences of ICGLR member states indicate that legacies and cycles of violent conflict are interconnected across national borders. Prevention must therefore be implemented by member states collectively at the policy and institutional levels, while also involving civil society (which works best at the communal, academic, religious and cultural levels), if it is to be sustained over time. While the role of nation states is prominent in this process, that of international organizations and communities is particularly crucial. At each level, efforts should be marked by clear intentions and a commitment to deploy political, legal, material and human resources to achieve enduring preventive effects. Knowing whom to engage, where, and when is crucial.

The Great Lakes region is currently a leading example of a binding commitment to state-led initiatives to prevent genocide and mass atrocities, despite enduring hostilities within and between states and communities. However, as Semboja and Therlkildsen have argued, the mechanism is unlike the traditional state-centric approaches in which non-state initiatives are often construed as potential threats to regimes.[22] Although it emerges out of an inter-governmental arrangement, it does not position states as the motor of prevention, but instead creates room for the active participation of non-state institutions and the masses in prevention initiatives. To this extent, it provides a shared space for learning and practice by state and civil society leaders. So far, this has brought to life legal frameworks, along with institutional and operational norms and practices that translate into practical, observable and measurable achievements in countries like Tanzania, Uganda and Kenya, where national committees are functional.

With this regional mechanism and legal instruments in place, together with other international and regional instruments, the remaining challenge lies not in developing structures and enforcement mechanisms, but in promoting goodwill for implementation and compliance at national and regional levels, with the active support of the international community.

Challenges

Prevention of genocide and mass atrocity is a topic that has attracted interest among scholars and civil society organizations, but prevention has yet to be fully integrated into member states' policies and programs.[23] The African Task Force Report states that sub-regional cooperation for prevention and conflict resolution is born out of the vested interests of members. However, often these interests are not necessarily compatible with the quest for peace. Juma further maintains that, even if they are compatible, powerful nations within the alliance tend to hijack the process.[24] This view explains why, despite Burundi being a member state of the ICGLR, heads of state were constrained in their response to the violent conflicts in the country, much as they were with the M23 in the DRC. The non-conformity and violations of constitutional order have created undue tensions among some member states in the region, leading to an escalation of conflict and violence, as recently witnessed in the DRC and Burundi.

Despite advances with the formation of national and regional committees, the region's major setback is the lack of resources, capacity and sustained commitment of member states to implement the agreed programs and projects under the respective Protocols for prevention, and to meet its overall objectives for the peace, stability and development of the Great Lakes region.

The emerging regional mechanism is not equal to a regional early-warning and rapid-response mechanism. Despite a few country-level projects, for example the Uwiano Peace Platform in Kenya,[25] focusing on peaceful elections, there are no dedicated systems for effective early warning or with appropriate response capacities to effectively prevent situations like that in South Sudan. Bruce also observed that "whereas Rwanda is viewed as a failure of early warning and conflict prevention, the events instead reflect a failure of concerted conflict management efforts: not a failure of action, but a failure of actions taken."[26]

One of the challenges is the multiplicity of organizations and competing initiatives, often termed a "spaghetti bowl" that lacks coherence and coordination.[27] From this perspective, prevention work remains fragmented both at regional and country levels, both among committees and among other relevant stakeholders. The existence of diverse national committees with competing mandates, and various civil society organizations, leads to a competition for resources to implement projects as partners and collaborators.[28] This situation is worsened by the fact that national committees do not yet conceive of themselves as legal and well-defined stakeholders whose work is to complement governments' efforts to achieve stable societies through peaceful means.

The Regional and National Committees remain unable to influence political decisions of the leaders or communities they work in, because their relationships with political institutions and organizations has not been developed even to consultative levels. This is related to the sensitivity of their work, but also lack of capacity within the membership of committees to think about prevention, act politically and thus influence and complement their work with the actions of political leaders.

Despite complementary programs, common mandates and positions on prevention and shared operational problems, there are few or no opportunities for collective learning to promote best practices for prevention in the region. There are enormous difficulties in linking the work of prevention across communities and state together. This is despite the fact that the region is interconnected culturally, ethnically, socially, economically and, to some extent, politically.

Opportunities

There is a growing recognition that a regional or sub-regional approach should be the primary response mechanism for atrocity prevention in Africa. According to Khadaigala, regional organizations like the ICGLR, because of their proximity, are more likely to have a better understanding of the situation than external actors, and can often take decisions and implement responses much faster than the UN, because their members have direct interest in regional stability.[29] From this perspective, the emerging genocide and mass atrocity prevention mechanism in the Great Lakes region provides the framework within which prevention policies, programs and projects can be planned and executed. The mechanism is the outcome of distilled insights and wisdom gained from regional experiences, and creates the space to engage with historical, contemporary and emerging factors that influence war and mass violence in the region. In the same spirit, the ICGLR and its array of protocols and projects, despite constraints in human capacity and material resources to prevent setbacks like the ongoing situation in Burundi, provide a viable framework and enshrine the twin principles of ownership and international partnerships necessary for states to build effective national and regional preventative mechanisms.

Emerging capacities and capabilities at the national and regional levels, incorporating research, training and education by academic institutions and civil society organizations, constantly engage with causes and prevention of wars, human rights abuses, genocide and discrimination. Increasingly, therefore, actors within the ICGLR genocide prevention framework are learning to analyze and identify the underlying causes of conflicts in the region, in order to develop and implement appropriate interventions. To reduce failures of prevention, capacity building helps leaders and other stakeholders to apply a preventive lens when contemplating, preparing and implementing regional strategies, national policies and community programs aimed at responding to causes of violence and war. This promises to strengthen technical and operational opportunities for prevention, for example through the sharing of best practices and lessons learned from early warning and response (EWR).

Lijphart and Ulrich both assert that consensus-building mechanisms are often preferable to guarantee political participation, especially in pluralistic communities, and are therefore necessary to respond to state-based conflict situations.[30] The ICGLR is currently known for its insistence on dialogue and negotiations between member states, and also, at the national and community levels, as participative processes to address conflicts in the region. This presents a unique opportunity to transform chronically unstable situations and terminate the cycles of mass atrocities that currently engulf the region through consensus and compromise.[31] Dialogue and mediation also enhance consensus building by facilitating interactions between adversaries and creating conditions for actors to work together to prevent hostilities or their escalation, as a necessary condition to arrive at more sustainable solutions to identified causes of conflicts.

The demand for local ownership of prevention strategies is enmeshed with the requirement for local solutions to local problems.[32] Up to this point in the work of the regional and national committees, none of the activities implemented, e.g. in Tanzania, Kenya or Uganda, has been counterproductive, which reflects the fact that the activities are perceived as locally owned and tailored to address local problems. Much as local ownership is the policy ideal at regional and national levels, it also has an important function in driving local cooperation and participation for prevention. Various scholars have argued that, in modern states, the state remains the locus of power, while identity is the locus of self-esteem. The influence of both must be exploited when seeking to effectively transform conflicts.[33] To this end, local ownership of processes helps to build confidence and reinforce the self-esteem of affected communities, thus contributing to greater state stability. Therefore, collaboration among states, donors and communities should ensure that local ownership continues to be cultivated through meaningful and locally-relevant partnerships to achieve more effective prevention strategies at regional, national and local levels.

We submit that with such regional and national mechanisms in place, as well as legal instruments, the remaining challenge lies not in the structures and in the enforcement mechanisms, but in the political will to implement them and ensure compliance at national and regional levels, with the active support of the international community. The various initiatives taken at the international and regional levels will have no effect if they work in isolation from local initiatives. Without local ownership and sustainable commitment, the prevention of mass atrocities and genocide in the Great Lakes region will remain a daunting task.

Notes

1 "Member states" refers to the International Conference on the Great Lakes region's 12 member states: The Republic of Angola, The Republic of Burundi, The Central Africa Republic, The Democratic Republic of Congo, The Republic of Congo, The Republic of Kenya, The Republic of Rwanda, The Republic of the Sudan, The Republic of South Sudan, The United Republic of Tanzania, The Republic of Uganda and The Republic of Zambia. The majority of these countries emerged from long years of conflicts and wars, while others have been suffering the effects of persistent conflicts in their neighboring countries, thus making the brokering of peace and security very difficult in the region.
2 See, e.g., Mahmood Mamdani, *Politics and Class Formation in Uganda* (Kampala: Fountain Publishers, 1999); Tarsis B. Kabwegyere, *The Politics of State Formation and Destruction in Uganda* (Kampala: Fountain Publishers, 1995); Peter Mutibwa, *Uganda since Independence: A Story of Unfulfilled Hopes* (Trenton, NJ: Africa World Press, 1992).
3 Victoria Passant, "The Great Lakes Refugee Crisis and the Dilemma of Contemporary Humanitarianism," *POLIS Journal*, 2 (Winter 2009), p. 6.
4 Sidney Tarrow, *Power in Movement: Social Movements and Contentious Politics* (New York: Cambridge University Press, 1998), p. 18.
5 Henri Tajfel, "Social Psychology of Intergroup Relations," *Annual Reviews*, 33: 1 (1982), p. 3; Karina V. Korostelina, *Social Identity: Structures, Dynamics and Implications* (London: Palgrave MacMillan, 2007), p. 4.
6 Richard Sezibera, "International Conference on the Great Lakes Region(IC/GLR): Inception, Process and Achievements," *Journal of African Conflicts and Peace Studies*, 1: 1 (2008).
7 *Ibid.*
8 Luc Reychler, "Proactive Conflict Prevention: Impact Assessment-Limits of Conflict Prevention," *Journal of Peace Studies*, 3: 2 (July 1998).
9 Ronald J. Fisher, "Interactive Conflict Resolution: Dialogue, Conflict Analysis, and Problem-Solving," in Dennis J.D. Sandole *et al.*, eds., *Handbook of Conflict Analysis and Resolution* (New York: Routledge, 2008), p. 329.
10 Ould-Abdallah, Burundi on the Brink, p. 111.
11 Frank Dukes, "Public Conflict Resolution: A Transformative Approach," *Negotiation Journal*, 9: 1 (January 1993), p. 46.
12 The Movement of 23 March is a Congolese rebel group created in May 2012 following the difficulties of the implementation of the peace agreement signed between the Congolese government and the rebellion of the National Congress for the Defence of People (CNDP) of Laurent Nkunda on 23 March 2009, after the Kivus war. The M23 was mainly composed of ex-rebels of the CNDP.
13 The Press Release issued by the ICGLR Communication Officer, dorine.nininahazwe@icglr.org, described the holding of the Extraordinary Summit on DRC on 7 and 8 October as the fourth hosted by ICGLR within a period of four months.

14 The signing of the peace agreement between the government of DRC and M23 in Nairobi, Kenya on 12 December 2013 under the ICGLR Chairmanship of President Museveni of Uganda following a year of protracted negotiations was described as a landmark deal to end rebellion and hostilities in Eastern DRC. Press release issued by Uganda government: www.statehouse.go.ug/media/news/2013/12/12/landmark-pea ce-agreement-between-m23-rebels-and-democratic-republic-congo-sign

15 African Task Force on the Prevention of Mass Atrocities, *African Regional Communities and the Prevention of Mass Atrocities* (Budapest: Foundation for the International Prevention of Genocide and Mass Atrocities, 2016).

16 See African Task Force on the Prevention of Mass Atrocities (op. cit.), Chapter 2, "ICGLR Case Study: Burundi," pp. 18–19, 21.

17 Lewis A. Coser, *The Functions of Social Conflict* (New York: The Free Press, 1956), p. 36.

18 Other representatives are from the Ministry of Foreign Affairs, the Ministry of Justice, the Ministry of Internal Affairs, the Ministry of Defense, the Ministry of Gender, the Uganda High Commission, the Uganda Human Rights Commission, the Uganda Police Force, Care International, the International Refugee Rights Initiative, the Uganda Law Reform Commission, the Uganda Civil Society Fund, Regional Associates for Community Initiatives and other civil society groups and human rights organizations.

19 Fisher, "Interactive Conflict Resolution," (op. cit.), p. 329.

20 *Training Resource Manual for Genocide and Mass Atrocity Prevention in the Great Lakes Region of Africa.* www.auschwitzinstitute.org/training-resource-manual/

21 Uganda National Committee on the Prevention and Punishment of Genocide and Mass Atrocities (UNCP-GMA), 13 February 2014, http://uncpgma.wordpress.com/icglr/

22 Ole Therkildsen, *Service Provision under Stress in East Africa: The State, NGOs and People's Organizations in Kenya, Tanzania and Uganda* (London: James Currey, 1995), p. 77.

23 African Task Force on the Prevention of Mass Atrocities Report (2016).

24 Laurence Juma, "Regional Initiatives for Peace: Lessons from IGAD and ECOWAS/ECOMOG," *Africa Quarterly*, 40: 3 (2000), pp. 85–107.

25 *Uwiano Platform: A Multi-Stakeholder Strategy for Peaceful Elections*, www.ke.undp.org/con tent/kenya/en/home/operations/projects/peacebuilding/uwiano-peace-platform-pro ject.html

26 Bruce D. Jones, *Peacemaking in Rwanda: The Dynamics of Failure* (Boulder, CO: Lynne Rienner Publishers, 2001), p. 163.

27 The analogy of the "spaghetti bowl" of Regional Organizations and countries' multiple initiatives competing for attention, finances and not least human capacity is well explained in the article on "A New Dawn for Africa? The Conference on the Great Lakes Region Analyzed," jn *SIGNAL: The Official Magazine Representative Association of Commissioned Officers*, 19: 2, p. 30.

28 African Task Force on the Prevention of Mass Atrocities Report.

29 Gilbert M. Khadiagala, *Eastern Africa: Security and the Legacy of Fragility* (New York: International Peace Institute, 2008).

30 Arend Lijphart, *Democracy in Plural Societies. A Comparative Exploration* (New Haven, CT: Yale University Press, 1977); Ulrich Schneckener, "Making Power Sharing Work: Lessons from Successes and Failures in Ethnic Conflict Management,".*Journal of Peace Research*, 39: 2 (2002), p. 203.

31 Jeffrey Laurenti, *The Preparedness Gap: Making Peace Operations Work in the 21st Century* (AC Policy Report of the United Nations Association of the USA, 2001), p. 14.

32 Hannah Reich, *Local Ownership in Conflict Transformation Projects: Partnership, Participation or Patronage?* (Berlin: Berghof Research Center for Constructive Conflict Management, 2006), p. 3.

33 See, e.g., Jon Pierre and B. Guy Peters, *Governance, Politics and the State* (New York: St. Martin's Press, 2000); Ronald Cohen and Elman R. Service, *Origins of the State: The Anthropology of Political Evolution* (Philadelphia, PA: Institute for the Study of Human Issues, 1978).

12

ROOTS OF AMBIVALENCE

The United Nations, genocide, and mass atrocity prevention

Edward C. Luck

Introduction

The signs of disconnect, even discomfort, came early. Despite the liberation of the Nazi death camps, the Holocaust was not a subject of the founding conference of the United Nations in San Francisco in the spring of 1945. The delegates were ready to talk about almost anything else. The United Nations that they produced was designed to prevent armed conflict, not atrocity crimes. Though the 1948 Genocide Convention was negotiated in its halls, the United Nations took more than half a century to appoint its first official—on a part-time basis—to address the prevention of genocide. Sixty years after the liberation of Auschwitz-Birkenau, the UN General Assembly established the International Holocaust Remembrance Day.[1] What accounts for this disconnect and for the decades that saw so little effort to implement the Genocide Convention? What steps have been taken to correct these gaps, and what are the prospects for the future? Those are the core inquiries of this chapter.

Founding ambivalence

Two factors, above all others, drove the creation of the United Nations. One was the refusal of the United States to join its predecessor, the ill-fated League of Nations. The other was the League's failure to prevent World War II, the most destructive conflagration the world had ever seen. Many observers drew the somewhat simplistic conclusion that the lack of US participation had doomed the League to impotence in the face of Axis aggression. So, the planning for a successor organization was led by the United States and began shortly after it entered the war in December 1941.[2] In order to gain the support of the American people, it was decided that the post-war organization was to have more muscle and conviction than its predecessor, as well as a more pronounced respect for basic human rights.

This determination to project publicly the combination of military strength and respect for human rights echoed the 1 January 1942 Declaration of the United Nations, the name preferred by President Franklin Roosevelt for the anti-Axis alliance.[3] The allies asserted, among other things, that:

> complete victory over their enemies is essential to defend life, liberty, independence and religious freedom, and to preserve human rights and justice in their own lands as well as in other lands, and that they are now engaged in a common struggle against savage and brutal forces seeking to subjugate the world.[4]

When it came to shaping the new world organization, however, the Big Three—the US, USSR, and UK—were more circumspect about how it should pursue human rights, beyond asserting the responsibility of Member States to respect rights within their borders.

Though the most bullish about including human rights provisions in the Charter, US delegates to the Dumbarton Oaks conferences were concerned about international criticisms of American civil rights and immigration practices, as well as about possible Congressional reactions. These concerns had been raised, as well, in earlier planning sessions for post-war organization led by the State Department.[5] At Dumbarton Oaks, the British representatives were more cautious on this score, given sensitivities about international, as well as American, critiques of their colonial policies and practices. The Soviet team had few reservations about the expression of general human rights principles, but cautioned against diverting attention from the core peace and security purposes of the new body.[6] Like the others, they were keen on having provisions in the Charter to avoid interference in matters traditionally considered to be domestic concerns.

Compared to other, supposedly more substantial, matters, human rights received relatively modest attention either at Dumbarton Oaks or at the more inclusive deliberations that followed in San Francisco. On several occasions, however, Presidents Roosevelt and then Truman did call for the inclusion of human rights references in the Charter, especially among its animating purposes. They ensured that a sizeable group of consultants and representatives of non-governmental organizations, many of them rights advocates, were given access to the San Francisco proceedings. Among their achievements was working with Virginia Gildersleeves, a Barnard College Dean and the only woman on the US delegation, on making the Preamble more rights and people friendly.[7] Beginning with the Preamble's expressed determination "to reaffirm faith in fundamental human rights, in the dignity and worth of the human person, in the equal rights of men and women and of nations large and small," the Charter is peppered with references to human rights. Three times, the Charter calls for "fundamental freedoms for all without distinction as to race, sex, language, or religion."[8]

No references to genocide or other mass atrocity crimes, however, made it into the Charter. Indeed, no delegation made a determined effort to insert such

158 Edward C. Luck

language. Why was this, when so much human rights language was included? There are both readily apparent and more subtle explanations, though the lack of candor on all sides makes a definitive explanation impossible:

- One obvious reason was the matter of timing. "Genocide," a term Raphael Lemkin coined publicly only when *Axis Rule in Occupied Europe* was published in 1944, was not in 1945 a generally accepted term with a specific legal meaning and was not used as a basis to convict Nazi criminals at the Nuremberg Trials that commenced in November 1945. Once the UN was up and running, he did lead the effort to get the General Assembly to pass a resolution the next year, 1946, mandating the UN's Economic and Social Council (ECOSOC) to negotiate an international convention on the crime of genocide to be submitted to the Assembly for review and approval.[9]
- A second was the distinction between the focus of human rights on the individual victim and of genocide on crimes against a group. This had been a matter of ongoing debate between Lemkin and much of the growing human rights community from the 1930s on. It helped explain the reluctance to employ the notion of genocide at the Nuremberg Trials.[10] Also, as Mark Mazower has argued, the emphasis on crimes against groups raised concerns about reigniting the debates on minority rights that had proven so divisive in the era of the League of Nations.[11] Likewise, it highlighted questions of national identity and Wilsonian notions of self-determination that were prominent matters of contention in the shaping of both the League of Nations and the United Nations.
- A third plausible explanation was that the inclusion of genocide or other mass crimes against groups might have raised uncomfortable questions about the limits of national sovereignty, seen as a fundamental pillar both of the new world body and of the larger inter-state system based on Westphalian principles. None of the references to human rights implied the need for any particular course of international action and certainly not the employment of enforcement measures. The commission of genocide on the scale of the Holocaust might have had implications for international peace and security that would be undeniable, however much political leaders in other countries might prefer to look the other way. As discussed below, only New Zealand, hardly a world power and located far from the European theater, pressed this issue at the San Francisco conference.
- Fourth, by the time of the San Francisco meeting, the four convening powers—the US, UK, USSR, and China—were determined to push for broad international acceptance of the draft Charter as quickly and painlessly as possible. Given the priority on sustaining the wartime alliance, which was a primary rationale for convening the conference before the war was concluded, the conveners were quick to set aside matters that could prove unnecessarily divisive. The big exceptions, of course, were matters relating to their veto power and privileged position as permanent members of the Security Council,

The UN and mass atrocity prevention **159**

which were enormously controversial with the larger membership but seen as essential to maintaining their ongoing working relationship or compact.[12]

- Fifth, it was quite plausible, given the existential wartime struggle with the Axis powers and the core peace and security purposes of the organization, to conclude that the surest way to stop ongoing genocide was to defeat militarily those states that were committing such horrific acts. As noted above, the Declaration of United Nations had, some three years before the San Francisco conference, made precisely this linkage between unconditional victory in the all-out war effort and the restoration of respect for human rights. To the limited extent that genocide was recognized and acknowledged, it was in the context of Nazi Germany's aggression and flouting of international law and organization.

- A sixth possible rationale—though the author has not seen any historical evidence to directly document this conjecture—would have been that the numerous references to human rights and fundamental freedoms, without distinction to race, sex, language, or religion, in the Charter could have been seen as sufficient. As discussed below, the contention that genocide and other mass atrocity crimes are simply the most extreme end of a human rights continuum continues to fuel debates to this day about how genocide prevention and the responsibility to protect (R2P) should be institutionalized within the United Nations system. The second point in this list—that there should be a distinction between crimes committed against individuals and those against groups, as the debates over the basis for the Nuremberg Trials illustrated—would seem to suggest that some differentiation was needed here, but it would not have been unreasonable for delegates at San Francisco to have reasoned that where human rights were respected, mass atrocity crimes were unlikely to occur.

- Seventh, it should be recalled that Raphael Lemkin himself favored keeping genocide prevention on a separate track. In his determination to move this agenda forward, he apparently paid relatively little attention to the proceedings in Dumbarton Oaks and San Francisco. Though he was a tireless advocate for his cause, he did not make the US delegations to these historic meetings priority targets for his lobbying efforts. He was trained as a lawyer, not a political scientist, and he was far more interested in law than organization.[13] Once the United Nations was established, he frequented its chambers as a place where norms could be developed and propagated, not as a place where the operational work of preventing genocide might be pursued rigorously.

- Eighth and finally, it is quite possible that the convening powers and others were reluctant to have their lack of response to the Holocaust questioned or highlighted on the highly visible stage of the San Francisco conference. US delegates, for instance, would not have been eager to address why their country had been so unwilling to admit large numbers of Jewish refugees during the war. The French probably would not yet have been ready to come to grips with the acts of the Vichy government in such a global forum, and so

160 Edward C. Luck

on with other delegations, including some of those from Eastern Europe and Latin America.

Whatever the explanations, it is important to acknowledge and understand the implications of the ambivalence with which the world body took up the question of genocide. In some ways, this initial reluctance—even avoidance—still undermines the efforts of the United Nations to prevent genocide and other mass atrocity crimes. There are, of course, real questions of capacity and some of these are addressed below. But the formative experience of ignoring the Holocaust in the creation of the United Nations and its Charter speaks to a pervasive but unspoken lack of will to tackle genocidal impulses and actions in a frontal, unambiguous manner. In *"A Problem from Hell,"* Samantha Power concluded that it was, over the course of the twentieth century, deliberate US policy to look the other way and not respond to genocidal violence.[14] Perhaps reflecting the positions of its most powerful members, the same might have been said about the United Nations and, particularly, the Security Council.

The lack of attention to genocide and mass atrocity prevention has had broader and persistent institutional effects as well. For one thing, the prevention of genocide and other mass atrocity crimes lacks a clear and specific mandate in the Charter. That omission leaves efforts to curb atrocities more vulnerable to political challenge than other related peace, security, and human rights pursuits. Second, the failure to address atrocity crimes in the Charter has made it harder to establish and maintain institutional, substantive, and working relationships among these related policy priorities. There is, for instance, no Charter basis for determining who should have responsibility for what in this area, either among inter-governmental organs or among secretariat entities. Third, and most fundamentally, the conscious or unconscious choice to leave out any references to mass murder and the attempt to eliminate whole populations based on their identity implied that these were secondary or even tertiary concerns when it came to maintaining international peace and security. That was not the lesson that one should have wanted would-be perpetrators to have learned from efforts at post-war international organization.

Adaptability

It should be underscored, in any case, that the fact that the Charter did not mention genocide or other mass atrocity crimes did not preclude the possibility of the United Nations trying to prevent or curb them, even within sovereign borders. Its failure to act in any number of specific situations, from Cambodia to Rwanda to Srebrenica to Syria, was, again and again, because of political, not legal, constraints. The Charter was shaped to give the organization and, most critically, the Security Council substantial leeway in determining why, when, where, and how to act. The founders regularly asserted that the Council was to be a political body, making judgments about the best course in each situation. It was to "act in accordance with the Purposes and Principles of the United Nations," as Article 24 (2) put it.

Those provisions, however, did not significantly limit the ways in which the Council could interpret how to carry out its primary responsibility for the maintenance of international peace and security.

The Council was to be flexible and adaptable. As this author has written elsewhere, "the founders ... as pragmatic diplomats and policy-makers in the midst of a world war, wanted a Security Council for all contingencies."[15] Though the San Francisco conference pre-dated the first atomic explosion, the agenda and work plans of the Council quickly adapted to the demands and dangers of the nuclear age, as well as to the tensions of the subsequent Cold War. Those permanent members of the Council that were leading colonial powers—France and the United Kingdom—hardly welcomed the organization's growing focus on decolonization. Yet, with the United Nations in the vanguard, this movement was to radically alter the political dynamics of the world body.[16] There was nothing in the Charter, moreover, about peacekeeping or terrorism, which have become major preoccupations of the Council, the Secretariat, and, to a lesser extent, other principal organs. And, with the turn of the century, the Council has finally devoted an increasing portion of its time and attention to human protection issues, including genocide prevention and the responsibility to protect (R2P).

As noted above, the only delegation at San Francisco that was vocal about its mass atrocity concerns was New Zealand. Its representatives questioned whether the restrictive language of what became Article 2 (7) of the Charter would prevent the world body from responding to violent atrocities committed against national minorities, as had been the case with Nazi Germany.[17] Their concerns centered on the oft-quoted wording of the first half of the Article:

> Nothing contained in the present Charter shall authorize the United Nations to intervene in matters which are essentially within the domestic jurisdiction of any state or shall require the Members to submit such matters to settlement under the present Charter.

Indeed, the convening powers had seen this clause as a way of discouraging other Member States from prying into matters within their borders that would have traditionally been considered domestic affairs.

Yet, the delegates from Wellington were reassured by the rest of the text of Article 2 (7): "but this principle shall not prejudice the application of enforcement measures under Chapter VII." On the one hand, this wording allowed the permanent members of the Council to have it both ways. They could veto attempts to interfere in what they considered to be their domestic affairs, yet they could vote to take enforcement measures triggered by actions or developments within another state's borders that they believed constituted a threat to international peace and security. On the other hand, the delegates from New Zealand could report back to their capital that these provisions would give the Council the authority to respond to mass atrocity crimes if sufficient votes could be gathered within the Council.[18]

Several other caveats also suggest a broad interpretation of Article 2 (7):

- One, there is a suggestive piece of evidence about the legislative history of Article 2 (7) that has been completely overlooked by scholars, as well as by policy-makers. At San Francisco, the drafting committee, in explaining how it produced the language of 2 (7), told the plenary that it was its understanding that if fundamental freedoms and rights are "grievously outraged so as to create conditions which threaten peace or to obstruct the application of the provisions of the Charter, then they cease to be the sole concern of each State."[19]
- Two, under Article 39, "the Security Council shall determine the existence of any threat to the peace, breach of the peace, or act of aggression" and then decide how to respond to it. There is no set of rigid guidelines to inhibit the Council's decision-making in this regard, and it has tended to perceive situations of intra-state conflict as threats to international peace and security more frequently since the early 1990s.
- Three, Article 34 gives the Council the authority to:

  investigate any dispute, or any situation which might lead to international friction or give rise to a dispute, in order to determine whether the continuation of the dispute or situation is likely to endanger the maintenance of international peace and security.

  That is very broad language, which, though rarely invoked, could be useful in giving an opening for the early engagement of the Council in investigating situations of potential mass atrocity.

- Four, Article 99 gives the Secretary-General the authority "to bring to the attention of the Security Council any matter which in his opinion may threaten the maintenance of international peace and security." This author, as the UN's first Special Adviser to the Secretary-General on the Responsibility to Protect, suggested to a working group of the Council that warnings of the imminent commission of mass atrocity crimes should be included as an integral part of the Secretary-General's Article 99 responsibilities.[20] This interpretation of the scope of Article 99 now appears to be widely accepted.

Nevertheless, sovereignty does remain a neuralgic issue for many Member States. This may not always be for the reasons assumed by many observers, however. True, territorial sovereignty is often an acute concern of smaller and/or developing states wary of militarily powerful countries invoking principles such as genocide prevention or R2P as a pretext for intervention in their domestic affairs. But when this author served as Special Adviser, he found that it was often the case that territorial sovereignty was at best a secondary concern. There were several reasons. In some situations, it was non-state armed groups that were committing the mass atrocity crimes and the government gave its consent to international assistance, whether global, regional, or both. Often, UN and/or regional peacekeeping operations were already in place in the country of concern, suggesting that security conditions had already caused some diminution or adjustment of sovereignty claims. In some instances, the government lacked the capacity to take the steps it agreed were needed to prevent an escalation of domestic violence. In such cases, it was not unusual for government leaders to complain instead that international assistance was not sufficiently forthcoming when it was most needed.

At the same time, countries with the capacity to make a difference may resist doctrines or principles, such as R2P or even the Genocide Convention, which may seem to suggest that they have an obligation to act when mass atrocity crimes appear imminent in distant countries where their perceived interests are modest. The reluctance of US officials to publicly acknowledge the commission of genocide—the "G" word—in Rwanda spoke volumes in this regard. Yet, less than a decade later, Secretary of State Colin Powell was willing to speak of genocide in Darfur without feeling any compulsion for the US to take further action to stop it. The collective action dilemmas presented both by the Genocide Convention and by responsibility to protect principles are real and persistent. When something is everyone's responsibility, it may be seen in capitals as no one's responsibility.[21]

When John Bolton was representing the United States during the preparations for the 2005 World Summit that endorsed R2P, he voiced acute concerns about the need to preserve American decision-making sovereignty in the face of potential R2P claims.[22] As his pointed comments underscored, states expected to act in such situations, as well as those that feared being the object of interventionist actions, have had reservations about the possibility of different aspects of their sovereignty being compromised by the application of atrocity prevention principles. Sensitivity about decision-making sovereignty, in fact, helps to explain the inconsistent and selective manner in which these principles have been applied both by governments and by inter-governmental organizations, such as the UN's Security Council. Ambivalence about atrocity prevention may thus flow, in part, from antipathy about decision-making sovereignty.

The long road from words to deeds

It is an axiom that the United Nations is better at words than deeds. This widespread impression may be as much a tribute to its unsurpassed capacities for producing and disseminating all sorts of global norms, declarations, and legal conventions as it is an indictment of its myriad operational deficits. Like so many other axioms, however, this one is too simplistic and too sweeping. It ignores the ways in which normative and operational progress are often symbiotic. The primary purpose of normative measures is to provide standards for acceptable behavior, as well as to establish a measure for determining when behavior is unacceptable. It is a time-tested proposition that, the more broadly that normative principles are accepted and considered legitimate by international actors, the more likely they are to encourage acceptable behavior and to discourage unacceptable actions. This is a core rationale for the enunciation and propagation of norms against genocide and other mass atrocity crimes. Likewise, if the norms are widely and regularly flouted, then their legitimacy and efficacy would come into question. Thus, normative and operational progress should feed off each other in a symbiotic manner, as steps to insure more extensive and consistent implementation of norms against genocide and mass atrocities should enhance their generic persuasive power as rules of behavior as well as offer greater protection in specific situations.

As the world's only virtually universal political forum, the United Nations is a natural place for norm builders to gather, as Raphael Lemkin, like so many others, recognized. It holds irresistible attraction to such norm entrepreneurs. By all accounts, he was an indefatigable proponent of achieving international legal status for the notion of genocide. In that, he succeeded brilliantly with the drafting and acceptance by the General Assembly of the Genocide Convention. As instrumental as he was in creating an international legal norm, however, Lemkin seemed much less sure of himself when it came to next steps, other than seeking sufficient ratifications for it to go into effect.

One reason for the lack of sustained and effective follow-up was that there was no twin for Lemkin on the implementation side, no one to develop the policy and institutional dimensions of genocide prevention. It appears that he gave relatively little thought to what it actually would take to prevent genocide and to protect populations in imminent danger. That was understandable, given the legal lens through which he viewed the issue. More disconcerting is why it took policy makers, policy analysts, and scholars so many decades to give serious and sustained attention to these practical policy questions. We are still at a learning stage when it comes to implementation.

The Convention became, to put it a bit harshly, something of a paper promise. The critical first step of getting broad acceptance of the notion that genocide was not acceptable behavior was achieved, but little was done either in governments or in international institutions to insure that cross-national lessons learned, training, and educational programs were underwritten, that compliance was measured and monitored, that deviations were reported, that incentives and/or pressure for remedial steps were undertaken, that timely and pointed messaging was communicated, that perpetrators were prosecuted and impunity was eliminated, and that pressure was generated, as needed, by neighbors, peers, powerful governments, and regional and global institutions, including, if necessary, a range of possible enforcement and protection measures. For half a century, preventing genocide became what people said, not what they did.

In this regard, it would be useful to see how the normative experience of genocide prevention matched the classic model of norm development proposed by Martha Finnemore and Kathryn Sikkink in 1998.[23] Under their model, norms evolve in a patterned "life cycle" through three stages: 1) norm emergence; 2) a norm cascade; and 3) internalization. Between stages one and two, there is a "tipping point" when a critical mass of states have adopted the new norm and peer pressure begins to work on the hold-outs, who seek "legitimation, conformity, and esteem." In the case of genocide, Raphael Lemkin and other civil society actors helped greatly to facilitate the emergence of the new norm under stage one. There appeared to be a tipping point during the negotiations of the Convention that helped propel its relatively expeditious acceptance and then ratification by a sufficient number of states to permit it to enter into force in January 1951. Thus, stages one and two of the model were largely accomplished.

Peer pressure, however, did not have much effect on the United States, which did not complete the ratification process until 1988 (under President Ronald Reagan), almost four decades after the Convention's adoption. It was not the only laggard. China did not come aboard until 1983, Bangladesh and South Africa until 1998, Switzerland until 2000, and Nigeria until 2009. Even some prominent human rights advocates, such as Ireland in 1976 and New Zealand in 1978, were slow to accede to the Convention. More importantly, there is reason to believe that Cold War politics hindered the process of dissemination and internalization. Given the widespread domestic violence that, at points, accompanied the political development of the Communist regimes in the Soviet Union and China, they were undoubtedly concerned with the possible extension of genocide principles and standards to what Barbara Harff and Ted Gurr identified in 1988 as "politicides."[24] In the United States, the ratification of many human rights instruments was delayed by opposition from legislators concerned about the linkages between international human rights and internal civil rights, as well as about sovereignty and states' rights implications.[25]

Moreover, as this chapter argues, the process of internalization under stage three has been incomplete and superficial. This is so even in comparison to the slow movement toward internalizing many human rights norms, a process that has also been affected both by international politics and by domestic constraints in many parts of the world.[26] The willingness of national leaders, particularly those of major powers, to look the other way during the massive violence in Cambodia during the late 1970s attested to the derivative and subsidiary nature of the claims of genocide prevention compared to those of geopolitics. The same was true in Rwanda in 1994 and, to a lesser extent, in Srebrenica the next year. It was not until 1998–1999, when the dilemmas inherent in responding forcefully to mass atrocities without Security Council authorization came into sharp focus in the case of Kosovo, that there was concerted and high-level attention to the question of genocide and mass atrocity prevention as a first-order policy problem.[27]

More generically, there were also significant gaps in the way the Genocide Convention was crafted. These contributed to its limitations as a framework for the prevention of mass atrocities and the protection of vulnerable populations. According to the Convention, the targeted populations include those of "a national, ethnical, racial or religious group."[28] As Barbara Harff has pointed out, "the Convention does not include groups or victims defined by their political position or actions."[29] She terms cases of mass violence "with politically defined victims" as "politicides." In her research, she identified many more cases of politicides than of genocides between 1955 and 2001.[30] Some of these situations, such as in Cambodia and East Pakistan, resulted in very large numbers of victims.

The Convention also speaks of prevention and punishment, but not of protection.[31] "The Contracting Parties … undertake to prevent and to punish" genocide

166 Edward C. Luck

as "a crime under international law."[32] This sounds more like a statement of law than of policy.[33] There is no indication of which entities—if any—are to be responsible for responding to the commission of genocide, nor mention of monitoring or reporting mechanisms. The Convention does not have any system for periodic review or for adapting its provisions to changing circumstances and the lessons of experience. It requires that intent be established, which generally requires some level of inquiry and discovery or research after the fact. This inhibits the ability of policy makers to make such a determination while the crimes are underway, unless the perpetrators have declared their intent to eliminate an identified group "in whole or in part" before or during the campaign of extermination.

In light of these multiple liabilities, it perhaps should not have been surprising that genocide and mass atrocity prevention was not in the vanguard of the human security and human protection issues taken up by the United Nations from the mid-1990s.[34] Launched in the 1994 *Human Development Report*, the notion of human security sought to reorient prevalent conceptions of security to give priority to the security of people as well as of states.[35] This reflected a growing interest, in the post-Cold War environment, in addressing intra-state as well as inter-state conflict. Yet, a range of subjects were addressed by the world body under the human security umbrella before it turned to genocide prevention and the responsibility to protect. Among these were humanitarian assistance, internal displacement, children and armed conflict, sexual and gender-based violence, post-conflict peacebuilding, security sector reform, election violence, women, peace and security, and protection of civilians in peacekeeping missions. The genocidal violence in Rwanda in 1994 and Srebrenica in 1995 led to two 1999 lessons-learned reports that contained sweeping indictments of international inaction.[36] Yet, as discussed below, they did not lead to immediate or even early implementation steps. The United Nations, it seems, was still having trouble coming to grips with genocide and mass atrocity prevention as core strategic, doctrinal, policy, and institutional challenges.

Sadly, it took the tenth anniversary of the genocide in Rwanda to spur action in the world body. Until that point, no official, and certainly no unit, in the UN Secretariat had a mandate to address the prevention of genocide or other mass atrocity crimes. At the tenth anniversary commemoration convened by the Human Rights Commission in Geneva in April 2004, Secretary-General Kofi Annan announced his intention to appoint a Special Adviser for the Prevention of Genocide.[37] This step was part of the UN's first Action Plan to Prevent Genocide that he unveiled there.[38] The plan included five parts:

- "First, preventing armed conflict" based on the assertion that "genocide almost always occurs during war;"
- "Second, protection of civilians in armed conflict" through bolstering respect for international humanitarian law and for the protection mandates already being assigned to peacekeeping missions by the Security Council;
- "Third, ending impunity" through international tribunals, such as the ad hoc one for Rwanda and the International Criminal Court (ICC);

- "Fourth, early and clear warning" by working with civil society groups and the Human Rights Commission, including its Special Rapporteurs, as well as by the appointment of the Special Adviser; and
- Fifth, "the need for swift and decisive action when, despite all our efforts, we learn that genocide is happening or about to happen." Such action, he continued, could include

a continuum of steps, which may include military action. But the latter should always be seen as an extreme measure to be used only in extreme situations. We badly need clear guidelines on how to identify such extreme cases and how to react to them. In that regard, he referred to the guidelines for the use of force proposed by the International Commission on Intervention and State Sovereignty (ICISS) that had coined the phrase "responsibility to protect" and by his High-Level Panel on Threats, Challenges and Change.[39]

According to the Secretary-General, the Special Adviser was to:

report through me to the Security Council and the General Assembly, as well as to this Commission. This adviser's mandate will refer not only to genocide but also to mass murder and other large-scale human rights violations, such as ethnic cleansing. His or her functions will be:
- First, to work closely with the High Commissioner to collect information on potential or existing situations or threats of genocide, and their links to international peace and security.
- Second, to act as an early-warning mechanism to the Security Council and other parts of the UN system;
- And third, to make recommendations to the Security Council on actions to be taken to prevent or halt genocide.

None of this, it should be recalled, was mandated by the Member States. The Plan, in that sense, was the personal initiative of a Secretary-General still seeking remedies to the inaction of the world body during the Rwandan genocide, which unfolded when he was Under Secretary-General for Peacekeeping Operations. Therefore, while Annan deserves personal credit for undertaking this initiative and appointing a Special Adviser, it was not evident either that these measures had wide and deep political support among the membership or that they were the result of extensive consultations with them. There were signs that some of these proposed steps had not been vetted sufficiently or fully thought through. The next section of this chapter addresses some of the ways in which their implementation has not fully matched Annan's original conception and the implications this has had for the development and operationalization of the mandates, both for genocide prevention and for the responsibility to protect.

Open questions and continuing challenges

In two important respects, the proposed mandate that Annan submitted to the Security Council three months later differed from the contents of his Geneva announcement, suggesting pushback from some Member States, especially members of the Council, and/or further reflections by the Secretary-General and his top aides.[40] First, the Special Adviser's mandate was narrowed to the prevention of genocide, as references to "mass murder and other large-scale human rights violations, such as ethnic cleansing" were deleted.[41] It is not known whether specific members of the Council objected in 2004 to the wider scope of crimes to be addressed, but, three years later, Russia reportedly objected to Secretary-General Ban Ki-moon's effort to add mass atrocities to the title of the Special Adviser for the Prevention of Genocide. Second, the prominent references to working closely with the High Commissioner for Human Rights, to providing early warning to "other parts of the UN system," and to reporting through the Secretary-General to the General Assembly and the Commission on Human Rights, as well as to the Security Council, were also excised. In the end, only references to the Security Council remained.

It is also striking how far Annan was willing to stretch earlier texts of Security Council resolutions and Secretary-General's reports to try to find a mandate for his Action Plan. He asserted that the mandate for the Special Adviser for the Prevention of Genocide derives from Security Council resolution 1366 (2001), which actually focuses on conflict prevention, not genocide or mass atrocities, which are not mentioned in any of its operative paragraphs.[42] In turn, resolution 1366 (2001) is a response to an earlier report by the Secretary-General on conflict prevention that only makes a passing reference to the Rwandan genocide.[43]

These questions about scope and context continue to shadow the implementation and institutionalization of mass atrocity prevention in the UN system. These are not just theoretical or conceptual matters, because they define and shape how the world body goes about both prevention and response. There are three related challenges that need further reflection and clarification. One is the relationship between preventing mass atrocities and preventing armed conflict. A second is the relationship between genocide prevention and the responsibility to protect. And a third is the relationship among mass atrocity prevention, humanitarian affairs, and human rights. As of this writing, it remains to be seen how Secretary-General António Guterres will approach these matters, but the current situation is suboptimal and, at times, dysfunctional.

In his Action Plan, Annan contended that "genocide almost always occurs during war ... So one of the best ways to reduce the chances of genocide is to address the causes of conflict." There is something to this, as upstream structural prevention may be helpful in avoiding both intra-state conflict and the commission of mass atrocities, though cause and effect are necessarily hard to establish in such situations. Also, it is true that, more often than not, atrocities occur in situations of armed conflict. Yet a substantial number of mass atrocities, including genocide, take place outside of armed conflict. The early stages of the Holocaust were launched before the onset of World

War II, the killing fields of Cambodia came after the civil conflict, and the genocide in Rwanda took place in the midst of a peace process overseen by UN peacekeepers. More recently, the mass violence in Kenya in late 2007 and early 2008, in and around Osh, Kyrgyzstan in June 2010, and in Guinea (Conakry) in the fall of 2009, among others, occurred during peacetime.[44] Preventing conflict may reduce the chances of mass atrocities in some cases, but it would not eliminate them. It would be overly sanguine and potentially distorting to believe that improving conflict prevention is the best way to prevent mass atrocities. The UN has spent decades trying to perfect its conflict prevention capacities, but they remain insufficient for that task and have hardly proven to be a panacea for curbing mass violence.

Through his service from 2008 to 2012 as Special Adviser for the Responsibility to Protect, this author discovered a more pernicious effect of giving priority to conflict prevention over atrocity prevention: in operational situations, the two mandates often pull in different directions. On a tactical level, especially when it comes to messaging, timing, and access, what looks like the right thing to do for one mandate may seem counterproductive to the other. On the one hand, having Special Advisers or the Secretary-General issuing warnings about possible atrocity crimes, for instance, may appear disruptive to those, such as the Secretary-General's Special Representatives, who are engaged in sensitive peace negotiations. On the other hand, playing down growing threats to groups within societies while conflict resolution efforts are being held hostage by potential perpetrators could prove disastrous. That was clearly the case in Rwanda in 1993–1994 and, to some extent, in Srebrenica in 1995.

In that regard, the UN's self-generated inquiry on Srebrenica reached some brutal conclusions about the organization's peace-making culture.

> The men who have been charged with this crime against humanity reminded the world and, in particular, the United Nations, that evil exists in the world. They taught us also that the United Nations global commitment to ending conflict does not preclude moral judgments, but makes them necessary.[45]

According to the Secretary-General, the international community had conducted negotiations that "amounted to appeasement," resisted the use of force, and applied "a philosophy of impartiality and non-violence wholly unsuited to the conflict in Bosnia."[46] This was, of course, a particularly dramatic clash of distinct institutional cultures. In the author's experience, there also have been a number of situations in which there has been a more substantial convergence of perspectives. But the bottom line is clear: if you want to prevent mass atrocities, go about it in a forthright way, do not approach it through the backdoor provided by other disciplines and mandates. The wrong questions will not provide the right answers.

The relationship between genocide prevention and the responsibility to protect is multi-layered, complicated, and dynamic. The two Special Advisers have shared a joint office since 2009, each pair has worked well together on a personal basis, and, on the whole, this has been a symbiotic relationship. But there are conceptual, political, and institutional anomalies that need to be addressed by Secretary-General Guterres and the Member States. As Scott Straus has put it, "genocide is a specific, somewhat rare form of violence."[47] In this author's years as Special Adviser, he did not see any unambiguous cases of genocide, compared to many instances of crimes against humanity, ethnic cleansing, and war crimes. As noted earlier, preventing something—genocide—that cannot be established until after the fact because of the "intent" requirement is problematical. Over that period, experience appeared to confirm Barbara Harff's conclusions from earlier times that there are more "politicides" than genocides, given the political motivations for so much mass violence.

Yet, at the UN, the higher-level post (and the only one with a full salary) has been assigned to the smaller and less politically contentious mandate of genocide, while the R2P post is still unpaid and with very little staff support. Moreover, genocide prevention is the responsibility of both Special Advisers, creating an unnecessary redundancy. The posts either should be combined or differentiated on tasks to be performed, such as field versus headquarters, rather than on atrocities to be addressed. Secretary-General Ban Ki-moon's initial proposal to the Security Council in August 2007, envisioning a Special Representative focused on direct prevention in situations of concern and a Special Adviser on the conceptual, political, and institutional work in New York and Geneva, had it about right.[48] Though Juan Méndez, the first Special Adviser on the Prevention of Genocide, has reportedly expressed concern about the lack of direct access to the Security Council, that has become less of a problem over the years both because the members of the Council have become more attuned to these issues and because of growing acceptance of the work of the joint office.[49]

The relationship between mass atrocity prevention and humanitarian and human rights agendas is largely mutually reinforcing, but here, too, there are nuances and situations where they point in different directions in terms of policy choices. They share a devotion to building respect for international law and institutions, as well as to advancing human security and human protection. All three mandates are facing rising challenges from non-state armed actors and those who employ the tactics of terror. But there are differences as well. International humanitarian law and policy applies in situations of armed conflict and, therefore, not in all environments in which mass atrocities occur. The possibility of using coercive sanctions and/or coercive military force to stop mass atrocity crimes, particularly under R2P principles, is awkward for humanitarians whose practices call for a separation from military activities.[50] Many human rights advocates also find this connection uncomfortable, as do those in the peacekeeping and peacemaking realms who stress impartiality and resist the appearance of taking sides. The biggest division, however, has come in relation to the understandable emphasis by some humanitarian actors on keeping political access and maintaining humanitarian space. Often that has not been an issue, but in the brutal endgame to the Sri Lankan civil war in early 2009, it was a difference that divided the UN Secretariat and led to the sidelining of acute concerns about potential mass atrocity crimes, to no good end.[51]

None of these conceptual, institutional, and operational hurdles are insurmountable. Slowly but purposefully, the international community is learning lessons about how to advance prevention and protection purposes. The conceptual and legal dimensions have progressed more rapidly than the policy and operational ones. But that was to be expected. In many ways, the United Nations has been in the vanguard of both sides of these efforts, despite its limited operational capacities. That gap between prominence and capacity may be one reason why its failures along the way have been so visible and disconcerting. Yet, the brief rendering of this history in this chapter is, overall, a cautiously hopeful narrative. The ambivalence that weighed so heavily on Raphael Lemkin's struggle to gain acceptance and legal standing for the crime of genocide has not disappeared, but it has faded substantially over time. The task today and tomorrow is finding a way to turn his legal vision into practical strategies, doctrines, institutions, policies, and practices to prevent genocide and all other mass atrocity crimes and to provide real protection to real people. As these pages suggest, a fuller and more sustainable marriage between genocide prevention and R2P offers the best route for getting there.

Notes

1 United Nations, General Assembly, Resolution 60/7, 1 November 2005. The commemoration is on 27 January, the day in 1945 that the Auschwitz-Birkinau camp was liberated. The San Francisco conference to negotiate the UN Charter and establish the new world body was convened a few months later in April 1945.
2 Of the many accounts of the early post-war planning efforts, particularly helpful are Townsend Hoopes and Douglas Brinkley, *FDR and the Creation of the U.N.* (New Haven, CT: Yale University Press, 1997) and Ruth B. Russell, *A History of the United Nation's Charter: The Role of the United States, 1940–1945* (Washington, DC: Brookings Institution Press, 1958). The United Kingdom and the Soviet Union, and to a lesser extent China, also played significant parts in shaping the draft Charter that was presented to the delegates in San Francisco, of course. The fullest account of the preparatory meetings in Washington, DC during the late summer and early fall of 1944 involving the four powers in two conferences (one including the Soviet Union and the other China) is Robert C. Hilderbrand, *Dumbarton Oaks: The Origins of the United Nations and the Search for Postwar Security* (Chapel Hill, NC: University of North Carolina Press, 1990).
3 Initially the Declaration was signed by twenty-six countries, but twenty-one additional nations signed on over the course of the war.
4 They also ascribed to the Atlantic Charter proclaimed by the United States and the United Kingdom on 14 August 1941, prior to the US entry into the war.
5 See, for instance, Russell, op. cit., pp. 328–329 on the uneven treatment of human rights in State Department planning efforts in 1943–1944. For a sense of the continuing tension between international human rights goals and domestic differences over civil rights during the first two post-war decades, see Edward C. Luck, *Mixed Messages: American Politics and International Organization, 1919–1999* (Washington, DC: Brookings Institution Press, 1999).
6 Hilderbrand, op. cit., pp. 91–93 and 135. Though the Chinese delegation had limited leverage, one of its most consistent themes—the need to assert racial equality—did make it into the Charter at several points. For reactions to the Chinese position at Dumbarton Oaks on this matter, see Hilderbrand, op. cit., p. 93.
7 Stephen C. Schlesinger, *Act of Creation: The Founding of the United Nations* (Boulder, CO: Westview Press, 2003), pp. 122–123.
8 Articles 1 (3), 13 (1b), and 55 (c).

9 United Nations, General Assembly, Resolution 96 (I) of 11 December 1946. For discussion of the course of negotiations, with a focus on the essential role played by Raphael Lemkin, see James Waller, *Confronting Evil: Engaging Our Responsibility to Prevent Genocide* (Oxford, UK: Oxford University Press, 2016), pp. 15–21 and Samantha Power, *"A Problem from Hell:" America and the Age of Genocide* (New York: Harper Collins, 2002), pp. 51–60.

10 For Lemkin's unsuccessful efforts to influence the Nuremberg prosecutions, see Waller, op. cit., pp. 14–15 and Power, op. cit., pp. 49–50.

11 Mark Mazower, *No Enchanted Palace: The End of Empire and the Ideological Origins of the United Nations* (Princeton, NJ: Princeton University Press, 2009), pp. 122–133.

12 For detailed accounts of the views and positions of the convening powers and France, see Russell and Schlesinger, op. cit., and Edward C. Luck, "A Council for All Seasons: The Creation of the Security Council and Its Relevance Today," in Vaughan Lowe, Adam Roberts, Jennifer Welsh, and Dominik Zaum, eds., *The United Nations Security Council and War: The Evolution of Thought and Practice Since 1945* (Oxford: Oxford University Press, 2008), pp. 61–85. On the Council's continuing role as a compact among great powers, see David L. Bosco, *Five to Rule Them All: The UN Security Council and the Making of the Modern World* (New York: Oxford University Press, 2009) and Edward C. Luck, "The Security Council at Seventy: Ever Changing or Never Changing?" in Sebastian von Einsiedel, David M. Malone, and Bruno Stagno Ugarte, eds., *The UN Security Council in the Twenty-First Century* (Boulder, CO: Lynne Rienner Publishers, 2016), pp. 195–214.

13 In an April 1946 article, he suggested that states that practice genocide "should be held accountable before the Security Council of the United Nations Organization" and commented that "the Council may request the International Court of Justice to deliver an advisory opinion to determine whether a state of genocide exists within a given country before invoking, among other things, sanctions to be leveled against the offending country." Raphael Lemkin, "Genocide," *American Scholar*, vol. 15, no. 2 (April 1946), p. 230. But these points, voiced after the new world organization had been launched, were secondary to the largely legal thrust of his argument.

14 Power, op. cit., p. 508.

15 Luck, "A Council for All Seasons," op. cit., p. 63.

16 The shifting political dynamics with the post-colonial surge in UN membership, of course, were not welcomed by all of the founders. As Winston Churchill lamented to the American Bar Association in 1957: "the shape of the United Nations has changed greatly from its original form and from the intentions of its architects. The differences between the Great Powers have thrown responsibility increasingly on the Assembly. This has been vastly swollen by the addition of new nations ... It is anomalous that the vote or prejudice of any small country should affect events involving populations many times exceeding their numbers, and should affect them as self-advantage or momentary self-advantage may direct." Quoted in Luck, *Mixed Messages*, op. cit., p. 32.

17 New Zealand Delegation to the United Nations Conference on International Organization, San Francisco, *Report on the Conference* (Wellington: Department of External Affairs, 1945), p. 28.

18 Ibid. Also cited in Edward C. Luck, "Change and the United Nations Charter," in Ian Shapiro and Joseph Lampert, eds., *Charter of the United Nations* (New Haven, CT: Yale University Press, 2014), pp. 128–129.

19 The US Department of State, Proceedings of the United Nations Conference on International Organization, San Francisco, Volume 6 (Washington, DC: US Government Printing Office, 1945), pp. 684 and 705. Also cited in Russell, op. cit., p. 780. As drafted by this author, UN Secretary-General Ban Ki-moon included a reference to this statement in his Cyril Foster Lecture at Oxford University, "Human Protection and the Twenty-First Century United Nations," SG/SM/13385, 2 February 2011.

20 United Nations Security Council, "Letter Dated 30 December 2008 from the Permanent Representative of South Africa to the United Nations Addressed to the President

of the Security Council," S/2008/836, 31 December 2008, p.13. Also see Simon Chesterman, "Relations with the UN Secretary-General," in von Einsiedel et al., op. cit., p. 453.

21 For further discussion, see Alex Bellamy, "Responsibility to Protect or Trojan Horse? The Crisis in Darfur and Humanitarian Intervention After Iraq," *Ethics and International Affairs*, vol. 19, no. 2 (2005); James Pattison, "Mapping the Responsibilities to Protect: A Typology of International Duties," *Global Responsibility to Protect*, vol. 7, no.2, pp. 190–210; and Edward C. Luck and Dana Zaret Luck, "The Individual Responsibility to Protect," in Sheri P. Rosenberg, Tibi Galis, and Alex Zucker, eds., *Reconstructing Atrocity Prevention* (New York: Cambridge University Press, 2016), pp. 207–248. The latter underscores the importance of individuals at many levels assuming responsibility for prevention and protection and argues that the initial conception of R2P was too statist.

22 This theme is developed in Edward C. Luck, "Sovereignty, Choice, and the Responsibility to Protect," *Global Responsibility to Protect*, vol. I (2009), pp. 10–21.

23 Martha Finnemore and Kathryn Sikkink, "International Norm Dynamics and Political Change," *International Organization*, vol. 52, no. 4 (Autumn 1998), pp. 887–917.

24 Barbara Harff and Ted Robert Gurr, "Toward Empirical Theory of Genocides and Politicides: Identification and Measurement of Cases since 1945," *International Studies Quarterly*, vol. 32, no. 3 (September 1988), pp. 359–371.

25 Luck, *Mixed Messages*, op. cit., pp. 95–96 and 124–126.

26 The evolution of human rights norms has also followed a contested and lengthy path, though the internalization process under stage three started earlier and has progressed much further. The acceleration of UN capacities has been much more pronounced for human rights than for genocide prevention, for instance, with the appointment of the first High Commissioner for Human Rights in 1993. In *The Justice Cascade: How Human Rights Prosecutions Are Changing World Politics* (New York: W.W. Norton, 2011), Kathryn Sikkink contends that the internalization process has been spurred in recent years by international prosecutions, loss of impunity, and peer pressure. For a discussion of the role of civil society, see Margaret E. Keck and Kathryn Sikkink, *Activists Beyond Borders: Advocacy Networks in International Politics* (Ithaca, NY: Cornell University Press, 1998). This author has argued that the model is too uni-directional and takes insufficient account of how the content of norms themselves are shaped by the give-and-take politics that characterize more contentious normative developments, such as the responsibility to protect. See Edward C. Luck, "Building a Norm: The Responsibility to Protect Experience," in Robert I. Rotberg, ed., *Mass Atrocity Crimes: Preventing Future Outrages* (Washington, DC: Brookings Institution Press, 2010), pp. 108–127.

27 For a series of eloquent statements in 1998 and 1999 by UN Secretary-General Kofi Annan on these dilemmas, see the United Nations, *The Question of Intervention: Statements of the Secretary-General* (New York: United Nations Department of Public Information, DPI/2080, December 1999). For an analysis of Annan's approach to these matters, see Alex J. Bellamy, *Responsibility to Protect: The Global Effort to End Mass Atrocities* (Cambridge, UK: Polity Press, 2009), pp. 27–32.

28 United Nations, Convention on the Prevention and Punishment of the Crime of Genocide, Approved and Proposed for Signature and Ratification or Accession by the General Assembly, Resolution 260 A (III) of 9 December 1948, Article II. The Convention entered into force on 12 January 1951.

29 Barbara Harff, "No Lessons Learned from the Holocaust?: Assessing Risks of Genocide and Political Mass Murder Since 1955," *The American Political Science Review*, vol. 97, no. 1 (February 2003), p. 58.

30 Ibid., Table 1, p. 60.

31 Under Article VIII, "any Contracting Party may call upon the competent organs of the United Nations as they consider appropriate for the prevention and suppression of acts of genocide or any other acts enumerated in article III." The term "suppression" is not defined, nor used elsewhere in the Convention.

32 Convention, Article I.

33 Under Article V, "the Contracting Parties undertake to enact, in accordance with their respective Constitutions, the necessary legislation to give effect to the provisions of the present Convention, and, in particular, to provide effective penalties for persons guilty of genocide or any of the other acts enumerated in article III."

34 Alex J. Bellamy and Edward C. Luck, *The Responsibility to Protect: From Promise to Practice* (Cambridge, UK: Polity Press, 2018), Chapter One.

35 As it put it, "the concept of security has for too long been interpreted narrowly: as security of territory from external aggression, or as protection of national interests in foreign policy or as global security from the threat of nuclear holocaust. It has been related more to nation-states than to people." United Nations Development Programme (UNDP), *Human Development Report 1994* (Oxford, UK: Oxford University Press, 1994), p. 22.

36 United Nations, Report of the Secretary-General, *The Fall of Srebrenica*, A/54/549, 15 November 1999 and United Nations, Security Council, Letter Dated 15 December 1999 from the Secretary-General addressed to the President of the Security Council, S/1999/1257 16 December 1999, to which the *Report of the Independent Inquiry Into the Actions of the United Nations During the 1994 Genocide in Rwanda* is annexed.

37 The timing was ironic, in that the Commemoration preceded the World Summit that adopted the broader concept of the responsibility to protect by just sixteen months. If the timing had been reversed, the first appointment might have been that of a Special Adviser for the Responsibility to Protect, an appointment that followed when this author was named in early 2008. This point was made in Edward C. Luck, "Getting There, Being There: The Dual Roles of the Special Adviser," in Alex J. Bellamy and Tim Dunne, eds., *The Oxford Handbook of the Responsibility to Protect* (Oxford, UK: Oxford University Press, 2016), pp. 289–316.

38 United Nations, Secretary-General, *United Nations Secretary-General Kofi Annan's Action Plan to Prevent Genocide*, SG/SM/9197, AFR/893, HR/CN/1077, 7 April 2004.

39 International Commission on Intervention and State Sovereignty, *The Responsibility to Protect* (Ottawa: International Development Research Centre, 2001) and United Nations, Report of the Secretary-General, *In Larger Freedom: Towards Development, Security and Human Rights for All*, A/59/2005, 21 March 2005.

40 For the Secretary-General's proposal to the Security Council, see United Nations, Secretary-General, Letter Dated 12 July 2004 from the Secretary-General Addressed to the President of the Security Council, S/2004/567, 13 July 2004.

41 These points are addressed in Luck, "Getting There, Being There," op. cit., pp. 294–296.

42 The only relevant passages are in the resolution's preambular paragraphs, the language of which actually would have been a better fit for the responsibility to protect than for genocide prevention. Ibid.

43 United Nations, Report of the Secretary-General, *Prevention of Armed Conflict*, A/55/985-S/2001/574, 7 June 2001.

44 For a useful account of the crisis in Guinea, see Naomi Kikoler, "Guinea: An Overlooked case of the Responsibility to Protect in Practice," in Serena Sharma and Jennifer M. Welsh, eds., *The Responsibility to Protect: Overcoming the Challenge of Atrocity Prevention* (New York: Oxford University Press, 2015). For a discussion of the Kenyan case from an R2P perspective, see Luck and Luck, "Individual Responsibility," op. cit., pp. 233–237.

45 Secretary-General, *The Fall of Srebrenica*, op. cit., p. 108, para. 506.

46 Ibid., p. 107, paras. 500, 497, and 499, respectively.

47 Scott Straus, "What Is Being Prevented? Genocide, Mass Atrocity, and Conceptual Ambiguity in the Anti-Atrocity Movement," in Rosenberg et al., *Reconstructing Atrocity Prevention*, op cit., p. 21.

48 United Nations, Secretary-General, Letter Dated 31 August 2007 from the Secretary-General Addressed to the President of the Security Council, S/2007/721.

49 Waller, *Confronting Evil*, op. cit., pp. 247–248. Though both sets of Special Advisers have had a number of informal contacts with the Security Council over the years, the first formal briefing of the Council was performed by the Special Adviser on the Prevention of Genocide, Adama Dieng, in 2014, after his trip with the High Commissioner on Human Rights to South Sudan.
50 Hugo Slim, "Saving Individuals from the Scourge of War: Complementarity and Tension between R2P and Humanitarian Action," in Bellamy and Dunne, *Handbook*, op. cit., pp. 545–560.
51 Luck and Luck, "Individual Responsibility," op. cit., pp. 237–241.

13

WHO IS IN CHARGE?

Emerging national and regional strategies for prevention

Andrea Bartoli and Tetsushi Ogata

Making a serious commitment and sustained efforts to prevent the occurrence or recurrence of mass atrocity crimes needs to be the default orientation of any state. Many member states of the United Nations have come to share this stance today, as evinced by their increasing interest and participation in state-led initiatives that focus on building national architectures for genocide and mass atrocity prevention. One of the most recent manifestations of such initiatives is the Global Action Against Mass Atrocity Crimes (GAAMAC). It is the latest of many responses to a longing that has been explicitly articulated since the coining of the term "genocide" by Raphael Lemkin and the adoption – even prior to the Universal Declaration of Human Rights – of the Convention on the Prevention and Punishment of the Crime of Genocide in 1948.

Launched after four regional fora on the prevention of genocide (Argentina in 2008; Tanzania in 2010; Switzerland in 2011; and Cambodia in 2013), GAAMAC aims to provide a platform of collaboration and cooperation among states and civil society organizations that are already working on or are interested in preventing mass atrocities today. The initial participants included representatives of Argentina, Switzerland, Tanzania, Australia, Costa Rica, and Denmark; the UN Office of the Special Adviser on the Prevention of Genocide (OSAPG); regional organizations; non-governmental organizations; and experts in the fields of genocide prevention (GP) and Responsibility to Protect (R2P). The effort was to explore the commonalities between the two communities – GP and R2P; "the gaps at national and regional levels to preventing mass atrocities and mechanisms to overcome these gaps; and finally, key elements for the development of national architectures and programmes for the prevention of mass atrocity crimes."[1]

The emergence of such a "forum" itself reflects several shifting trends in the field of preventing genocide and mass atrocities, regarding our own conceptions about genocide, ways in which responsibility is taken, and available tools and resources.

More fundamentally, it demonstrates an emerging process through which states are reorienting how they address challenges of respecting peoples' diversity and maintaining stability within their own societies. The states and the organizations that are involved in GAAMAC are sending a message that the prevention of genocide and mass atrocities is no longer a task for only "failed" or "fragile" states, but is a collective project. This signal is a critical reminder at a time when record numbers of humans are forced to flee their homes from mass atrocities, when divisions along identity and ideological boundaries polarize and radicalize extremist groups who commit atrocities, when those crimes are left unaddressed, and, more importantly, when no one state alone can fix these problems. It is also important to amplify this signal when we stand at the crossroads in our efforts in prevention. On the one hand, we should be reassured by the good news that, especially during the last two decades, the international community has advanced norms and standards in preventing genocide and protecting human lives, so much that the trends are not easily reversible. This means that, although far from ideal, the upward trajectory to keep developing and institutionalizing prevention and protection mechanisms will continue in the coming years and cannot be rolled back by the whim of a few governments. Institutionalization creates bureaucracy, but also provides continuity.

On the other hand, there is still a lack of translating these norms and standards into "national" strategies, architectures, or policies of genocide and mass atrocity prevention at the local and national levels. The fact that states recognize genocide and mass atrocity prevention as a collective project does not provide them with tailored responses and remedies; the task still hinges on states' proactive steps in implementing their own national strategies. When such responsibility is called for, but states are not penalized for *not* taking those extra steps – which is all too common in the international system – the collective agenda of genocide and mass atrocity prevention can easily stagnate.

GAAMAC is now a decade-long effort to establish a network of governments from African, Asian, European, and Latin American states willing to take responsibility for the prevention and protection agendas at the national level. It may be seen as a contribution to an emerging global architecture that aims at strengthening national policies and architectures. As with the United Nations that was – in the famous words of Dag Hammarskjöld – "not created to take mankind to heaven, but to save humanity from hell," GAAMAC is also not going to serve as the panacea to genocide and mass atrocity prevention. Still, it can provide additional guardrails where there used to be none. The following sections trace the roots of this progress.

From neglect to commitment

"Atrocity prevention" as a field is rather a novel approach that can be distinguished from "genocide prevention," or, to be more precise, "genocide-only" prevention. At its core, the legitimacy of genocide prevention is derived from the legal mandates of the 1948 UN Genocide Convention. However, this means that, like any other international treaties, genocide prevention is effective only insofar as the states are willing to accept the terms of the Genocide Convention and live up to the letter and spirit of the law. Just as the Convention's definition of genocide has allowed room for interpretation – stirring much debate among scholars and practitioners – the *idea* of operationalizing genocide prevention has long occupied an equally ambiguous space, its meanings dependent on who sees it and who speaks about it. Article V of the Genocide Convention illustrates a case in point. It mandates that "[t]he Contracting Parties undertake to enact, in accordance with their respective Constitutions, the necessary legislation" to prosecute persons guilty of the crime of genocide, but it falls short of providing a precise sanction or penalty for the acts of genocide defined in Articles II and III. Consequently, while some states have enacted provisions to establish the criminal accountability of genocide, other states, among them Australia, Belgium, Ecuador, Egypt, Greece, Iceland, India, Iraq, New Zealand, Norway, Pakistan, Senegal, Turkey, and Ukraine, have taken the view that no new domestic legislation is required because their domestic penal codes already cover crimes of killing or causing serious physical or mental harm.[2]

Article V and Article VIII (which calls for interventions in cases of genocide) are the clauses that outline state obligations for the "prevention" side of the Convention's objectives. However, the efficacy of genocide prevention has been subject to states' discretion, just as the Convention's legal definition allowed states to willfully choose – and therefore neglect – when to invoke the term "genocide" and hold themselves accountable for taking action. "Willful neglect" of states is thus linked to the narrow legal definition of genocide and to the strictly contractual obligations under the Convention. For so long, the field of genocide prevention was without the power of moral suasion other than states' self-interest of national security, and therefore the climate of willful neglect has pervaded the security structures in the post-Cold War era. Willful neglect was as much *intentional* as any other acts of states.

The World Summit Outcome Document in 2005, which adopted the Responsibility to Protect doctrine as the UN consensus (A/RES/60/1), further popularized the notion that the four crimes (genocide, crimes against humanity, war crimes, and ethnic cleansing) constitute the rubric of mass atrocities. In attempting a conceptual synthesis, "mass atrocity" was suggested to include "genocide, crimes against humanity (the emerging crime of ethnic cleansing), and serious war crimes … meriting timely and effective responses in political, military, and judicial terms."[3]

The concept of mass atrocity has since gained more recognition and wider acceptance, because it captured the multifaceted nature of the genocidal phenomenon in a single label. Though without a formal consensus, the term set the common standard as "large-scale, systematic violence against civilian populations."[4] It allowed reference to the phenomena of genocide, crimes against humanity, ethnic cleansing, politicide, cultural destruction, or rape without the limits of overly-restrictive distinction. Put differently, the lack of a legal definition of mass atrocity actually reflected both the *impracticality* of trying to define a genocidal phenomenon by one label or another, and the *practicality* of freeing ourselves from getting mired in the definitional debate about genocide. The use of the term "mass atrocity" thus enables greater emphasis on the *likelihood* of genocide, which, in and of itself, warrants timely and effective response measures, even before anyone can generate a definitive genocide determination or formal classification.

In parallel, even the concept of genocide itself has undergone a noticeable shift towards contextualizing genocidal intent and action as part of broader social structures and political violence. Feierstein discusses genocide in terms of "relational" systems in which genocide is one "technology of power," engineering social identities and establishing new social relations in the image of the perpetrators.[5] Shaw extends the sociological and historical analysis of the definitional debates that began with Fein and Chalk and Jonassohn, and discusses genocide as a "hybrid" phenomenon of both "structure of conflict" between or among the actors involved, and in "structural contexts" where such genocide-as-action is only a part of wider systems.[6] In a similar vein, Verdeja places genocide in the spectrum of political violence in order to uncover variations of genocidal violence temporally and spatially and contextualize them in the overall continuum of violence.[7]

Recent scholarship certainly does not define the entirety of genocide studies, but these studies share an important characteristic. They show that, while genocide does entail its own peculiar processes of manifestation, distinct in size and magnitude, genocide is never completely remote from us, is sometimes invisible, and can never be separated from its broader contexts. From this comes an understanding that it is possible for genocidal violence to emerge and submerge at varying points in a given episode, regardless of whether we can see tangible evidence of it or not. This view stands in contrast to a generation of comparative genocide scholarship that focused on singling out tangible and identifiable causes of genocide that are distinct from other forms of conflict.[8]

So far, genocide as a legal term has been essentially a retroactive concept. One comes to know of genocide after the fact. Paradoxically, the prevention of genocide suffers from a circular logic in that the determinant of genocide requires that prior evidence – clear or circumstantial – of intentional group destruction has been established, while its prevention requires taking actions before the phenomenon in question rises to the level of genocide. But, if we come to know of genocide after the fact, that defeats the purpose of prevention. To this conundrum, the notion of mass atrocity and our broader reconceptualization of genocide help us *see* genocide without actually having to see it. The shifts in our use of the lexicons help us move beyond the intentionality debate and genocide-only focus that have caused more harm than good. As Scheffer notes, our answer to whether genocide has or has not occurred or whether the evidence of genocide intent is or is not specific enough, should be "We don't care!"[9] – that is, if we take seriously precursors of genocide.

In so doing, we exercise more flexibility in defining and preventing genocide. On the one hand, we keep what we generally mean by genocide as "the intent and action to annihilate a human group as such, as defined by the perpetrators, in whole or in part";[10] on the other hand, we recognize greater fluidity and mutability of genocidal violence in human groups' relations, social structures, and types of violence. The field of atrocity prevention is therefore an *epistemic community* whose active participants are able to distinguish genocide conceptually and prevent

180 Andrea Bartoli and Tetsushi Ogata

it pragmatically. They are drawn to each other precisely because of their shared, overriding concern to prevent atrocities – however a given "atrocity" may be defined. The term "atrocity" itself has ambiguous – and perhaps indefinable – space, and yet this *ambiguity*, and hence flexibility, enables this epistemic field to be expansive and inclusive.

Doctrinal and operational shifts in the praxis

The trends towards framing genocide and mass atrocity prevention in larger contexts are also evident in the discourse of the Responsibility to Protect (R2P) and ways in which data gathering and verification are done to assess atrocity risk factors. In other words, the praxis of prevention is similarly moving beyond a genocide-only focus, but without losing sight of the fundamental aim of preventing genocide and mass atrocities.

Since its inception, R2P has passed through several conceptual and operational phases. When the International Commission on Intervention and State Sovereignty (ICISS) introduced a positive reframing of state sovereignty in its final report, from "*sovereignty as control* to *sovereignty as responsibility*" (2001: 13), the initial set of R2P entailed three forms of state responsibilities – to prevent, to react, and to rebuild. However, these original formulations were extremely unwieldy as they purported to protect populations from "serious harm, as a result of internal war, insurgency, repression or state failure," and the way to achieve that was seen as addressing "both the root causes and direct causes of internal conflict and other man-made crises" (2001: XI). It was at the UN General Assembly World Summit in 2005 that the scope of R2P was refined to protecting populations from four mass atrocity crimes – genocide, crimes against humanity, war crimes, and ethnic cleansing (A/RES/60/1). The operational trigger for invoking R2P situations was also limited to when states are "manifestly failing" to discharge such responsibility, as opposed to when they are "unwilling and unable" to do so, as it was framed in the ICISS report. Then, the former UN Secretary-General Ban Ki-moon released his report in 2009, outlining three pillars of operational modalities to implement R2P under the auspices of the UN authorities (A/63/677). The third pillar, which involved the international community's responsibility to respond collectively in a timely and decisive manner, stirred much debate among the critics and proponents alike. But the three-pillar approach remains an authoritative framework today, and has clarified legally legitimate and politically permissive forms of foreign interventions – coercive and non-coercive, military and non-military, lethal and non-lethal – under the strict guidance of the UN.

However, especially after the Libya and Syria debacle in 2011 and beyond, which caused an uproar of discontent and dismay criticizing double-standards of R2P applications and the mismatch between means and ends of R2P, prevention and protection agendas shifted towards the first and second pillars. These touch upon the need to strengthen state-building measures and capacity-building mechanisms. This turn of attention to a pre-crisis phase revived the idea of "responsibility to prevent," which was part of the initial conception of R2P by the ICISS. In the original ICISS report, it was declared that "prevention is the single most important dimension of the responsibility to protect,"[11] and "responsibility to rebuild" was *sine qua non* of such formulations. Although the original formulation of "responsibility to rebuild" focused on external powers' responsibility to engage in rebuilding, recovery, and reconstruction efforts following their military interventions, the Secretary-General's seventh report on R2P in 2015 revisited this notion of "rebuilding," this time in the name of "preventing recurrence of atrocity crimes" (A/69/981–S/2015/500). He emphasized that a long-term commitment to rebuilding the post-atrocity societies, coupled with assistance in transitional justice, ending impunity, strengthening governance, and broader peacebuilding processes, is central to atrocity prevention agendas. This is consistent with his first report in 2009, in which the Secretary-General said that the prevention scope should be "narrow" in terms of mass atrocity crimes, but the response options "deep," in terms of employing a wide variety of tools and resources available.[12] What underlies this revisiting of the notions of "rebuilding" (from 2001) and a "narrow but deep" approach (from 2009) is our increasing recognition that we cannot prevent genocide only by looking at its tangible signs.

Furthermore, there are trends in early warning and risk assessment models that explore non-genocidal contexts in order to assess atrocity risks. With the few exceptional studies establishing predictive, forecasting models of genocide and politicide,[13] there is a trend shifting in orientation from early *warning* and more towards early *detection*, engaging in a much broader contextual analysis than a genocide-only (or even atrocity) focus. The early detection of atrocity risks pays attention to all potential structural risk factors, as does the UN Framework of Analysis for Atrocity Crimes.[14] The Framework of Analysis categorically identifies an all-encompassing set of 147 indicators that together constitute 14 "common" and "specific" risk factors warranting assessment for atrocity risks. A more recent example along this line of development is an epidemiological approach, which does not necessarily seek a potential genocide onset-point, but ascertains *non-randomness* in event distribution, so that it is possible to identify the potential systematic nature of violence (see Chapter 4). Waller encapsulates these trends in the praxis of prevention by saying that atrocity prevention today entails a "continuum of prevention strategies" that aim to prevent the occurrence of mass atrocities in the first place ("upstream"), further escalation once they take place ("midstream"), and recurrence of future atrocities ("downstream").[15]

The field of atrocity prevention is now predicated on holistic engagement in multilateral dimensions, such as education, security sector reforms, transitional justice, human rights protection, and dealing with the past, to name just a few. Experts, lawmakers, and practitioners who engage in those areas do so without necessarily knowing that they are engaged in "atrocity prevention." Atrocity prevention is therefore mainstreaming measures of peacebuilding and state-building more explicitly for the purpose of preventing genocide and mass atrocities. It is an epistemic community today.

GAAMAC is one expression of such trends, further substantiating the needs of multilateral and collective engagement that is at the heart of atrocity prevention. From willful neglect to intentional commitment, from a genocide-only focus to the spectrum of political violence, the scope of prevention and protection agenda is expanding. Genocide and other mass atrocities are concerned with a swath of human affairs and societies; prevention of such violence requires a no-less-complex agenda. It is clear that, as will be discussed below, the national-level engagement will be at the forefront of implementing the praxis of prevention, and spaces for such an exchange will be key.

Emergence of GAAMAC

GAAMAC is a "global, inclusive, state-led voluntary network of partners that support, are interested in or are involved in atrocity prevention." An analogy of "big tent" is applicable here, to which are invited all states and organizations, regardless of their size or power, that share an interest in mutual learning and good practices of atrocity prevention. This is a working principle of this emerging epistemic community that intends to assist states, in collaboration with other relevant atrocity prevention networks and actors, to design and develop national architectures for the prevention of mass atrocity crimes.

A decade before GAAMAC was conceived, the Stockholm International Forum on Preventing Genocide in January 2004 was the first major inter-governmental conference that dealt with issues of genocide prevention. Hosted by the government of Sweden, delegations from 55 states and 14 international organizations participated in this gathering, the last in a series of four symposiums. Together they adopted the Stockholm Declaration, reaffirming their commitment to R2P, the fight against impunity, and education and awareness-raising about genocidal dangers. It was also at this conference that the former UN Secretary-General, Kofi Annan, shared his plan to strengthen the UN's capacity and move it from a culture of reaction to one of prevention. One result was the appointment of the first Special Adviser on the Prevention of Genocide, Juan Méndez, in July 2004.

Another notable precedent to GAAMAC was the series of "regional fora" on the prevention of genocide, as mentioned earlier, organized by the governments of Argentina, Switzerland, and Tanzania. Each forum represented the first region-wide discussion of genocide prevention at the state level, and one of the most remarkable moments in each was when regional experiences for "successful" genocide prevention were shared. In the 2008 Latin American forum, for instance, the Union of South American Nations (UNASUR) mechanism was highlighted as an example of facilitating mediations and negotiations; it was credited with resolving four cases of interstate conflict in Latin America. In the 2010 African forum, the African delegates themselves affirmed that the constitution of the African Union replaces the principle of non-interference with that of non-indifference. Also, having adopted the Dar-es-Salaam Declaration on Peace, Security, Democracy, and Development in 2004, 11 member states (now 12, with South Sudan) of the

International Conference on the Great Lakes Region (ICGLR) pledged to launch Regional and National Committees for genocide prevention (which later materialized in September 2010) as a mechanism to domesticate the ICGLR's Protocol on the Prevention and Punishment of the Crime of Genocide, War Crimes, Crimes against Humanity, and All Forms of Discrimination (see Chapter 11). In the 2011 European forum, the Organization of Security and Cooperation in Europe (OSCE) shared experiences of developing in-house guidelines to facilitate the work of early warning and conflict prevention. In the 2013 Asian forum, participants underlined the role that the Association of Southeast Asian Nations (ASEAN) would play in the regional architecture, as well as a network of national human rights commissions.

The overarching aim throughout the four fora was to highlight how genocide prevention is conceptualized and practiced in different national contexts and across different regions. It was designed to be a space for the delegates of the governments and organizations to share their own examples and stories of good practices and successes, while exploring ways to mainstream a genocide prevention agenda.

The list of recommendations discussed at the fora reflected their regional character. One of the recurring items, across all the four fora, was to designate a focal point in each country for the prevention of genocide at local, national, and regional levels and develop their institutional mandates, as well as mechanisms for interaction among them. In fact, by the end of the last Regional Forum in Phnom Penh in 2013, there was a recognition that at least two parallel networks of focal points were being developed – one on genocide prevention, the other on R2P. The Global Network of R2P Focal Points was launched in September 2010, at the initiative of Denmark, Ghana, Costa Rica, and Australia and in close collaboration with the Global Centre for the Responsibility to Protect. As of September 2016, 57 focal points who are senior level representatives of the governments had been appointed, and regular global coordination meetings had begun.

The proliferating work of the focal point networks in both genocide prevention and R2P was a testament to governments' growing interest and commitment to engage with these topics, but at the same time there were real and logistical challenges associated with scarce resources and bureaucratic complexity. Given overlapping mandates between the four regional fora and the R2P Global Network of Focal Points, often the same individual represented his or her country as the focal point person for both genocide prevention and R2P issues. In other cases, two focal points participated in the two networks separately and did not necessarily coordinate with each other. While officials representing the foreign ministries often participated in the meetings on genocide prevention or R2P, the prevention work on the ground or at the community level would require active participation from the ministries of internal affairs, as well as other national agencies and civil society, who were less visibly represented. Furthermore, an official who would represent the government at one meeting did not always occupy the same position when the next meeting came around. Discussions on building national strategies or architectures for preventing genocide or atrocities require a longer commitment, but internal cohesion, as well as institutional memory among different ministries and officials, were left up to each government.

Against this backdrop, a group of six states and civil society organizations, who had been taking leading roles in the regional fora for genocide prevention (Argentina, Switzerland, and Tanzania) and the R2P Global Network (Australia, Costa Rica, and Denmark), came together in Tanzania in 2013 to discuss mutually-reinforcing and complementary methods of collaboration. It was acknowledged that national efforts for *both* genocide prevention and R2P are integral components for successful and effective prevention and protection. In the end, the states and the civil society organization agreed that we need a common working language and "community of commitment" through which national actors can share and exchange information, experiences, knowledge, and expertise for preventing atrocities at the national level. To this end, this ad hoc working group of six states and civil society organizations decided to launch the Global Action Against Mass Atrocity Crimes.

Subsequently, the first international meeting of GAAMAC was held in San José, Costa Rica in 2014, with the involvement of more than 50 states and 127 participants, including civil society representatives. The second international meeting took place in Manila, Philippines in 2016, with the participation of 53 states (37 of which were represented by officers coming from their respective capitals), more than 50 non-governmental organizations, and ten international bodies. At the time of writing, GAAMAC III is planned to take place in Africa in 2018.

GAAMAC is not a conventional organization or government agency; it is a service organization in which GAAMAC seeks to supplement and encourage, but not supplant, the work of other organizations and states. The interested governments and civil society organizations now constitute the Steering Group, with the government of Switzerland as its current Chair. They produced the "Founding Document" of GAAMAC, delineating the overarching mission for this global cooperation network, as well as the roles and responsibilities of the Steering Group. As articulated by the Founding Document,[16] the working premises of this atrocity prevention community are:

- *States are the ones to bear primary responsibility for prevention.* This is consistent with the legal obligations to prevent genocide for state parties to the 1948 Convention on the Prevention and Punishment of the Crime of Genocide. It also acknowledges the commitment to upholding the fundamental state responsibilities as articulated in the 2005 World Summit Outcome Document.
- *No state is immune.* This is based on the recognition that atrocity crimes can occur in any state, and therefore it is a task of every state to engage in manifold and multilevel preventive efforts within their domestic territory.
- *Prevention starts at home.* Our efforts to identify and understand root causes, risk factors, and dynamic processes of atrocity crimes, and to implement timely and efficient responses, are more effective when they are informed by local and national contexts.

- *Prevention requires inclusive participation.* This acknowledges that effective prevention policies and national architectures need the support and active participation of local civil society actors and society at large.
- *Prevention takes time and effort, different forms, different actors, and varying contexts.* This includes a wide array of prevention measures, including awareness-raising of atrocity risks, mechanisms to inhibit them, national policies for early decision and early action, and institutional capacity building.
- *Prevention requires deep reflection on the past.* Impunity for past atrocity in one place increases the risk of atrocity in another. This recognizes that protection, prevention, and prosecution are linked with each other to ensure the guarantee of non-recurrence of atrocity crimes.
- *Prevention requires will, resources, capacities, and knowledge.* Precisely because of this, GAAMAC seeks the most optimal cross-fertilization so that no state is alone in cultivating the necessary will or expending resources.
- *Prevention needs to be ingrained as part of national policy frameworks.* This reaffirms that atrocity prevention perspectives need to be embedded within the existing design and implementation of policies concerning broader human rights protection, rule of law, governance, and the security sector. It also highlights the need for education and training of public officials to enable them to develop such policy frameworks.

Ways forward

Unlike many other international symposiums, GAAMAC meetings have placed greater emphasis on small group working sessions, with an aim to maximize peer-to-peer exchanges among the state delegates, experts, and practitioners. And, unlike many academic conferences, speakers and panelists were encouraged to focus more on sharing pragmatic lessons learned, exchanging practical tools and knowledge, and making policy relevant recommendations for atrocity prevention. One of the concrete examples of these exchanges was the creation of regional working groups during the GAAMAC II meeting in Manila 2016. At the suggestion of the UN Special Adviser on the Prevention of Genocide, Adama Dieng, the delegates who were present during the meeting spontaneously constituted regional groupings in Asia, Africa, Europe, North America, and Latin America in a self-organizing manner, in order to brainstorm and formulate concrete proposals specific to their respective regions. Most notably, the African regional working group proposed "to produce a manual through country consultative meetings, research and peer review workshops in order to facilitate formulation of and strengthen the management of national architectures towards atrocity prevention." As of January 2017, the African regional working group of GAAMAC held its inaugural workshop, convening 16 experts and practitioners working in the fields relevant to atrocity prevention. They began organizing a continental online survey to collect information and stories of prevention activities from various organizations, the work of which will certainly be featured in the upcoming GAAMAC III.

The Global Action Against Mass Atrocity Crimes is a "community of commitment," developing the knowledge, practices, and experiences of atrocity prevention through national dialogues and regional configurations. There were two moments of global consensus within the UN system relevant to this effort: the approval of 1948 Genocide Convention and the 2005 Outcome Document. Both clearly stressed national responsibilities as the key cornerstone of the emerging system. Officials of Argentina, Costa Rica, Denmark, Switzerland, and Tanzania, as well as civil society organizations, are enacting those responsibilities today, recognizing that true integration of local, national, regional, and international networks must include robust national architectures.

Notes

1 www.gaamac.org/about-gaamac/history#.WW4EldPyvq0
2 William Schabas, *Genocide in International Law: The Crime of Crimes*, 2nd ed. (Cambridge, UK: Cambridge University Press, 2009), p. 407.
3 David Scheffer, "Genocide and Atrocity Crimes," *Genocide Studies and Prevention*, 1: 3 (2006), p. 237.
4 Scott Straus, *Fundamentals of Genocide and Mass Atrocity Prevention* (Washington, DC: United States Holocaust Memorial Museum, 2016), p. 31.
5 Daniel Feierstein, *Genocide as Social Practice: Reorganizing Society under the Nazis and Argentina's Military Juntas* (New Brunswick, NJ: Rutgers University Press, 2014).
6 Martin Shaw, *What is Genocide?*, 2nd ed. (Malden, MA: Polity Press, 2015); Helen Fein, *Genocide: A Sociological Perspective* (London: Sage Publications, 1990); Frank Chalk and Kurt Jonassohn, *The History and Sociology of Genocide: Analyses and Case Studies* (New Haven, CT: Yale University Press, 1990).
7 Ernesto Verdeja, "On Situating the Study of Genocide within Political Violence," *Genocide Studies and Prevention*, 7: 1 (2012).
8 Scott Straus, "Review: Second-Generation Comparative Research on Genocide," *World Politics*, 59: 3 (2007), pp. 476–501.
9 Scheffer, "Genocide and Atrocity Crimes," op. cit., p. 237.
10 Yehuda Bauer, Memorandum in preparation for 2013 GPANet Stockholm Program, 2013.
11 International Commission on Intervention and State Sovereignty, *The Responsibility to Protect* (International Commission on Intervention and State Sovereignty, 2001), p. XI.
12 See J.M. Welsh, "The 'Narrow but Deep Approach' to Implementing the Responsibility to Protect: Reassessing the Focus on International Crimes," in Sheri P. Rosenberg, Tibi Galis, and Alex Zucker (eds), *Reconstructing Atrocity Prevention* (New York: Cambridge University Press, 2015), pp. 81–94; Alexander Mayer-Rieckh, Karim Kamel, and Sabrina Stein, *Atrocity Prevention in a Nutshell: Origins, Concepts and Approaches* (Social Science Research Council, Conflict Prevention and Peace Forum, 2016).
13 Barbara Harff, "No Lessons Learned from the Holocaust? Assessing Risks of Genocide and Political Mass Murder since 1955," *American Political Science Review*, 97: 1 (2003), pp. 57–73; Benjamin E. Goldsmith et al., "'Forecasting the Onset of Genocide and Politicide,' Annual Out-of-Sample Forecasts on a Global Dataset, 1988–1003," *Journal of Peace Research*, 50: 4 (2013), pp. 437–452.
14 Adama Dieng and J. Welsh, "Assessing the Risk of Atrocity Crimes," *Genocide Studies and Prevention*, 9: 3 (2016), pp. 4–12.
15 James Waller, *Confronting Evil: Engaging our Responsibility to Prevent Genocide* (New York: Oxford University Press, 2016).
16 GAAMAC. (n.d.) GAAMAC Documents. Available from: www.gaamac.org/resources/documents.

14

GUIDELINES FOR PREVENTION OF GENOCIDES AND OTHER MASS ATROCITIES

An overview

Ted Robert Gurr

Foreknowledge

What do we know about causes and responses? Yehuda Bauer lays out reasons, rooted in human evolution, why the potential for mass killings is always with us, but at the same time capable of containment (Chapter 1). Ideologies play a major role in justifying contemporary genocides and mass murders, though typically they are invoked to cloak the perpetrators' political objectives. They can be contained by acting on norms – international morality, if you will – that justify preventive action, responding to mass violence once it is underway, and reconstructing traumatized societies in its aftermath.

Our annual global risk assessments, based on Barbara Harff's empirical research, make it possible to identify the countries and situations at greatest risk of genocides and mass political violence in the near future (Chapter 3). For other kinds of mass atrocities, we have historical data but lack models and means to forecast them (Chapter 5). A half-dozen structural, or persisting, conditions that determine genocidal risks have been identified in empirical research and are used in Table 3.1 to identify high-risk countries as of 2016–2017, with specifics about the driving conditions in each country and how they are measured in historical analysis. In addition, Harff has designed a system for tracking early warning signs – the flurry of political events and actions that should help policy-makers recognize when high-risk situations are about to erupt in mass killings (Chapter 3).

In another empirical chapter, Birger Heldt describes a statistical procedure adapted from its use by epidemiologists for early detection of disease outbreaks. He shows how the Poisson distribution can be used by analysts to determine whether the killings that often forewarn of mass atrocities are random or patterned, thus indicative of intent. And he illustrates its use through analysis of data from Darfur for 2003–2004 (Chapter 4).

188 Ted Robert Gurr

Risk assessment and early warning jointly could give national, regional, and international decision-makers the analytic means to deploy preventive policies before the onset of mass killings – should they chose to use them. As far as we know, none of these empirical analyses are regularly done or used by policy makers, except maybe by the US intelligence community and the State Department. And if they are carried out by those agencies, the results are classified. The risk assessments prepared for GPANet are cost-free to the users, based on empirical research, and can be used by states and their agencies, and by any other actors.

Organizing preventive action

Virtually all genocides and political mass murders since 1955 have occurred during or in the aftermath of violent civil conflict, or the disintegration of democratic political institutions. Thus, the preventive approach often urged by activists and observers is to use conflict-resolution strategies to resolve civil wars before they have devastating humanitarian consequences. But, as I showed in Chapter 5, there are a large number of civil wars at any given time, many international efforts to contain them, and usually no certainty that genocides and other mass atrocities have been thereby prevented. It seems inevitable that the most effective contra-genocide strategies are those employed midstream, to use James Waller's term (Waller 2016, Chapter 5).

As a guiding principle, when civil wars begin in countries that have three or more of Harff's genocide/politicide risk factors, those places should be the focus of international preventive measures.

In this book our authors, all members of GPANet, describe organizations and programs that aim at anticipating and responding to genocides and other mass atrocities.

Edward Luck, the UN's first Special Adviser on the Responsibility to Protect (2008–2012), shows in Chapter 12 how and why the UN has been from the outset ambivalent about prevention of genocide and other mass atrocities. He identifies eight considerations that in his view discouraged the founders of the UN system from referring to such events in its founding Charter. Prevention nonetheless became a significant issue in the first decade of the twenty-first century. In 2004, on the tenth anniversary of the Rwandan genocide, Secretary-General Kofi Annan appointed a Special Adviser on the Prevention of Genocide, the Argentine lawyer (and survivor of the country's Dirty War) Juan Méndez. Since then, three successive Special Advisers and their small staffs have wrestled with the ambiguities of their mission, including the relation between genocide prevention and implementing the Responsibility to Protect (the two share offices and staff). The Prevention of Genocide office has identified a rather long list of factors and events that suggest a genocide may be in the making, and monitors them on a near-global scale. But the framework is not theoretically driven, nor does the Special Adviser regularly report high-risk or escalating situations. Luck concludes that:

the task today and tomorrow is finding a way to turn [Raphael Lemkin's] legal vision into practical strategies, doctrines, institutions, policies and practices to prevent genocide and all other mass atrocity crimes and to provide real protection to real people.

Roy Gutman contends in Chapter 6 that international humanitarian law was widely invoked in the 1990s to justify interventions, particularly in response to war crimes and atrocities in Bosnia. A great deal of journalistic attention was focused on these events, not least his own Pulitzer-prize-winning reporting on the Balkan wars from their beginning: "I am convinced that war crimes are the prelude to crimes against humanity, and these, if they go unchecked, lead to the ultimate crime … Genocide." He also argues that, more recently, there is less attention to atrocities, in Syria in particular, and thus a lesser response. Preoccupation with international terrorism from 2001 onwards is mainly responsible for the shift away from concern about humanitarian crises. The decline in public awareness and concern thus undercuts the international will to invoke humanitarian law. He cites a litany of war crimes and mass atrocities from Afghanistan and Iraq, as well as Syria, and the lack of international action.

Gutman argues that journalistic reporting is key to reviving public concern. How to do so in places where authorities block the entry of international journalists? He advocates tapping local journalists and citizen-journalists, and pairing them with editors operating remotely; he is trying this out on a small scale in Syria.

The US and UN are the principal international actors who might be expected to take the lead in responding to mass atrocities. But, as Edward Luck observes in his Chapter 12, the UN has been ambivalent virtually from its founding about taking action in response to genocide and other mass atrocities. The US has relied since the Obama administration on the analyses and recommendations of the Atrocities Prevention Board, but, as James Finkel shows in Chapter 9, reviewed below, the APB is hamstrung by turf wars among agencies and variable access to the President. There is little reason to expect that the Trump administration will support action in humanitarian crises.

Prevention in Africa: Examples

To find examples of "real protection for real people," to use Edward Luck's phrase, we need to look at other actors, ones that face fewer international and institutional constraints than do the UN or the US policy community. Let me begin with Africa, which has been the site of more genocides and mass atrocities in the last half-century than any other world region. In principle, preventive action should begin before – long before – the onset of atrocities. James Waller calls this "upstream prevention, focusing on the underlying causes of genocide, with an aim toward understanding the ways in which a society can be inoculated against the risk of its occurrence."[1] One of our essays, by Ekkehard Strauss, reports a project for overcoming identity conflicts that contributes directly to this objective (Chapter 7, reviewed below). The other preventive strategies considered later in this chapter take higher-level approaches.

In Chapter 7, Dr. Strauss describes a promising local initiative at prevention in Mauritania, a country that is third-highest on our list of countries at risk of genocide – should civil war break out. His project, sponsored by the Office of the UN High Commissioner for Human Rights, focuses on the village level. The aim is to bridge ethnic and clan divisions by establishing representative community committees that deal with administration of local development projects – often funded by outside agencies – ethnic inequalities and resentments, access to water points and pastures, and many other issues. Preliminary research identified 26 villages in the country's southeast that had divisive internal conflicts, aggravated by conflict with refugees from conflict in neighboring Mali; plus 30 villages elsewhere. Committees have been established in all, with the conflict-mitigating aim of forming alliances and cooperation among people of different identity groups. The ethnic mix in the country includes Afro-Mauritanians (comprised of multiple ethnies), a minority ethnic elite, the Beydane (White Moors), and Black Moors (Haratin), who are the most numerous and the most subject to deliberate discrimination. Exacerbating tension is the Beydane elite's support for an Arabization policy in state institutions and the military. The project is said to be effective at the local level. We strongly endorse Dr. Strauss's hope that similar approaches can be developed and applied in other countries where violent identity conflicts could have disastrous consequences, as they have in Mauritania's recent past.

Eric Reeves, a long-time observer of genocide and its human costs in Sudan, identifies a half-dozen situations since the 1990s in which a vigorous international response might have deterred the militantly Arabist Khartoum regime from its murderous policies toward the peoples of Darfur and the Nuba mountains (Chapter 8). International action, if taken at all, was ineffective. In broad perspective, there were two underlying reasons for the feckless international responses. One was the lack of general public concern and demands for action in the Western countries that had the means to act. The second was the decisional constipation of the UN and regional international entities that have had the means to act. Edward Luck, whose Chapter 11 is summarized above, analyzes the "roots of ambivalence" that have constrained the UN, and the Security Council in specific, from a coherent preventive response to genocidal conflicts. Neither the Genocide Convention of 1948 nor the widely-touted doctrine of Responsibility to Protect (R2P), endorsed by the UN in 2005, led to any clear, purposive action in Sudan or anywhere else – though R2P was used to provide a fig-leaf of justification for European and US intervention in the first Libyan civil war of 2011. The potential of the R2P doctrine for international prevention is examined more closely by Andrea Bartoli and Tetsushi Ogata in Chapter 13.

The US has potentially greater means to act than the UN in genocidal crises, and has often been a leader in organizing and providing humanitarian assistance. In August 2011, the Obama Administration established the Atrocities Prevention Board (APB) to coordinate the intelligence and policy recommendations of the multitude of federal agencies that had information on and interests in emerging crises. Five Cabinet-level departments were to be represented plus five other agencies – for example, the Joint Chiefs and the US Mission to the UN. In Chapter 9, James Finkel, a former high-level official with first-hand knowledge about the APB's work, provides a detailed assessment of how it did – and did not – work in response to humanitarian disasters.

Finkel reviews the constraints faced by the APB that led to what Finkel summarizes as "calculated decisions (not to intervene) rather than lack of political will." It was a given that President Obama would not support any new military action in the Middle East, for example in response to the genocidal civil war in Syria. The ABP itself had no funding. Moreover, it represented agencies with different expertise and policy agendas, and consensus was difficult to reach about how the US might respond to escalating crises such as mass atrocities in Central African Republic. The APB representatives included many – especially more junior officials – who were intensely committed to recommending preventive action. But at a higher level, agency heads often had competing agendas that were difficult to overcome – turf wars were common. If action was to be taken in any given situation, it required a White House decision, and in the early years that was helped by the personal relationship between the first APB head, Ambassador Samantha Power, and President Obama. Her successor had no such advantage. In the CAR case, the belated US response was to provide diplomatic and logistic support for French and African peacekeepers already on the ground.

The most effective peacemaking action in CAR was that of the lay Catholic organization Sant'Egidio, which in June 2017 brokered a ceasefire among 16 warring factions. Andrea Bartoli, a long-time member of Sant'Egidio, and Mauro Garofolo, its representative on the ground in Bangui, describe in Chapter 10 the principles and practices by which Sant'Egidio gains the confidence of warring antagonists, persuading them to agree to meet, discuss, and sometimes negotiate a conclusion. The organization had been active in CAR since the 1990s and had credibility with the governments *du jour* and many of the contenders. It had the further advantage that it could convene meetings of the parties to conflict in Rome as well as in Bangui. One object lesson is that NGOs on the ground can be more effective in peacemaking processes than the UN and the major powers.

The fragile states of Africa's Great Lakes region have been devastated by some of the world's deadliest conflicts and mass atrocities since the 1970s, exemplified by the Rwandan genocide. The US government and its APB are far away, NGOs like Sant'Egidio are limited in the number of countries in which they can be effective. Between them are regional organizations, representing the international political efforts of the governments most affected. The African regional responses aimed at prevention in the Great Lakes region are reviewed in Chapter 11 by Ambassador Liberata Mulamula of Tanzania and her collaborator Ashad Sentongo. Their working assumption is that "prevention involves linking available knowledge about causes, processes and manifestations, with policies, practices and programs that may be implemented at different levels to respond, deescalate or terminate hostile conditions and situations." In diplomatic practice, this has meant agreement on ten protocols and programs of action. National Committees focused on prevention of genocide and mass atrocities have been established in most states in the region. An International Conference on the Great Lakes Region (ICGLR) of state representatives can convene a Summit in response to the emergence of crises. In an ironic comparison, in Washington, DC, decisions about preventive action have to overcome turf wars among agencies; in Africa, the hurdle is competing international interests of member states. The ICGLR is also hampered by the proliferation of related entities that has been characterized as "a spaghetti bowl" of initiatives competing for attention, finances, and human capacity. The ICGLR, young and handicapped though it may be, has one success to its credit: it convened year-long negotiations that led to a December 2013 peace agreement between M23, a rebel Congolese movement, and the government of the Democratic Republic of Congo, a deadly conflict in a region that had a tragic history of mass atrocities.

Global Action Against Mass Atrocities Crimes (GAAMAC)

Last, and especially promising, is the recent emergence of a global alliance of regional government fora that have agreed on principles and policies to prevent mass atrocity crimes. GAAMAC is "a global, inclusive, state-led voluntary network of partners" focused on the prevention of mass atrocities, broadly conceived to include genocide and war crimes. In Chapter 13, Andrea Bartoli and Tetsushi Ogata describe the evolution of GAAMAC from regional fora held in, first, Buenos Aires in 2008, followed by others in Africa (2010), Europe (2011), and Asia (2013). Each forum included representatives of the governments of the region and civil society organizations. Officials of Switzerland, Argentina, and Tanzania took the lead in promoting these fora and their shared commitment to prevention. These regional fora provided the setting in which working principles for prevention could be worked out, and future cooperation among states ensured. GAAMAC built on these initiatives, holding its first global meeting in Costa Rica in 2014. The second was held in Manila in 2016 with 53 states and more than 50 nongovernmental organizations. The next, in 2018, will be held in Africa where plans for prevention are ahead of the curve, thanks to the work of the ICGLR.

A final comment

The chapters reviewed here show just how far researchers, activists, and governments have come in the last 20 years when confronting the threats and fact of genocide and other mass atrocities. On the ground, we have examples of local conflict-avoidance initiatives in Mauritania (Chapter 7) and a journalistic approach that can bring atrocities to global attention (Chapter 6). The UN and major powers face internal constraints in organizing responses on the ground (Chapters 9, 11), but at least they exemplify the international norms that condemn mass killings by states and violent factions. Two developments are especially encouraging. One is the impact of NGOs like Sant'Egidio in negotiating peace in conflict zones. The other is the emergence of regional fora for consultation, planning, and action against mass violence. The African experience is illustrative (Chapter 11). The founding of an international network of governments and civil society organizations, Global Action Against Mass Atrocities, shows there is a common, global commitment to avert mass killings (Chapter 13). And, thanks to the work of empirical social scientists (Chapters 4, 5, and 6), we have tools to anticipate and act in situations of high risk.

Note

1 James Waller, *Confronting Evil: Engaging Our Responsibility to Prevent Genocide* (Oxford, UK: Oxford University Press, 2016), p. 137.

INDEX

Note: Page numbers in *italic* type refer to figures
Page numbers in **bold** type refer to tables
Page numbers followed by 'n' refer to notes

Afghanistan 17, 75, 76, 79, 80–81, 82, 90, 117, 122, 189; internal wars 80, 81; war on terror 80, 81, 82
Africa, prevention examples 189–192
African Union (AU) 108, 109, 111, 146, 182
African Union Mission to Sudan (AMIS) 49, 50, 52
Afro-Mauritanians 94, 95, 96
al-Assad, B. 83, 84, 85, 86, 87, 89
Al Qaida 22, 75, 79, 80, 81, 82, 83, 86, 88, 89, 90, 106
Albright, M.K. 78; and Cohen, W.S. 4
Albright-Cohen Genocide Prevention Task Force Report (GPTF) 120, 131
Aleppo 85, 86, 89
alliances 13–14
American Civil War (1861–1865) 14
American Political Science Review 29
Annan, K. 166, 167, 168, 182, 188
antecedent conflicts, and mass atrocities **61**, 62
Arab Spring 66, 84, 122
Armenian genocide 5, 15, 19, 23
assassinations 32
Association of Southeast Asian Nations (ASEAN) 183
at-risk countries, genocide 33, **34–36**, 37

Atrocities Documentation Project (ADP) 48, 49
Atrocities Prevention Board (APB) 8, 66
Atrocities Prevention Interagency Working Group 116, 117
Atrocity Forecasting Project (University of Sydney) 42, 45
atrocity prevention: doctrinal/operational shifts 182–184; field 177, 179–180
Atrocity Prevention Board (APB) 114–116, 118–122, 123, 125–126, 128, 129, 130, 131, 190–191; bureaucracy 119; expectation management 119; hurdles 119–122; member turnover 124–125; resources 119
attachment 15
Auschwitz Institute for Peace and Reconciliation 149
autocratic governments, and genocidal violence 30

Bahrain 37
Ban Ki-moon 109, 168, 170, 180
Bangui National Forum (2015) 136, 139
Banka Luka 77, 78
Barnard, A. 74
Bartoli, A.: and Garofalo, M. 135–143; and Ogata, T. 9, 176–186
Bauer, Y. 2, 7, 11–24, 187

beheadings 88
bin Laden, O. 79, 80, 81, 82, 106
Bolshevism 20
Bolton, J. 163
Bosnia-Herzegovina 5, 8, 77, 78, 79, 81, 82, 84, 102, 113, 169, 189; Croats 65
Brandt, W. 76
Brown, C. 123–124
Buddhism 19
Bureau of Conflict and Stabilization Operations (US) 120, 127
Bureau of Democracy, Human Rights and Labor (DRL, US) 120–121
Burundi 6, 115, 116, 131, 145, 147, 148, 155, 157
Bush, G.W. 75, 80, 81, 82, 116, 117

Cambodia 6, 22, 61, 62, 74, 160, 165, 169, 176
Carayannis, T., and Lombard, L. 141
Carthage 18–19
Castro, F. 61–62
ceasefires 32, 64
Central African Republic (CAR) 8, 31, 32, 37, 66, 115, 122–124, 191; Bangui National Forum 136, 139; and Community of Sant'Egidio 135–143, 191; DDRR process 136, 137; genocide risk 33, 37; peace process drivers 138
Central Intelligence Agency (CIA) 131
Chechnya 64
China 16, 17, 23, 30, 64, 108, 111, 158, 165; and Sudan 16–17
Christianity 21
civil wars 14, 64–65
Clarke, R.D. 46
climate change 97, 98
clusters, disease 44
co-operation 15
Cohen, W.S., and Albright, M.K. 4
Cold War, and humanitarian law 75–79
collateral damage 40
collective moral norms 16
colonial experience, impact 7
Colvin, M. 88
Community of Sant'Egidio 8, 31, 32; and Central African Republic (CAR) 135–143, 191
conflict analysis 60–70; early prevention 63
conflict prevention, versus atrocity prevention 169
coordination, degree 47
count data 44; randomness 45–46
coups d'état 32
crimes see war crimes

Croatia 64, 65, 77, 78, 79
Cuba 61–62

Darfur 8, 16–17, 19, 48–52, 62, 105–112, 163, 187, 190; civilian conflict-related fatalities 50, 51; Doha Document for Peace in Darfur (DDPD) 110; inaction explanation 111–112; Liberation and Justice Movement (LJM) 110; National Islamic Front/National Congress Party (NIF/NCP) 105, 106; Obama administration 109–110; Rapid Response Forces (RSF) 105, 111; relief organizations expulsion 108–109; and self-determination referendum 109; Severe Acute Malnutrition (SAM) 109; Trump administration 111; UN Department of Peacekeeping Operations 107–108; UN/African Union Mission in Darfur 108, 109, 111
Darfur Peace Agreement (DPA) 107
data: count 44, 45–46; genocide/politicide victims 6
Dayton Peace Conference (1995) 81
DDRR process, Central African Republic (CAR) 136, 137
de Waal, A. 107
de-accelerating events, early warning models 32
death tolls, mass atrocities 62
Declaration on National Minorities (1992) 102
Declaration on the Rights of Indigenous Peoples (2007) 102
definitions 2–3, 11, 12, 60–61
Democratic Republic of Congo (DRC) 148, 151, 192
Deng, F. 147
Dieng, A. 185
discrimination, systematic 29, 30
disease surveillance systems 44–45, 53
Djotodia, M. 136, 137
Doha Document for Peace in Darfur (DDPD) 110
Dostum, A.R. 81
Dukes, F. 147

early detection: civil conflicts and systematic atrocity crimes 46–52; count data randomness 45–46; epidemiology 44–45; risk assessment and early warning 41–44; and statistical approach 40–59
early warning (EW): atrocity crimes 41–44; genocidal violence 27; political

196 Index

considerations 32; versus risk assessment 28
early warning models, accelerators 31–32
Early Warning Project (US Holocaust Memorial Museum) 42, 45
education 5
elite: ethnicity 30; ruling 29, 30
empathy 4
empirical theory, genocide causes 28–30
Entente de Sant'Egidio (2017) 137, 140, 141–142
epidemiology, early detection 44–45
Ethiopia, genocide risk 33
ethnopolitical wars 61; mass atrocity prevention 63–65
exclusionary ideology 29, 30, 67

Facebook 96
failed states 67
Feierstein, D. 179
Fein, H. 1, 67, 179
female life expectancy 29
Finkel, J.P. 8, 113–134, 189, 191
Finnemore, M., and Sikkink, K. 164
Fisher, R.J. 145, 149
Framework of Analysis for Atrocity Crimes 42–43
Francis, Pope 139

Gaddafi, M. 66
Garofalo, M., and Bartoli, A. 135–143
Geneva Conventions 74
genocidal violence 27–28, 29, 30
Genocide: Its Political Use in the 20th Century (Kuper) 23
genocide: and anthropology 14; Armenian 5, 15, 19, 23; background 14–20; concept 179; debate past and present 4–5; definitions 2, 11–12, 13; empirical theory and causes 28–30; and International Law 17; and mass atrocities 3–4; term 11
Genocide Convention (1948) 2, 3, 4, 6, 11, 12, 13, 23, 47, 52, 60, 74, 102, 156, 163, 164–165, 177; Article V 178; Article VIII 178; gaps 165–166; late ratifiers 165
Genocide Memorial Museum (Kigali) 47
Genocide Prevention Advisory Network (GPAnet) 93, 188
genocide studies, evolution 1
George, A., and Holl, J. 124
George Mason University 149
Georgia 64
Gildersleeves, V. 157
Global Action Against Mass Atrocity Crimes (GAAMAC) 9, 149, 150, 152, 176–177;

emergence 182–185; first international meetings 184; Founding Document 184–185; regional fora 182–183; regional working groups 185; working premises 184–185
Global Network of R2P Focal Points 183, 184
global risk assessments 18
Goldhagen, D.J. 5
governments, autocratic 30
Great Lakes region, regional prevention perspective 144–157
Grotius, H. 14
group: interaction 4; membership 4–5; racial 11–12; rights and human rights law 102
Guantánamo Bay detention camp 75, 80
Gurr, T.R. 8, 9, 42, 45, 60–70, 187–193; and Harff, B. 6
Guterres, A. 168, 170
Gutman, R. 8, 73–92, 189

Hague Conventions 14
Hammarskjöld, D. 177
Haratins 94, 95, 190
Harff, B. 1–10, 13, 21, 27–39, 41, 42, 45, 60, 67, 68, 94, 187; and Gurr, T.R. 6
Heldt, B. 8, 40–59, 65, 187
Helsinki Final Act (1975) 76–77
Helsinki process 76
Hilal, M. 105
Hinduism, Radical 19, 21
Holl, J., and George, A. 124
Holocaust 13, 15, 16, 19–20, 22, 156, 158, 159, 160
human behavior, and ideology 18–20, 21
Human Development Report (1994) 168
human evolution 187
human rights 102, 105, 110, 163–165, 166, 167, 168; law 102
Human Rights Watch 105, 110
humanitarian law 74; Cold War 75–79; norms 75; and war crimes 73–92
Hussein, S. 62, 82
Hutu 13, 15, 22
hybrid peacekeeping force, Darfur 108
hypotheses, and typologies 6–7

ideology 187; exclusionary 29, 30, 67; and human behavior 18–20, 21
intent 47, 54
internally displaced person (IDP) 85, 88
International Commission on Intervention and State Sovereignty (ICISS) 167, 180, 181

Index   197

International Conference on the Great Lakes Region (ICGLR) 144–155, 183, 191–192; challenges 151–152; collective responsibility and learning 150–151; Executive Secretariat 147, 148; Expanded Joint Verification Mechanism (EJVM) 147; genocide and mass atrocity prevention mechanism 147–148; Joint Intelligence Fusion Centre (JIFC) 147; National Committees 149, 150, 152; opportunities 152–154; protocol implementation 148–150; Regional Committee 148, 152; Regional Inter-Ministerial Committee (RIMC) 147; Security Pact (2006) 146; Summit 147, 148; violence prevention 145–146
International Criminal Court (ICC) 17–18, 74, 78, 81, 117, 166
international engagement, and success 65–66
International Holocaust Remembrance Day 156
International Law (IL), and genocide 17
International Red Cross 14
Internet 102
Iraq 62, 75, 82, 83, 84, 90, 107, 113, 115, 117, 122, 189
Iraq War (2003–2011) 75, 82–83, 107, 117, 122
ISIL 7
ISIS 22, 68, 75, 83, 87, 88, 89; beheadings 88
Islam, Radical 20, 21, 22
Israel, genocide risk 33
Ivory Coast 31

Jabhat al Nusra 86, 88, 89
Jacobs, S.L., and Totten, S. 1
Japan 14, 23
Jones, A. 28
journalism, and war crimes 73–92, 189
Judaism 21

Kampuchea 62
Karadzic, R. 77, 78, 79
Kenya 150, 151, 153
Khmer Rouge 6, 61, 62
Khosla, D. 63–64
Kosovo 5, 79, 81, 165
Krain, M. 68
Kuper, L. 6, 23
Kurdish People's Protection Force militia (YPG) 87, 90
Kurdistan Workers Party (PKK) 64, 83, 87, 89

law: of armed conflict 74; human rights 102; humanitarian 73–92; International Law (IL) 17
Law of Unintended Consequences 66
League of Nations 14, 156, 158
Lemkin, R. 11, 158, 159, 164, 171, 176
lethality, level 47
Liberation and Justice Movement (LJM) 110
Libya 17, 37, 66, 122, 180, 190
life expectancy, female 29
Lijphart, A. 153
literacy rate, Mauritania 104n17
local level: identity-based conflict prevention 96–98; mass atrocity prevention 93–104
Lombard, L., and Carayannis, T. 141
Luck, E.C. 8–9, 156–175, 188–189, 190
Lupel, A., and Verdeja, E. 32

Macedonia, Albanians 65
Malawi 62
Mali 94, 97, 98, 99, 100, 101, 190
Marxism-Leninism 20
mass atrocities 12–13; definitions 2, 12–13, 60–61; and genocide 3–4; term 180–181
Mass Atrocity Response Operations Military Planning Handbook 134n16
Mauritania 8, 37, 93–104, 190, 192; Afro-Mauritanians 94, 95, 96; Haratins 94, 95, 190; identity-based conflict general risk factors 94–96; literacy rate 104n17; local level identity-based conflict prevention 96–98; media and false rumors 95–96; social-political context 94; village community committees 93–104, 190; village tribal structure 97
Mazar-i-Sharif 81
Mazower, M. 158
midstream intervention 8, 65, 67, 68, 181, 188
Milosevic, S. 77
moral norms, collective 16
Mosul 83, 84
Mozambique 135
Mulamula, L. 8; and Sentongo, A. 144–155, 191–192

National Intelligence Estimate (NIE), Global Risk of Mass Atrocities 126
National Islamic Front/National Congress Party (NIF/NCP) 105, 106
National Socialism 20
natural disasters 32
New York Times 107

198 Index

New Zealand, San Francisco Conference (1945) 161
Newsday 77, 78
Nicaragua 62
Nigeria 37, 62, 64, 89, 165
norm development model 164–165
norms: humanitarian law 75; moral 16
North Atlantic Treaty Organization (NATO) 32
nowcasting 53
Nuremberg Trials 3, 74, 158, 159

Obama, B. 8, 32, 75, 83, 84, 86, 87, 113, 114, 115–117, 119, 122, 124, 132, 191, 192, 193; and Darfur 109–110
Ogata, T., and Bartoli, A. 9, 176–186
Omarska 78
Onanga-Anyanga, P. 136, 137, 142
Organization for Security and Cooperation in Europe (OSCE) 183
Oromo 33
Ould-Abdallah, A. 145–146
over-dispersion 46

Park, R. 47
past genocides, and genocidal violence 29, 30
Patassé, A.-F. 136
peace accords 32
peace processes, drivers and characteristics 138–139
Peace of Westphalia (1648) 14
peacekeeping forces 64, 107–108
Pinker, S. 24n6
Pioneers of Genocide Studies (Totten and Jacobs) 1
Poisson distribution 44, 45, 46, 48, 50, 52, 54, 187
Political Instability Task Force 6, 37–38n1
political prisoners, release 32
politicide 13, 28–29, 42, 43, 60, 61, 62; concept 6, 7
post-trauma reconstruction 22–23
Powell, C. 48, 49, 52, 163
Power, S. 114, 120, 121, 122, 124–125, 160, 191
Prague Spring (1969) 76
preventive action, organization 188–189
primary education 29
Prosper, P. 116–117
Protestantism, Radical 21

qualitative analysis: current crises 20–21; and genocide 18–19

quantitative analysis: genocidal violence 27–28; risk assessments 18

racial groups 11–12
racism 12
Radical Hinduism 19, 21
Radical Islam 20, 21, 22
Radical Protestantism 21
Radio Dabanga 109
Rapid Response Forces (RSF), Darfur 105, 111
Raqqa 83, 84, 90
reconstruction, post-trauma 22–23
Reeves, E. 8, 105–112, 192
regime type, and genocide 29, 30
regional wars, mass atrocity prevention 63–65
religion 18–20, 21
Responsibility to Protect (R2P) 3, 8–9, 66, 93, 110, 159, 161, 162, 163, 166, 167, 168, 169, 170, 171, 176, 178, 180, 181, 183, 184, 190
revolutionary regime changes 61, 62
revolutionary wards 61
Richardson, L.F. 46, 48
rights, human 102, 105, 110, 161–163, 164, 165, 166
risk assessments: atrocity crimes 41–44; global 18; political considerations 32; and prevention 7–9, 18, 27, 28; versus early warning (EW) 28
Rosenberg, S.R. 47
ruling elite, ethnic character 29, 30
Rummel, R. 6
Rwanda 6, 8, 13, 15, 18, 19, 22, 40, 47, 53, 62, 74, 78, 102, 113, 116, 123, 144, 145, 147, 148, 149, 150, 152, 160, 163, 165, 166, 167, 168, 169, 188, 191–192

Saudi Arabia 37
Scheffer, D. J. 3, 4, 12, 116, 117, 121, 179
scope 47
seasonality, data 52, 53, 54
Security Council (UN) 11, 12, 73, 74, 108, 111, 114, 135, 137, 158–159, 160, 161, 162, 163, 165, 166, 167, 168, 170, 190
Séléka 66
Semboja, J., and Therkildsen, O. 151
Sentongo, A., and Mulamula, L. 144–155, 191–192
separatist wars 61
September 11th attacks (2001) 80
Serbia 77
Shaw, M. 179
Sierra Leone 22, 74

Sikkink, K., and Finnemore, M. 164
slavery 12
Slovenia 77
South Africa 30, 167; Truth and
  Reconciliation Commission 22
South Sudan 17, 64, 68, 106, 115, 121,
  122–123, 145, 154, 184
Soviet Union 20, 64, 76, 79, 80, 165
Srebrenica 78, 79, 160, 165, 166, 169
Sri Lanka 170
State Department (USA) 85, 87, 109, 116,
  118, 120, 121, 123, 126, 127, 131–132,
  157, 188
State Failures Task Force 4, 6, 7
statistical approach, early detection 40–59
Stockholm Declaration (1972) 182
Stockholm International Forum on
  Preventing Genocide 182
Straus, S. 170
Strauss, E. 8, 37, 93–104, 189–190
structural variables, and early action guide
  30–31
Sudan 6, 16, 16–17, 17, 49, 62, 64, 105–
  112, 190
Swiss Peace 149
Syria 6, 8, 17, 32, 37, 73, 74, 75, 82, 88, 89,
  90, 113, 115, 118, 121, 122, 180, 189,
  191; atrocity crimes 83–87
Syrian Network for Human Rights 85
systematic atrocity crimes, early detection
  46–52
systematic discrimination, and genocidal
  violence 29, 30

Taliban 17, 22, 79, 80, 81, 82
Tanzania National Committee for Genocide
  and Mass Atrocity Prevention 149, 150
terrorism: and humanitarian law 74–75; rise
  79–83
Therkildsen, O., and Semboja, J. 151
Tibet 17
torture 75
Totten, S., and Jacobs, S.L. 1
Touadéra, F.A. 136, 137
trade openness, and genocidal violence 29
Transnistria 68
Treaty of Vienna (1815) 14
Trump, D. 114, 115,
  117, 118,
  122, 125, 132, 191; and Darfur 111
Truth and Reconciliation Commission
  (South Africa) 22
Tutsi 13, 22, 40, 47, 62
Twitter 96
typologies, and hypotheses 6–7

Uganda 145, 147, 148, 149, 150, 151, 153
Ukraine 20, 178
Ulfelder, J. 43; and Valentino, B. 60, 62, 67
under-dispersion 46
Union pour la Paix en Centrafrique (UPC) 136
Union of South American Nations
  (UNASUR) 184
United Nations (UN) 11, 12, 48, 49; Action
  Plan to Prevent Genocide 166–167, 168;
  adaptability 160–163; /African Union
  Mission in Darfur (UNAMID) 108, 109,
  111; Article 2(7) interpretation 163–164;
  Article 34 wording 162; Article 39
  wording 162; Article 99 wording 162;
  Charter and human rights 159–161, 162,
  163, 164; conflict prevention versus
  atrocity prevention 171; Department of
  Peacekeeping Operations 107–108;
  Dumbarton Oaks conferences 157.159;
  early warning system 27; Economic and
  Social Council (ECOSOC) 136, 158;
  Framework for Analysis for Atrocity
  Crimes 181; genocide and mass atrocity
  prevention 156–175; High Commission
  for Refugees 78, 85, 149, 169, 170, 192;
  Human Development Report (1994) 166;
  national sovereignty 158, 162; Office for
  the Co-ordination of Humanitarian
  Affairs 85; open questions and continuing
  challenges 170–173; San Francisco
  Conference (1945) 157–159, 161, 162;
  Security Council 11, 12, 73, 74, 108,
  111, 114, 135, 137, 160–161, 162, 163,
  164, 165, 167, 168, 169, 170, 172, 192;
  Special Adviser for the Prevention of
  Genocide 168, 169, 170, 171, 172, 178,
  184, 187, 190; words and deeds 163–167;
  World Food Program (WFP) 109
United States of America (USA) 113–134,
  194–195; Agency for International
  Development (USAID) 85; Annual
  Genocide Prevention Conference 129;
  annual off-site meetings 127; Atrocities
  Prevention Interagency Working Group
  116, 117; Atrocity Prevention Board
  (APB) 114–116, 118–122, 123, 124,
  125–126, 128, 129, 130, 131, 192–193;
  Bureau of Conflict and Stabilization
  Operations 120, 127; Bureau of
  Democracy, Human Rights and Labor
  (DRL) 120–121; and Burundi 115, 116;
  and Central African Republic (CAR)
  115, 121, 122–124; conflict assessments
  128–129; country mission alerts 127–128;
  country task force creation 129–130;

200 Index

Holocaust Memorial Museum 114; ideal prevention proposal 118–119; and like-minded allies 129; National Intelligence Estimate (NIE) 126; Obama administration 8, 32, 75, 83, 84, 86, 87, 109–110, 113, 114, 115–117, 119, 122, 124, 132, 195, 196, 197; Office of the Ambassador-at-Large for War Crimes 116–117; Quadrennial Diplomatic and Development Report 121; recommendations 127–130; September 11th attacks (2001) 80; and South Sudan 115, 121, 122–124; State Department 121, 123, 126, 131–132; and Syria 115, 118, 121, 122–124; Trump administration 114, 117–118, 122

Universal Declaration of Human Rights (UDHR, 1948) 16, 182

upheaval 7, 29, 62; magnitude and genocidal violence 29

upstream intervention 8, 63, 65, 67, 68, 119, 170, 183, 191

urban population growth rate 29

Uwiano Peace Platform 153

Valentino, B., and Ulfelder, J. 60, 62, 67

Verdeja, E. 42, 44, 47, 179; and Lupel, A. 32

victims, data 6

village community committees (Mauritania) 8, 93–104, 194; basic functions 100; creation 99–101; election 100; priority location identification 99–100; public pledges 100–101; representative committee establishment 100–101; and state structures 98; and village tribal structure 97; vulnerable group representation 97, 98, 100

violence: genocidal 27–28, 29, 30; prevention 145–146

Waller, J. 32, 63, 67, 68, 189, 196, 197

war crimes 73–92; and humanitarian law 73–92; and journalism 73–92, 191; post-Cold War era 75–79; Syria 83–87; terrorism rise 79–83; tribunals 60, 74, 78, 117, 168

war on terror, Afghanistan 80, 81, 82

wars: civil 14, 64–65; ethnopolitical 61, 63–65; regional 63–65; separatist 61

Washington Post 107

West Bank 17

Wong, W.-K., *et al.* 44

World Summit Outcome Document (2005) 180, 188

World War 1 (1914–1918) 14

World War 2 (1939–1945), German V1/V2 bomb distribution 46, **47**

Yemen 37, 89

Yugoslavia, collapse 77–78

Zimbabwe 22

Zoellick, R. 107